AF253393

Sir Robert Meade who edited the
book after his brother's death.

First published in Great Britain in 1870 by John Murray under the title:
A Ride Through the Disturbed Districts of New Zealand; Together with Some Account of the South Sea Islands.
It is now in the public domain.

All additions, editing and annotations Copyright © 2017 Atlantis Group Limited.
Cover design Copyright © 2017 Atlantis Group Limited.

All rights reserved.
This book or any portion thereof may not be reproduced or used in any manner whatsoever without the express written permission of the publisher except for the use of brief quotations in a book review.

A copy of this publication is filed for legal deposit with the National Library of New Zealand.

This book was written in the 19th century by Herbert Meade and edited by his brother. It reflects the author's recollections, views and opinions at the time. These views and opinions do not necessarily represent those of the editor, nor of Atlantis Group Limited.

Trade Softcover ISBN: 978-0-473-39849-1
Epub Ebook ISBN: 978-x-xxx-xxxxx-x
Kindle Ebook ISBN: 978-0-473-39848-4

Typeset in Garamond

Front cover image:
Dahl, Carl. The Frigate Rotha. 1812–65. The Met Museum, New York.

TRAVELS IN SOUTHERN WATERS

Lieut. the Hon
Herbert Meade

1870

INTRODUCTION

Lieutenant the Hon. Herbert G. P. Meade was born in February 1841, the fourth son of Earl Clanwilliam. He entered the Royal Navy and first served in the Channel Squadron, before being assigned to the Australian Station in 1864. Here he served as lieutenant on HMS *Curaçoa* and HMS *Esk*. Both ships served in New Zealand: first with the Invasion of the Waikato, and then the subsequent Tauranga Campaign.

In December 1864, Meade accompanied a small party, sent by Governor Sir George Grey, to the Māori around Lake Taupō. HMS *Curaçoa* was then sent on a tour of the South Seas, visiting Norfolk Island, Niue, the Samoan group, Tonga, Fiji, Vanuatu, and the Solomon Islands. He then switched to HMS *Esk* and did much the same, before returning home to Britain.

In 1868 at the age of twenty-seven, Herbert Meade was tragically killed in an accident in Portsmouth, England. He was experimenting with a new torpedo design in the back room of a house on Union Street, Portsea Island. The torpedo exploded, causing fatal injuries to Meade and an assistant, and he died after "ten hours of intense suffering."[1]

During his travels in the New Zealand and the Pacific Islands, Herbert Meade kept a journal, and when he got the opportunity he sent copies back to his family to be printed for private circulation. Two of his fellow travellers also kept journals. One was the well-known adventurer Julius Lucius Brenchley, who tagged along as

---

1 Reported on page 5 of the Daily Southern Cross, 8 October 1868.

a guest of the Commodore, Sir William Wiseman. The other was Lieutenant Cecil Foljambe, Earl of Liverpool.

It is alleged that as Herbert Meade lay dying, he bequeathed his journals to Julius Brenchley, for him to publish them alongside his own. There was some contention over this, and Brenchley later returned the manuscripts to Meade's family. Meade's brother, Sir Robert Henry Meade, then published the journals in 1870 under the title *A Ride Through the Disturbed Districts of New Zealand; Together with Some Account of the South Sea Islands.*

Julius Brenchley regretted this, and a month before his own death in February 1873 he signed off on the preface of his book; *Jottings During the Cruise of H.M.S. Curaçoa Among the South Sea Islands in 1865.*[2] Brenchley's work drew heavily on both his own journal, as well as Meade's already published work, and Cecil Foljambe's journal, then only published for private circulation in 1868 under the title *Three Years on the Australian Station.*

This book is an annotated reprint of *A Ride Through the Disturbed Districts of New Zealand; Together with Some Account of the South Sea Islands,* by Herbert Meade. It also draws on information from the other two books, where necessary, to add depth to the text. These points have been added as annotations.

---

2 It is unlikely he ever saw the book published. Newspaper ads for the book run through May and June 1873, he died in February.

PREFACE

The following pages are extracts from my Brother's Journals which he kept while a Lieutenant of H.M. ships '*Curaçoa*' and '*Esk*' in Southern waters, four years before he was cut off by a fatal accident in the twenty-seventh year of his age. They were originally printed strictly for private circulation, but are now published at the request of friends connected with New Zealand, as serving to illustrate a curious phase in the history of that colony, and therefore likely to possess more than a merely personal interest. They have been edited in moments taken from the pressure of constant work and, with the exception of a few trifling corrections, are printed almost as they appear in my Brother's MS.[3]

For the revision of the proofs, so far as regards the Maori spelling and nomenclature, I am indebted to the kindness of Sir George Grey, at whose request, while Governor of New Zealand, the expedition to Lake Taupō was undertaken.

The object of this journey is fully explained in the subjoined letter from Sir George Grey, by whose permission I here insert it.

My Dear Meade, September 22, 1869.

I return you the proof-sheets of your poor brother's journal. I have read it with very great interest. From my knowledge of the country through which he travelled, and of the race who inhabit it, I can testify to the great accuracy of his descriptions. I have never read anything more spirited, and at the same time more

---

3 Manuscript.

faithful, than his descriptions alike of the country and its people are. I seemed, as I read them, to be living again in a country I know so well.

Your brother is quite right in saying that it was at my request he undertook the journey to Lake Taupō, although I did not contemplate his separating himself from Poihipi, or Busby, the native chief who accompanied him.

During the period of the war in New Zealand, no Europeans had visited the great Lake, and the friendly chiefs and tribes of that part of the island complained of their having been quite deserted by the Government. A cessation of hostilities had taken place, and I thought, as your brother states in his journal, that the confidence I should show, by sending Europeans again amongst them, would be productive of much good amongst those who had recently joined the Government, as well as amongst the tribes who had always been friendly to it.

You, who know so well how great was your brother's courage and love of enterprise, how winning was his manner, and how good his heart was, will understand what were the qualities in him which drew me to him, and made me think him the fittest person to undertake such a journey.

I would only add that very great benefits resulted from the expedition to Lake Taupō, which himself and Mr. Brenchley so successfully carried out.

Very truly yours,

(Signed) G. Grey.

I have added his account of two cruises, while on the same station, in the South Sea Islands, which, though not so full as that of the journey inland, will perhaps not be read without interest. The illustrations are from his own drawings.

R. H. Meade.
September, 1870.

A BRIEF NOTE

During his years on the Australian Station (which then included New Zealand and the Pacific Islands), the author served as lieutenant on HMS *Curaçoa* and HMS *Esk*. HMS *Curaçoa* was a 31-gun frigate while HMS *Esk* was a 21-gun corvette. Both used sail and steam for propulsion. HMS *Curaçoa* was slightly faster with a max speed under steam of 10.75 knots. HMS *Esk* managed 9.4 knots. HMS *Curaçoa* was broken up in 1869 and HMS *Esk* in 1870.

CONTENTS

CHAPTER I.

CHAPTER II.

CHAPTER III.

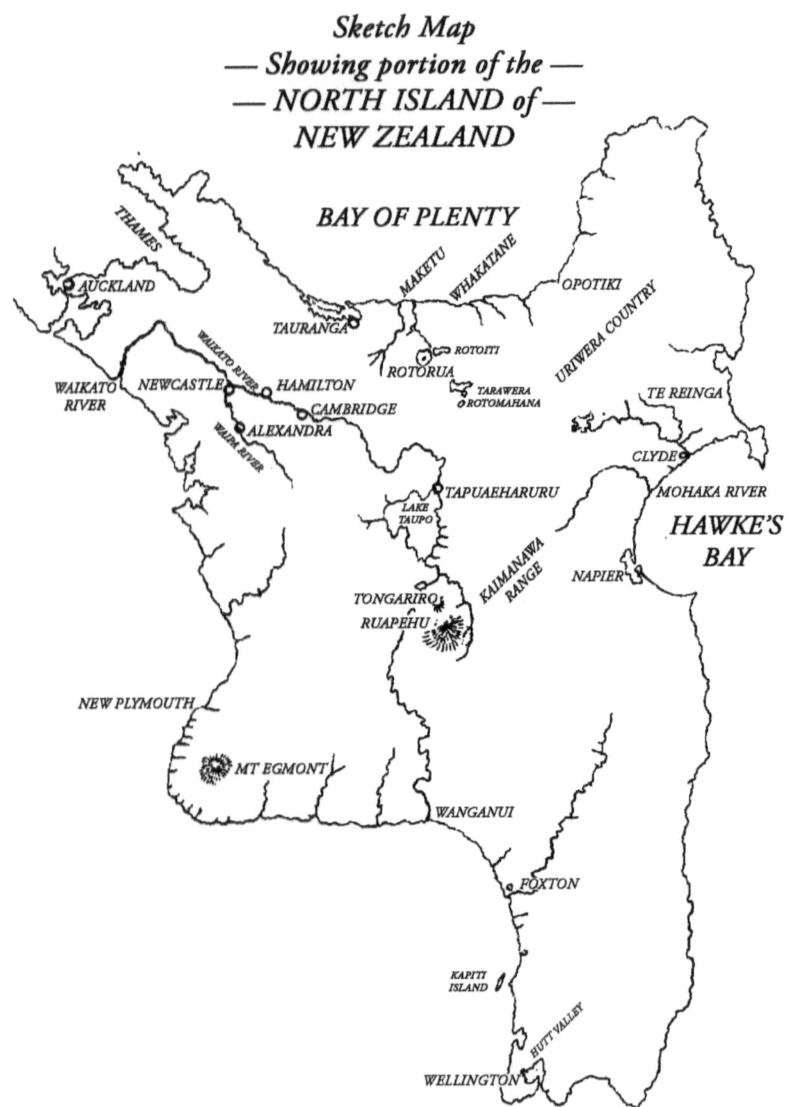

Sketch Map
— Showing portion of the —
— NORTH ISLAND of —
NEW ZEALAND
BAY OF PLENTY
THAMES
AUCKLAND
MAKETU
WHAKATANE
OPOTIKI
TAURANGA
ROTOITI
URIWERA COUNTRY
ROTORUA
WAIKATO RIVER
HAMILTON
TARAWERA
TE REINGA
WAIKATO RIVER
NEWCASTLE
CAMBRIDGE
ROTOMAHANA
WAIPA RIVER
ALEXANDRA
CLYDE
TAPUAEHARURU
MOHAKA RIVER
LAKE TAUPO
HAWKE'S BAY
KAIMANAWA RANGE
TONGARIRO
NAPIER
RUAPEHU
NEW PLYMOUTH
MT EGMONT
WANGANUI
FOXTON
KAPITI ISLAND
HUTT VALLEY
WELLINGTON

CHAPTER I.

Departure from Auckland — The party and object of the Expedition — Tauranga — Iguanas and Cuvier Island birds — Gate *pah* and Te Ranga rifle-pits — Penetake of Wairoa — Crossing the ford — Maketū — *Whare* for winter use — A Tangi — Holding the Runanga — The Treaty Stone and Arawa politics — Description of the *pah* — Maori toasts and races — Christmas at Maketū.

December 16th, 1864. — The little colonial war steamer '*Sandfly*,'[4] provided by the Governor of New Zealand for the conveyance to Tauranga of the party for Lake Taupō, steamed out of Auckland harbour shortly before midnight. The summer's night was calm and warm, the sea like glass.

We had stayed till the end of an opera, very fairly produced (or it seemed so in the absence of better) by an American company which had gone the rounds of the colonies, and the last strains of 'Maritana' left more pleasing impressions on our minds than the predictions of the numerous friends who ridiculed the idea of our ever reaching our destination, and prophesied every sort of disaster, from death at the hands of the Kingites[5] as foes or spies, to merely a year or two's captivity, relieved by regular and wholesome exercise, hoeing potatoes for our captors.

The Europeans of our party are three — Mr. Brenchley,[6] a well-known traveller, Mr. Mair, late Interpreter to the "Defence

---

4 A paddle gunboat, previously the Tasmanian Maid.
5 The context of this trip is the war between the "Queenites" (loyal to the colonial government) and the "Kingites" (loyal to the Māori king). These terms are used throughout the text.
6 Julius Lucius Brenchley.

Force" (Colonial cavalry) and the writer. With us also are a small number of natives, including two or three chiefs of note; and others are to join us on the road. By no means an ill-looking lot are they; and their European clothes hang not so awkwardly from their stalwart limbs as is usual with the "brown man" of other lands.

Let us make the acquaintance of the chiefs first, "Te Poihipi Tukairangi." The first part of the name of this chief, to whose especial care the Governor has consigned us, is Maori for "Mr. Busby" — the English Resident under whose auspices was signed the Treaty of Waitangi (our title-deeds to New Zealand).[7] Poihipi, then but a very young man, signed on behalf of his father, who lay ill at Taupō, and thus by virtue of representing the chief of one of the most powerful and distant tribes, assumed the name of the British signitary, in accordance with a custom, which we found common to most of the South Sea Islands, of complementing a distinguished host or guest by exchange of names. Amongst the whole of the "Queenites" (in contradistinction to the "Kingite" followers of the so-styled Maori king) Poihipi is probably the most influential chief, being only two removes from being patriarch or senior chief of the whole of the Taupō or Lake Country, and having succeeded in attaching to himself far more *Mana*" than either of the two chiefs who precede him in the Maori peerage — Kingites though they be.

That word *Mana*" is the most provoking stumbling-block to the stranger in the land of the Maori almost a language in itself, yet necessary to be mastered with all its ramifications before any just estimate of the character or customs of the natives can be formed. The new out-settler finds himself in continual danger of unforeseen hot-water in his relations with the natives, from ignorance of the *Mana*" of some powerful neighbour. So, being no wiser myself, I will merely say that in this instance it means influence, power, and prestige.

---

7 Signed 1840. While the topic is a controversial one, it is no longer generally considered a 'title-deed'.

Te Poihipi is the soul of loyalty, which quality administers alike to his interest and his pride, and he has rendered good service during the war. A bold navigator also is he, and said to be the only one who ventures to cross the broad waters of Taupō in the crazy lake-canoe.

But the gallant chief is more at home with paddle or tomahawk than with saddle and bridle, and is noted for his preference for a very little steed, on which his legs will nearly meet, and whence he has not far to fall. It was mounted on some such little "nugget" that he, last year, distinguished himself at Rotoiti, fighting against the Kingites, and galloping about between friends and foes, like the youngest A.D.C.[8] at a grand review — hard times though for his steed, for Poihipi is a jolly burly personage of some sixteen stone.

Wi Karamoa, native surname Takirau, is one of the chiefs of the Waikato (the battleground of the last campaign), and was one of the ministers (Chancellor of the Exchequer, or something of that kind) to his late Majesty Potatau I.[9] A clever-looking, gentleman-like man, very reserved in his manner, and making a favourable impression on better acquaintance. He surrendered at the storming of Ōrākau,[10] meeting the attacking party with a white flag in his hand, but was near being bayoneted by the excited soldiery, when Mair, who was present, interfered in his behalf.

His own account of himself is, that after the overtures which were made by William Thompson, consequent on the fall of Rangariri,[11] he and many others ceased to take any active part in the war against us; and that he found himself penned up, when the troops surrounded the Ōrākau *pah*[12] (to which he had gone

---

8 Aide-de-camp – assistant to an officer.

9 Pōtatau Te Wherowhero – the first Māori king. Died four years before this narrative.

10 Not far from Te Awamutu – the Battle of Ōrākau was fought in March that year.

11 November 1863.

12 Pā: a Māori fortified position, generally on high ground with concentric circles of palisade.

in search of some stolen horses), but took no active part in the defence — one of the most desperate of the whole war.

Reihana and Haeana were also taken after Ōrākau, whence with the rest of the gallant little garrison they had cut their way out of the *pah* through the 40th regiment, not, however, without suffering tremendous loss.

Haeana, a hoary old warrior, now one of four who are all that remain of a *"hapu"* which, at the commencement of the war, could muster forty fighting men.

Reihana, a shy young fellow, *"very well connected"* (at whose wedding fabulous numbers of fat pigs and cartloads of potatoes were devoured), was captured in a swamp by Mair himself. Both these two last levanted[13] with the other prisoners from Kawau, but returned next day, and remained on parole at Auckland. They have now both taken the oath of allegiance, and received permission to re-join their wives.

Besides these, we have Perenara, a native magistrate, a tall gentlemanlike-looking fellow; Wharetini and Moe, two strapping good-looking young Maories and some half-dozen more, of whom I know little.

We carry letters from the Governor to most of the principal chiefs of the interior, many of whom are Queenites, and, for our favourable reception by the others, His Excellency relies on his own personal *"Mana,"* which he acquired in former years, with some even of those who were most strongly opposed to British rule.

The Governor expects that the confidence which he shows by sending us amongst them will be productive of much good, as well as with the few and distant tribes who yet remain loyal in the country round the Great Lake, but complain that no official person coming from the Governor, nor any other white man, has visited them since the beginning of the war.

The Maories are to provide us with horses, as all our little journey will be on the saddle, with the exception of part of the

---

13 To run away/escape, in this case from Kawau Island, north of Auckland.

descent of the river Waikato on the way back, for which a steamer will be provided.

The natives are unable to pronounce some of our consonants, so in the letters to the chiefs we are described as "Te Peretiri" and "Te Mira," the former being the translation of Mr. Brenchley's name; the latter, that of the writer of this narrative.

December 17th. — Anchored off Tauranga this evening at dusk, the glorious weather all day having enabled us to enjoy the little archipelago of rocks and islands through which we passed on the eastern coast, — many of the most fantastic shapes one, for instance, pierced so as to form one large arch, surmounted by three smaller ones. On some of these islets, though only a few hundred yards in diameter, large iguanas are found, differing from any species existing either on the mainland of New Zealand or Australia.

On another, Cuvier Island, there are two species of birds which the natives say are not found elsewhere, and which serve them as barometers. The Maories assert that the peculiar note of one is an unfailing sign of fine weather, whilst the shrill cry of the other is a no less certain warning of storm. Those who live in the neighbourhood place implicit reliance on these signs, and invariably repair to the island to consult them before setting out on a fishing or other lengthened canoe expedition.

December 18th. — Tauranga is as yet little more than a camp and a mission station, but it must before long be a thriving settlement, for the harbour is a good one for small craft, and the land is rich. Here we found excellent quarters at Colonel H_______'s, an old shipmate of mine in the West Indies.

December 19th. — We rode out today to see the remains of the Gate *pah*[14] and of the Te Ranga rifle-pits.[15] The road to the former place, which is about three miles from the harbour, lies over

____

14 The Battle of Gate Pā was April 1864, months before the author visited.
15 June 1864.

fine open fern-land, flanked by gullies leading to the sea. On either side, little patches of luxuriant wheat and clover, accidentally sown by the troops and horses, bear witness to the fertility of the soil. Beyond this, and a few stray Armstrong percussion 104-pounder shells (which failed to explode at the bombardment of the Gate *pah*, and now lie harmless, half-hidden in the fern, some more than two miles beyond the *pah* they were fired at), there is little to call to mind the sanguinary[16] struggle of which this was the scene a few months since.

The Gate *pah* has been built up into a small sandbag redoubt, mounting an Armstrong field-piece. The *pah* is situated on the summit of a gentle rise, across which the Maories had dug a chain of rifle-pits, extending from each flank of the *pah* about 200 yards, to where the ground falls away on either side into swamps. It was this formation of the ground which allowed the assaulting party to keep under cover until within a very short distance of the *pah*, whilst a small body of men from the Naval Brigade and the 60th regiment were enabled to pass round and occupy a position in rear of the natives.

The rifle-pits, as well as the traverses and boltholes of the *pah*, are now filled in, and almost hidden by the rapid vegetation which conceals the little earthworks whereon our guns were placed.

Another half-hour's canter over the same sort of country brought us to the Te Ranga rifle-pits. They had all been filled in by our troops, but the ground was still strewn with ammunition and with natives' clothing, cast away for fight or for flight.

The skill with which the Maories usually make the best of the ground at their disposal for defence seems to have deserted them on this occasion for it would be difficult to find any position in the neighbourhood less adapted to withstand the advance of regular troops, or more favourable to the operations of cavalry. It is indeed difficult to understand why heavier loss was not inflicted on the enemy, after they had been driven from their pits.

---

16 Bloody.

Gate Pā Redoubt

The Maori entrenchment consisted of a ditch four or five feet deep, and about 200 yards long, stretching across a broad level piece of table-land, without an atom of cover but the low fern, and forming an obtuse angle in the centre, with the apex to the rear. From the half on their proper right having been easily enfiladed by an Armstrong on a neighbouring and convenient spur, they were forced to crowd into the remaining portion of the ditch on the left.

We say that the numbers on both sides were about equal. The 43rd and 68th charged right gallantly, reserving their fire till they got up to the pits, the Maories having delivered theirs when the English were within a few yards, but luckily nearly all firing high. An obstinate hand-to-hand fight ensued, resulting in the expulsion of the Maories, who, after a most plucky resistance, retreated, leaving a large proportion of their number dead in the pits. They were soon followed by the cavalry, and are said to have lost nearly 200 men.

They had the advantage of their entrenchment, such as it was; our side, that of the field-piece and the cavalry.

At the time when the tomahawks met the bayonets, each side had a reinforcement approaching to its assistance: 200 of the 1st Waikato regiment against a similar number of Maories, rumour said under William Thompson,[17] the New Zealand Earl of Warwick, or Wiremu Tamehana Te Waharoa, as his countrymen call him; but neither were in time to take any actual share in the fight.

The action over, every kindness was shown to the wounded Maories and the latter won golden opinions from our men and officers by the heroic stoicism with which they behaved, whilst suffering from the most frightful wounds. One poor fellow who was brought in, calmly smoking his pipe, on throwing open his blanket for the surgeon's inspection, disclosed four bullet holes and five bayonet wounds through his trunk and thighs. This man

---

17 "He [William Thompson] has written to all friendly chiefs, to say, he is driving all the Pakehas (English) into the sea, and intends to take Auck-land." (Foljambe, p.51)

was pointed out to me walking about the beach, having recovered, in defiance of every precedent in surgery.

After leaving Te Ranga we made for our redoubt at Judea, a strong position on the other side of the creek to the northward of Tauranga, crossing by the ford which it commands.

By the way we met, and made the acquaintance of, Penetake, the chief who built the Gate *pah*, now a "friendly native." These men fought well as long as they remained in arms against us, and then gave in thoroughly; they are now on very good terms with the troops.

From Judea we went on to Wairoa — Penetake's village — prettily situated on the banks of a river of the same name, which winds through a deep and beautiful valley,

Old Maori *pahs* are as common about here as feudal castles on the Rhine; some of them rather picturesque, especially that at Bethlehem, one of the largest that we saw, nearly covered with foliage and long drooping creepers, and moreover having, for a foreground to the picture, the only pretty Maori girl that I have yet seen.

Poihipi went on to Maketū to announce our arrival, and bring back horses.

December 20th. — Left this morning for Maketū, a native settlement and *pah* at the mouth of a river, about 17 miles farther south, where we are to remain for a day or two, in order to be present at a great meeting, or *"runanga,"*[18] where the Arawa chiefs from the lake and mountain tribes are to meet those of Maketū, for the purpose of deciding on measures for defence against an expected attack from their neighbours the Ngatiporos,[19] a very powerful tribe of Kingites; and for the discussion of other important matters. We crossed over in a boat to Matapihi, a native settlement on the southern side of the harbour, where saddle and pack horses had been sent to meet us. Whilst the latter were being packed with our provisions and slender stock of baggage

---

18 Rūnanga: meeting
19 Ngāti Porou

— no small share of which last was tobacco for presents — we inspected the court-house, or council-chamber of the village, a tolerably spacious "*whare*,"[20] substantially walled and roofed, and decorated inside with many coloured sinnet and *kakaho*, a slender and graceful species of flag-reed, which served for wainscoting to the wall — affixed to which we found a code of laws for the suppression of immorality.

Having saddled and bridled, we got a foretaste of the dilatoriness[21] of our native companions, but at last got clear of the village, our party consisting of eleven horsemen and three on foot.

Before reaching the beach we had to ford two swamps, each of them up to our saddles; but afterwards it was all glorious hard sand, alive with myriads of curlew, redbills, and graceful stilt-plover.

A few, very few, small patches of potatoes, scattered here and there at random through the fern-land, were the only signs of native cultivation that we met with.

Mair and I reached the river in time to ford it, and keep dry by crossing our feet between our horses' ears; but the heavy-weights — Brenchley and Poihipi — did not reach it till dusk had set in and the tide risen; so, their horses being small, the night dark, and the river deep and broad, they preferred to cross in a rather crank canoe, leaving their steeds to follow next morning. The rotten old canoe ended by capsizing, but luckily not till her last trip, after having safely transported the last of our packs.

Almost overhanging the ford is the *pah*, which presents an imposing appearance, and is strongly fortified both by nature and by art in every respect, save that it would be commanded by artillery from one neighbouring hill. But the Ngatiporos having no guns, and the hill in question being crowned by a redoubt garrisoned by our troops, the Arawas are safe enough for the present.

Leaving the *pah* on our left, we came to a settlement on a small hill, which is in process of conversion into another *pah*; here we

---

20 A house or building.
21 Slowness or tardiness.

found a *whare* prepared for our reception, among the dwellings of the natives from the Lake districts, who are to accompany us to Taupō.

As soon as we were discerned approaching, some of those within the palisades set up a long intoned shout or song of welcome, whilst others conducted us to our *whare*. These *whares*, or native houses, reflect scant credit on the race that remains content to live and die in them; for they are generally far inferior in size and appearance to the habitations of most of the South Sea Islanders, and are not such as might be expected from men so intelligent in most things as the Maories.

They are usually of an oblong shape, with an internal area of about 16 feet by 8, and the doorway too low to be entered without stooping; but the sloping roof gives greater height within.

The skeleton of the house is of wood, the posts, ridgepole and rafters being cut to fit into one another, and then securely lashed.

The roof is thatched with *raupo*, a plant which fills the marshes, and the walls are filled in with fascines of the same material, frapped in so tightly as to exclude both wind and water and keep the inmates warm.

On either side of the door a narrow board confines the loose fern or *raupo*, which, covered with a few mats, takes the place of bed and bedrooms; and in the centre, the fire-place, lined with a few stones, is sunk in the flooring.

In nearly every *"kainga,"* or native village, two or three *whares* of a much larger size are to be seen, the common property of all the village; but the Maories, when urged to increase the size of their domiciles, refuse, on the score of the difficulty of warming larger ones.

They have also a kind of *whare* specially designed for cold weather, which is sunken some three or four feet below the surface, the eaves of the roof alone being on a level with the ground.

In these dens as many natives as can find room assemble, and, after lighting their pipes round a hot fire, close every communication with the external air, till the atmosphere becomes inconceivably foul.

Our little *whare* was new and clean; fresh green *raupo*, thickly laid on the hard-trodden floor, made pleasant beds; and two staid matrons were told off to cook and "do for us."

As soon as we had supped and shaken down into our new quarters, we received visits from a number of the heads of families, bringing "salutations to the people from *Te Kawana*' (the Governor)."

They had expected us early in the day, and had accordingly prepared a great feast; but after waiting many hours, they concluded that we would not come that day at all, and so fell to, and demolished the viands themselves; an arrangement of which we very much approved.

The worthy females who are specially in charge of our domestic arrangements, were soon called away to perform a duty of a very different nature — that of acting as fugle-women at a *"tangi,"* or general wail, with which Karamoa and Reihana were received on their return from captivity.

When a Maori returns to his friends after a long absence, instead of smiles and joyous faces they receive him with tears and lamentations, intended to express the dreadfully painful state of their feelings while deprived of his company, sorrow for the death of such of his kindred as may have departed this life since he left them; and in this case, sympathy with his real or imaginary sufferings in captivity.

We found the two chiefs standing in an attitude of silent dejection, in the midst of a semicircle of their people, who performed the *"tangi"* for a good quarter of an hour. Commencing with an almost inaudible moaning, accompanied by a slight but increasing vibration of the head, they worked up their emotions till tears fell like rain — from men, women, and children — and the moaning became of the most doleful description. The *"tangi"* concluded, the quondam[22] captives solemnly pressed noses all round, and in ten minutes all hands were as jolly as ever.

---

22 Former.

December 21st. — Old Haeana, who was on foot, arrived during the night, so we were roused, from our slumbers at early dawn by the *"tangi"* renewed with fresh vigour and wind, and headed by an old lady with a shock head of hair and dreadfully powerful lungs.

The Runanga, at which we were duly invited to attend, was assembled at the great *pah* today.

Every precaution had been taken to ensure the comfort as well as the propriety of the meeting, but what tickled my fancy most was the posting of a small Maori member of the shoeblack brigade inside the gate of the *pah*, with his implements of trade, ready to serve anyone who might happen to wear shoes.

The chiefs assembled in a marquee, which covered a long table with seats around, from the centre of which rose a lofty flagstaff bearing an English ensign, and images typical of the political attitude of the Arawas. On each side of the mast was a head, carved of wood one looking north to the Governor for arms and troops, the other glaring defiantly southward and challenging their foes to come on. The eastern yardarm was ornamented with the frontispiece of some revered ancestor, gazing towards Hawaii (the supposed land of their forefathers) for assistance — a poetical, but not very practical idea. From the opposite yardarm another ancient hero, who seemed to have a better notion of the *"situation,"* was represented calling the lake and mountain Arawas to the rescue. And finally, the post of honour at the truck was occupied by a bust of the Queen.

The Maories were very anxious to impress upon us that these carvings were intended only for symbols, not portraits.

Close to the door were posted the bye-laws, which enjoined order and obedience to the directions of the chief who acted as chairman ruled that everyone on entering should uncover and make a sort of quarterdeck salute, by bowing in honour of the Queen and forbade the use of tobacco during the sitting of the Runanga.

About thirty chiefs were assembled round the table, which groaned under huge piles of bread and butter and biscuit, besides a small quantity of brandy, rum, and cider.

Most of these men were decently dressed in European clothes, but a few clung to the national and rather primitive costume.

The proceedings commenced by everyone in turn drinking the Queen's health. Now the only European present besides ourselves was a missionary, and having been helped first in virtue of the seats of honour where we had been courteously placed, we drank our "tots" in silence and ignorance of the etiquette; but afterwards, fearing that our omission might be ascribed to tepid loyalty, we asked for more, wherein we drank the *"Kuini Wikitoria"*[23] with all the honours. Yet I fear that our good intentions may have been misconstrued, and that we were looked on as men who had obtained a double allowance of grog under false pretences.

In the centre of the table stood a large wooden vase, handsomely carved out of a single block, which was much valued by the Maories on account of its antiquity, and made an excellent punch-bowl.

One of the chiefs explained that many years ago, before the *"pakehas"* had brought metals into use, the only means of boiling food was by continually dropping red-hot stones into wooden bowls of water. These urns were very carefully carved, and handed down from father to son; but since the introduction of European utensils, the art of carving the wooden vases has been lost.

The presiding chief, after requesting Mair to translate for us the speeches of the others (which he was kind enough to do and with great fluency), went on to explain the signification of a slab of stone at the foot of the flagstaff, bearing an inscription in Maori, "Let the peace be kept," deeply cut into the surface, with the date, Sept. 16, 1845. On that day peace was concluded, after long years of war, between the allied tribes of Maketū and Taupō on the one side, and the Tauranga and Waikato natives on the other; and this stone, to which they attach great value, is their treaty, a facsimile being kept by the men of Tauranga. It also serves in

---

23 Queen Victoria.

some degree as a sort of Maori temple of Janus, the stone being kept in its present position, with the fair side uppermost, as long as the "good principle remains in the ascendant" — that is, peace between these tribes; but so soon as fighting begins the stone is reversed.

The first resolution proposed at the meeting was one setting forth that the lands of all who have carried arms against the Queen ought to be forfeited to the Crown. This was agreed to, and passed, with all the decision and liberality which usually characterizes the actions of men who are dealing with the property of their foes.

The next subject was the proposed cession, or sale, of 20,000 acres of their own land to the Governor for the purpose of locating a large number of settlers, whom they had petitioned to be sent amongst them.

This was a very different affair, and not to be disposed of in the same summary manner. The object of the Arawas in asking for settlers is to make sure of the assistance of our naval and land forces in case of attack from the Ngatiporos, by identifying the interests of the settlers with their own.

In July last, the Ngatiporos crossed the boundary, a river a few miles farther south, and advanced to the ridge abreast of our redoubt and of the Maketū *pah*, where they threw up during the night two long lines of rifle-pits.

From these they were dislodged by shell from the guns of the '*Falcon*' and '*Sandfly*;' so, fording the Waihi river, close to its mouth, they retreated by the only route possible, a long strip of shingle which separates the sea from a large and impassable swamp. The Arawas turned out of their *pah*, and pursued their foes with great success, killing many and capturing others whilst fleeing along the beach. But they lost their great fighting chief, Wynard Beckham, a grand old fellow, in revenge for whom they tomahawked some prisoners.

The next morning, at daybreak, they surprised the Ngatiporos a little farther on, at Matata, routed them with great slaughter, and captured their chief. Beckham's wife, Mata (whose acquaintance we made today, a very determined-looking, but not repulsive woman), became terribly excited at the death of her husband, to whom she was much attached and being moreover covertly goaded on by a miscreant who thirsted for revenge for the loss of an eye caused by a recent wound, she seized a gun, and blew out the brains of the captive chief of the Ngatiporos. For this the Ngatiporos, whose numbers far exceed that of the Maketū natives, have sworn to have revenge, and have moreover allied themselves to other east coast tribes, who are hostile alike to the Arawas and to ourselves.

This murder cost Mata the pension which she would otherwise have enjoyed as the widow of a native magistrate. She was in the thick of the fight where her husband fell, and refused to desert his body.

The Arawas returned from Matata elated with victory and laden with plunder. They popped their dead chief into a bag, and carried him back along the beach towards Maketū; but on the way an alarm was raised that the enemy had rallied and were attacking in force; a panic and stampede ensued, and the shingle being at that place unusually heavy, the dead chief was dropped, and deserted by all save his sturdy old wife, who remained behind and buried him in the sand. The next day she returned alone, in spite of a storm of wind and rain, dug him up again, and carried him on till her strength failed her, when she buried him once more, and returned to report progress. At last some of the young men fetched him into the *pah*, where he was interred, and still remains. His daughter receives a small pension from Government.

But to return to the meeting. Many of the chiefs spoke in allegories and metaphors, and one of them applied the parable of the ten talents of silver to the land question. They all spoke with dignity and ease; their speeches were sensible, and many had a touch of grim humour. And here, as at every other Maori meeting which I have since witnessed, no abusive language was made use of, no speaker was interrupted, and the greatest courtesy was observed both between those who joined in the debate and the listeners.

One could not help drawing an unpleasant comparison between the behaviour of this assembly of *"savages"* and the scenes which are too frequently witnessed in one or two of our colonial parliaments.

But the meeting would not all agree to cede the land, notwithstanding their straits. After those who favoured the proposal had spoken, a man, named Fox I think, the principal fighting chief at Maketū, rose and opposed it, concluding by saying, "If land we must give, let it be the salt sea-beach you just have travelled by:" then he straightway left the meeting. When he had gone, up rose an old and hoary chief, in a full suit of mat and feathers, a man of broad acres and influence, who, when he spoke, and that was seldom, moved many with him. He bitterly opposed the bare notion of parting with a single rood of land and, stretching forth his shrivelled arms, he cried, "Oh that I could thus embrace the land of my forefathers, and, gathering it all within my arms, keep it whole and safe from the grasping Pakeha!" with a good deal more in the same strain.

Poihipi, who is in favour of the cession, made a speech which was much applauded, full of moderation, good advice, and moral maxims, which rather strangely contrasted with the gesticulations by which, revolver in hand, he emphasized his most telling points.

After this the Runanga adjourned to smoke, which gave me leisure to examine the *pah*. The stockade which encloses it is of an oblong shape, three sides resting on the edge of a steep cliff, partially scarped, and inaccessible except by the cut pathways to the gates. On the fourth or southern side only, the ground falls away at a gentle slope, and this face is therefore most strongly defended in other ways. The stockade, which is constructed with blinded gates and loop-holed flanking angles, consists of a double fence about 9 feet high, with a distance of 1 foot between the two fences. It is only at short intervals that the posts are stout and solidly imbedded in the ground the remainder consisting of tough and closely-placed, but slighter stakes, so secured with lashings of supplejack and horizontal stakes that the whole will give or bend, but never break. In the outer fence it is only the big posts (two or three yards apart) that are set in the ground at all the extremities of the intervening stakes, which are sharply pointed, are suspended so as to reach down to within about 18 inches of the soil. This allows the men in the rifle-pits within the stockade to point their muskets freely through the inner fence and, from its greater elasticity, the outside fence is in fact stronger than if every stake had been driven into the ground. In an obstacle of this description, shot or shell from great guns would make an opening no bigger than their own diameter.

All round the *pah*, and closely skirting the inner side of the fence, there is a chain of rifle-pits, with traverses and interrupted inner curtains, built of alternate layers of earth and fern. The gates, which are profusely ornamented with feathers and carved monstrosities, are too narrow to admit more than one man at a time; they are moreover commanded at all points from within by rifle-pits, and blinded without by zigzag double fences.

The interior is occupied by the family *whares*, the *whare-karakia*, or house of worship, and the store-houses and gardens; the latter all divided and subdivided by tall fences thickened with live green-stuff, so as to form a regular labyrinth, which a handful of determined men, who know their ground, could hold against five times their number.

Meanwhile the evening-bell was rung at the *whare-karakia*, and prayers were read by the native deacon.

Poihipi, though sanguine of ultimately carrying his point about the land, saw, with the other promoters of the meeting, that the day was going against them, and wisely postponed the question; and some more brandy having been sent for, pipes and grog became the order of the evening.

Each chief in turn had to propose a toast, and it was rather amusing to compare their remarks with similar specimens of post-prandial eloquence at home. The Queen was the most frequent toast, and one of the wildest-looking characters present said, whilst proposing Her Majesty: "... She is the fountain of all good — before her reign all things went wrong, but now we have good laws. It is she who gives us this brandy (a polite fiction). May she send us plenty of powder, plenty of rum, and may they both be strong! And may she send and open a public-house here." A voice: "And a jail." "Yes, and a jail, too, for that is good for some."

There was a good deal of light chaff, and we broke up in very orderly style about 9 p.m. The gatekeeper of the *pah* was found after some little trouble, and we returned to our *whare*.

December 22nd. — Some Maori horse-racing today, the ardour of the sportsmen and women being in no way damped by the torrents of rain which fell during the greater part of the morning. Several of the jockeys got spilt during the races, for no very apparent reason.

The natives much excited, dancing, shouting, and gesticulating at the success of their favourites. Foremost of all were the fair sex, who would frequently quite overpower with their most demonstrative caresses the fortunate quadruped which won.

December 23rd. — More racing today, but the ladies restrained the expression of their sympathies within more sober bounds, the levity of their conduct yesterday having called forth grave censure from some of the elder chiefs, who apparently do not approve of their daughters imbibing fast and horsey tastes.

December 25th, Christmas Day. — Still at Maketū, having been detained by delays in issuing the Government provisions to the natives of our party, as well as by the straying of our horses, with which last little misfortune the anxiety of our natives to pass their Christmas amongst the fleshpots of Maketū is probably in some degree connected.

Not a very lively Christmas, for it poured nearly all day, so we stopped in our *whare* (some 10 feet square) till the evening, when it cleared up a little, and we went to see the rifle-pits thrown up by the Ngatiporos when they came to attack Maketū, as has been already mentioned.

The advance parallel, about 800 yards from the redoubt, and the other, connecting two little *pahs* which had been just commenced, were all thrown up in two or three hours, just before daybreak, after marching all night.

At the foot of this hill flows the river Waihi, and beyond is a large swamp with excellent duck-shooting; but the hostile natives have given fair warning that any of the officers whose love of sport may induce them to cross the stream will be shot.

And a short time ago two officers from the re-doubt, who had gone after the ducks, had to run for their lives, the Ngatiporos peppering at them all the way to the hill, when the pursuit was abandoned — very fortunately, one of the officers having to lie down from exhaustion.

On our return we received the good news that all the horses had been caught, and safely pounded in the absent missionary's garden also a welcome invitation to eat our Christmas dinner with the officers of the garrison.

CHAPTER II.

December 26th. — A bright morning, with a sun whose searching rays lit up the depths of the forest, as the whole party for Taupō, now consisting of thirty horsemen, besides a few men and women on foot and some pack-horses, started in Indian file along the narrow path which at present represents the Queen's highway to the interior.

About three in the afternoon we reached the remains of a small shed, named Williams' House, from the Bishop having slept there many years ago. Here, finding some grass, we halted to feed and water our horses, and allow the rest of the party to overtake us, Wharetini and Moe alone being with us; but an hour or more having passed without any signs of our rearguard or commissariat, we saddled, and pushed on again for Rotorua.

Hitherto our route led along the crests of lofty ridges, showing on either side as far as the eye can reach a perfect network of rocky gorges and deep ravines.

We now entered the woods, and the road became more difficult — steep hills slippery from recent rains, with tangled roots crossing high above the path so the horses got many a fall, though they were led most of the way. At one time my nag entangled his legs in the bight of a tough supplejack, which hung from the overshadowing trees, and so thrown sideways off the path, he lighted on his back on a bush just below; but managed to kick his way down to the ground again unhurt.

The first lake we came to was Rotoiti ("Little Lake"), which, however, is nearly as big as Rotorua ("Second Lake"), of an irregular shape, and far prettier than the other. We crossed at a narrow place in a canoe, swimming our horses after us.

On a far hill-side on the opposite shore we sighted a steam-jet; one little link in the vast chain of volcanic action which stretches from Tongariro to White Island, a distance of some 150 miles. A queer little white cloud, bursting out of the ground at short intervals, like the firing of a minute-gun.

At the opposite end of the lake is a hostile *pah*, with the rebel flag flying.

After leaving this lake, from which the natives say the Maketū river takes its source, we crossed a high, fern-covered ridge, and before dark reached the Mouria *pah*, built on the stream which connects the two lakes of Rotorua and Rotoiti. The principal strength of this *pah* lies in the water with which its slight stockade is nearly surrounded.

As we rode across the ford we heard the cry to "put oh food," and the natives came running out of their *whares*, pressing us to pass the night at their *pah*, or at least to stop and eat; but the day was far spent, and we pushed on to Ngae, a settlement on the shores of Rotorua, where we purposed passing the night. Here we put up at a small house built in European style, though originally constructed for a Maori chief, and at present the residence of the gentleman who combines the functions of magistrate and doctor for this part of the country, but who is now absent. Close by the house we found a neat little waterfall tumbling over a low cliff straight into the lake, from a stream which once turned a mill, now deserted and fast going to ruin and decay; so also, the mission-house and the pleasant gardens and orchards which surround it are gradually getting smothered in creepers and weeds — a melancholy business altogether.

We had been over twelve hours on the road, but the rest of the party never arrived at all that night, having camped at the place where we crossed Lake Rotoiti.

The Mouria *pah* was the only place where we passed any dwellings or cultivations during the day's journey, but we met a small party of mounted natives, who brought news that an apostle of the new "Pai Marire," or "Te Hau," fanaticism, had arrived at Taupō with five followers, and had already produced a great effect among the dwellers by the Great Lake.

At present very little is known about the new creed, no white man having as yet witnessed their ceremonies or learnt their tenets.

They are called "Pai Marire," from the words which they subscribe to their signatures and use in greeting or parting from their co-religionists. The words literally mean "good! be appeased;" but the real tendency of the belief is to unite the Kingites of all sects in one common bond of fanatical hostility to the Pakehas. *"Te Hau"* means only "the hau (faith)."

The approaches to this *"kainga,"* or settlement, are defended by a double chain of rifle-pits, roofed over almost flush with the level of the ground, each roof being pierced with small loopholes.

A lamb having been killed for our supper, we were soon rolled up in our blankets, and fast asleep, on a heap of fresh-cut fern, in spite of the eloquence of a native assessor, who was endeavouring to extract from Mair a categorical answer as to how far his (the native's) little gallantries with the fair sex might endanger his situation under Government.

December 27th. — Next morning the rest of our party joined us, after we had enjoyed a long bathe in the lake, with a glorious *"douche"* under the waterfall. At midday we embarked in canoes and paddled across the lake to Mokoia, a little island, thickly inhabited and carefully cultivated, the sloping sides having been cut into terraces and built up to sustain the soil. It is best known as the scene of one of the most celebrated Maori legends —

that of Hinemoa, the ancestress of the present inhabitants of the island, and of the town of Ohinemutu on the mainland — a chief's daughter of the greatest beauty and the bluest blood in all New Zealand, who, finding her family (the powers that were, on the mainland) opposed to the marriage she longed for, answered the midnight trumpet of her island lover by swimming across the lake, supporting herself when tired by a string of gourds round her neck, and concealed herself in the warm bath, till her lover found her hiding beneath the rocks, and throwing her garments on her as she *"rose from the waters beautiful as the wild white hawk, and stepped on the ledge of the bath graceful as the shy white crane,"* took her home as his wife, and lived happily ever after, &c., &c., &c., &c.

The outer edge of the hot bath is separated from the lake by a wall of rocks artificially heightened, and the exact spot where the fair bride is said to have concealed herself is partitioned off, and "tapu."[24]

On the other side of the island we found Poihipi with canoes big enough to embark us all with our saddles and baggage, and made sail for Ohinemutu, a settlement on the southern shore of the lake, built in the very midst of the hot springs, which surround what is considered by one who has seen also those of Iceland, the largest geysers in the world, and an infinite number of hot springs; so that, except during a strong southerly breeze, the inhabitants live in a perpetual cloud of steam.

The Maories aver, however, that this atmosphere is by no means unhealthy for human beings, though it drives away all mosquitoes, sand-flies, and vermin whilst the warm and highly-mineral baths, which are close at hand, in every direction, are a sovereign remedy for cutaneous and many other diseases. And, in fact, some of the natives of our party who had left Maketū, suffering from Psora,[25] were cured by a single day's bathing.

This settlement has always been famed throughout Maori land for the beauty of the women, from the days of Hinemoa down to the present time and during our stay we saw a few young

---

24 To be sacred or set apart.
25 A skin disease. Obsolete as a term.

girls with complexions like southern gypsies, just fair enough to let the warm colour show through the clear olive skin, and large dark lustrous eyes, with great and ever-changing expression, rosy lips, as yet undefiled by the blue tattoo, and beautiful snow-white, regular teeth. But even the best-looking Maori girls rarely keep their beauty long — they have hardly reached womanhood or maternity, ere the once firm bust has lost its shapeliness, and the clear white of the eye becomes dimmed and tarnished.

Many are leaving off now the old barbarous unkempt shock head of hair, and comb their abundant locks in the more cleanly and becoming mode of the Pakehas. They have generally small and well-shaped hands and feet. The custom of tattooing is now falling out of fashion amongst the rising generation of both sexes, and it is to be hoped that before many years have passed, the nickname of "Blue-lips" will no longer be applicable to the native girls of New Zealand. Where the tattooing is confined to the slender lyre-shaped line on the fair one's chin, the effect is really not unpleasing; but the tattooed lip is an abomination.

The whole village is built on a thin crust of rock and soil, roofing over one vast boiler. Hot springs hiss and seethe in every direction; some spouting upwards and boiling with the greatest fury, others merely at an agreeable warmth. From every crack and crevice spurt forth jets of steam or hot air, and the open bay of the lake itself is studded far and near with boiling springs and bubbling steam-jets. So thin is the crust on which these men have built their little town and lived for generations, that in most places after merely thrusting a walking-stick into the ground beneath our feet, steam instantly followed its withdrawal.

Nature is here the public cook. Food is boiled by being hung in a flaxen basket in one of the countless boiling pools nature also finding salt. Stewing and baking are performed by simply scraping a shallow hole in the earth, wherein to place the pot, and covering it up again, to keep the steam in or by burying the food between layers of fern and earth in one of the hot-air passages. The great intermittent and annual geyser, "Waikite," bursts out of the midst of a narrow arm of the bay, which nearly divides the town.

In an open space in the middle of the settlement, stone flags have been laid down, which receive and retain the heat of the ground in which they are sunk. This is the favourite lounge; and here at any hour of the day, but especially when the shades of evening are closing round, all the rank and fashion of Ohinemutu may be seen wrapped in their blankets, luxuriously reclining on the warm stones.

Here the inhabitants met this evening, to hear what news the travellers had brought, and to have their usual *"korero,"* or debate, on passing events. From wars and rumours of wars, the discussion soon turned to the new fanaticism, which was ridiculed by all the speakers; yet some spoke as men who feared the object of their scorn, as though they had some lingering misgiving lest after all there might possibly be some truth in all these wonderful tales.

We hear that two emissaries from the headquarters of the new faith arrived here this morning, and are now actually in the settlement; but they keep quiet and out of our way, not showing even at the "korero" tonight, and bide their time till our departure probably understanding how small would be their chance when pitted against the influence and stubborn loyalty of men like Poihipi and his companions.

Before turning in for the night we went down to bathe in the warm lake, piloted by a native with a light for it is no easy matter to get about here in the dark, from the immense number of deep, boiling pools, and places where the apparently firm crust will not bear a man's weight. It is very lucky that there is no liquor to be had in the place fancy, after a jovial night, having to find one's way home, without a single false step, on pain of being boiled to rags!

Indeed, not long ago three unhappy people actually fell into one of these boiling caldrons, and were cooked in a trice. Stray horses frequently meet with the same horrible fate.

December 28th. — On exploring some of the adjacent shores of the lake we found many more hot springs of different sorts, with sulphur in great quantity and purity. Whilst walking on what seemed to be hard, dry, firm ground, the treacherous crust gave way and let me into a hot-water spring, luckily only knee-deep and not hot enough to take the skin off.

We have been very fortunate in the date of our arrival, for the great geyser commenced playing this very morning for the first time this season. It continues to increase in strength and frequency, till it culminates in February, and then gradually dies away again before the winter. At present the eruption occurs with great regularity every twelve minutes, and lasts about twenty-five seconds.

A vast volume of boiling water, surrounded by glittering jets of spray and curling wreaths of steam, rises in one grand bouquet to the height of 40 or 50 feet, an altitude which it retains for some seconds, and then slowly subsides into the bay whence it rose, where it dies away in a surf of seething foam, leaving huge banks of steam rolling slowly up the dark hill-side. An exceedingly grand sight!

Bathed again this evening, but this time at the fashionable hour of eight.

Young and old of both sexes meet in the lake every evening, almost the whole population taking to the water, which is of an agreeable temperature, like that of an ordinary warm bath, all over the bay except where the water boils. The whole lake seemed alive, for the rising steam prevented any more than the portion containing the bathers being visible, and the scene was a curious one.

From every side were heard Maori songs and shouts from the players at some native game and joyous peals of laughter came ringing along the surface of the water from beyond those misty veils.

Apart from these revellers, there were a few groups of staid old men, squatting up to their chins in water and smoking their pipes in conclave solemn. Poihipi, with his jolly face, fat corporation, and lighted pipe, looming through the steam, looked the very picture of enjoyment. We had not been in long, before one of the chiefs called on the girls to come and *"haka"* to the strangers, and in a few minutes a number of the prettiest young girls in. the settlement were seated in a circle in very shallow water, looking like mermaids, with the moonlight streaming over their well-shaped busts and raven locks.

They sang us a wild song, and beat their breasts to the changing time with varied and graceful gestures.

Others soon collected round us the fear of the Pakehas, which most of the girls had shown at first, had by this time passed away, and the choruses of the songs which followed were joined in by scores of voices.

But ever and again even these voices were hushed and stilled, while, with a weird and rushing sound, the great geyser burst from the still waters, rising white and silvery in the moonbeams which shone from the dark outlines of the distant hills, and dashing its feathery sprays high against the starry sky.

The scene was the very incarnation of poetry of living and inanimate nature. We remained in the water for about two hours, which we found quite long enough, though the Maories stopped much longer; for though very relaxing to us, it is just the sort of thing to suit their temperament.

Mair and I swam across the bay; but the ladies who piloted us across lived on the far side, and did not return so, being unable to find our way back clear of the boiling springs which abound at the bottom of some parts of the lake, we hailed for our clothes and returned by land.

December 29th. — In our saddles again this morning, and started for Motutawa, an island in Lake Roto-Kakahi. We went a little out of our way to examine the hot fountains and basins of Whakarewarewa.

Some of these fountains play in prettily-encrusted basins; others rise out of curiously-raised circular funnels, five or six feet in height and diameter, and formed of various kinds of stalagmite.

These fountains, the largest of which throws the water from 8 to 12 feet high, are all grouped together on a little hill, and the curious effect is increased by the brilliantly-varied colours of the water in the pools and basins.

The chemical colouring of the waters, produced by the decomposition of the subterranean rocks through which they have passed, causes the contents of some of these basins to assume a beautiful emerald green, while within a few yards are others of a brilliant turquoise tint, or cobalt blue, or pink, but all perfectly clear and transparent.

After leaving Lake Rotorua, the character of the country we passed through today was dismal in the extreme, the path winding along barren valleys and through vast crater-like basins of pumice-stone, sparsely covered with scattered tufts of a poor kind of buffalo grass.

In one of these terraced basins we found two little *whares*, one of which was surmounted by a cross. These were the church and dwelling of Father Boibeaux, a French Roman Catholic missionary, who has been out here about five years.

We gladly stopped for an hour or two, and partook of the good father's hospitality.

It would be difficult to conceive a life of greater devotion and self-denial than his. Wifeless, childless, with no companionship save that of his little congregation of natives, most of whom live at great distances from their priest, — no hope of ever again seeing his native land, or returning to the society of educated men, his life is passed in his Master's work, in a place where even the barest necessities of life are procured with the greatest difficulty. He spoke with affection of his native friends, and hopefully of the ultimate progress of civilization and Christianity amongst them though he confessed that, under the combined influence of the war and the new fanaticism, he, as well as the Protestant missionaries, have almost entirely lost the influence enjoyed in years gone by.

We reached Roto-Kakahi before sunset, a very pretty little lake, completely shut in by precipitous but verdure-clad, mountains, with the bright little island of Motutawa set like a jewel in the midst of the dark-blue waters.

Having dismounted and left our horses at Kaite-riria, a "*kainga*," or village, on the shore of the lake, where we were much pressed to stay, we procured canoes and passed over to Motutawa, the shouts of welcome from the thickly-peopled island arising long before we reached its shores.

After supper blazing bonfires were lighted in the open air, and by their fitful light the young people of both sexes danced and sang till long past midnight.

December 30th. — Landed from the island and walked through the Wairoa pass to Lake Tarawera, where a canoe awaited us on our way to Lake Rotomahana (or hot lake). This pass takes its name from a mill-stream which runs through it, and joins the two lakes of Tarawera and Roto-Kakahi. Midway we stopped to lunch at the house of a native magistrate, named Kepa; a good sample of the civilization which a thorough Maori will attain.

We found him living in a clean and orderly weatherboard house, with flooring, door, and windows, which, together with his furniture, had all been constructed by himself. Our host himself, an intelligent-looking fellow, was very decently dressed and there was an air of comfort and neatness about the place which forced us to confess that it was more like the residence of a civilized man than was the dwelling of any white man or Maori that we had seen since leaving Colonel H________'s hospitable house at Tauranga.

Near at hand is a native water-mill in full work. Some little energy must have been required to establish this branch of industry in the heart of a wilderness so difficult of access.

Our host provided, to wash down our lunch, some very palatable honey-beer homemade.

The natives expressed some fear lest wandering parties of Kingites might cross us about Rotomahana, and wished us to take our revolvers, which for various reasons we declined to do, and left them at the *whare*. After leaving the Wairoa we embarked on the western extremity of Lake Tarawera, and made sail to a fair wind for Rotomahana, whose seething floods pour into the former lake in a river of hot water. Tarawera is perhaps the most extensive as well as the most beautiful of the lower lakes. The shores are much indented, and covered with trees, whose luxuriously overhanging foliage droops to the water. At the easternmost end, from the midst of a chain of densely-wooded hills, rises a very remarkable and lofty mountain, whose summit is shaped like a truncated sugar-loaf, with symmetrical sides and upper edge — a huge, bare mass of rock 2000 feet high. After passing through some narrow straits we traversed Te Ariki, a part of the lake which is warmed by the current from Rotomahana, and landed on the southern shore, near the mouth of the hot river.

Here we left the canoe, for this being the close season for ducks, the passage up the stream is stopped by a fence, erected to prevent the thousands of wild fowl which breed in the warm lake from being disturbed by canoes.

This lake is one of the very smallest, but the most remarkable of the chain, from the immense number and variety of the geological phenomena which surround it.

We made a detour on foot, and crossed the hot river at a place where it was just fordable, by stretching ourselves full-length on the shoulders of the natives — three to each of us.

As I write, squatted on the crowded floor of a *whare,* with my saddle for a table and a twisted rag stuck into pork-fat for a candle, one of the natives, peering over my shoulder, discovers me representing in a vignette the elegant and dignified mode in which we crossed the river, and presses me to record the interesting fact that he (of the utterly unpronounceable name) was the proud man who marched first, in charge of my head and shoulders.

Having crossed the hot river we pushed through the fern and tea tree scrub to the edge of the little lake, skirted it for a short distance, and soon found ourselves at the foot of the great "ngawha," or hot spring, Te Tarata — a natural wonder, which surpasses everything of the kind that has yet been discovered in this or any other part of the world. To convey an idea of its beauty on paper is impossible; Hochstetter, the historian of the Austrian exploring expedition, got out of the difficulty simply by saying that it baffles description — and he is right.

The Te Tarata flows from a furiously-boiling pool which fills a deep crater opening on the side of one of the mountains surrounding the lake. The sides of the crater are lofty and perpendicular, and its dark and frowning walls afford a striking contrast to the huge, towering column of glistening white steam ever rushing upwards from its mouth.

The size of the crater at the level where the violence of the central action forces the boiling waves over the lower margin of the pool, is probably about 60 feet by 80. The water is of an intense and brilliant blue, the reflexion of which slightly tinges part of the column of steam; but the action of the vapour in escaping keeps the middle of the pool perpetually raised in a cluster of foaming hillocks, several feet above the general level.

From the mouth of the crater the wide-spreading waters fall in thousands of cascades, from terrace to terrace of crystallized basins. The water from each successive pool escapes in little curving jets to fill more numerous and broader pools below, or falls in a curtain of glittering drops from the fringes of crystals and glassy stalactites which form the margins of all the basins and terraces, and finally flows into Rotomahana over a smooth, hard flooring of a semi-transparent white glazed surface, which paves the shores of the lake for a considerable distance.

The water in the several basins is of the same deep blue as at the source, but the crystal margins, as well as the delicate crystallized tracery (reminding one of lace in high relief) which covers the whole of the broad flights of steps and curving terraces, are as white as driven snow, save in a few places, where, as if for the sake of contrast, a delicate pink hue is introduced. Anything so fairy-like I should never have dreamt of seeing in nature.

In shape most of the terraces somewhat resemble the curved battlements of ancient castles, though not so lofty, and the margins of the pools which they contain are disposed in almost symmetrical curves, each of whose extremities rests on the swell of those adjoining.

The traveller may here select a swimming-bath of any temperature he may prefer, from a mild tepid one in the basins nearest the lake to a heat several degrees above boiling point at the crater. The depth of these pools varies from 8 or 9 inches to as many feet but in all of them the chemical blue colouring of the water is strong enough to bring out a vivid contrast between the graceful patterns of the ridges which rise a *fleur d'eau* and the snow-white overhanging fringes. We could detect no smell arising from the cascade, but its taste brought to mind the "sky-blue" milk-and-water of school days.

The natives assured us that occasionally the Te Tarata discharges the whole of the water from the crater in one tremendous explosion, which must indeed be a magnificent sight, but rather dangerous to anyone in the neighbourhood. There is another "ngawha" of a somewhat similar kind, but inferior size and beauty, on the opposite side of the lake, which we unfortunately had not time to explore.

We could make out, however, that instead of the almost spotless white hue of the Te Tarata, its steps and terraces are all variegated with rose colour and a bright salmon tint, with a deep-orange terrace or basin at intervals.

Skirting along the eastern shore of the lake, every minute brought us to some fresh wonder, differing entirely from the last: here, a group of little mud volcanoes in full and rather comical action there, a furious, boiling pool, clear as crystal, with periodical geyser eruptions or again, a miniature lake of cold water of a brilliant green, surrounded by miniature cliffs of pumice-stone and silica.

Now a basin of boiling mud of a dull white, then a pink one, and then again a black.

Here a little geyser there a solfatara,[26] with sulphurous fumes issuing from a yawning orifice encrusted with crystals of sulphur or occasionally a fumarole, from whose crater escaped a few fitful wreaths of smoke while from a thousand cracks and crevices in the many-hued and decomposing rocks jets of steam hiss forth. There are about twenty-five large *"ngawha,"* as the natives term the

---

26 A shallow volcanic crater.

hot springs of the Te Tarata kind, scattered round the lake, and many hundred smaller ones.

The second in point of size on the eastern shore is to be found about half-way up the hill, but almost hidden in the bush, with a pool about 40 feet in diameter. We found the water in the centre rising to a height which varied from 8 to 10 feet, and driving the boiling waves over the rocky margin with a suddenness and fury which rendered both caution and agility necessary in approaching it.

At the time of Hochstetter's visit this *"ngawha"* threw its waters to the height of nearly 30 feet.

The mud volcanoes, of which there are a great number, might serve for miniature models of Mount Etna or Vesuvius, with boiling mud in lieu of lava. They are mostly of a sugar-loaf shape, rising from a flat surface covered with a very thin, smooth crust of naturally-baked earthenware some so small that, standing at the base, we could peep down the crater, wherein the mud or boiling fuller's-earth was being either violently thrown or "flopped" about in a manner which suggested the notion of its containing some living and sportive animal, or ejected altogether after having been boiled into an almost impalpable paste.

The red porcelain pavement extends to the cold lake mentioned above, whose shores and surface are so covered with floating and stranded pumice-stone that it is difficult to distinguish the outline of *terra firma*, till the floating pumice has actually given way beneath one's feet and let one into the lake beneath. Some of the earthenware is thinner and more brittle than a teacup.

There are two of these geysers about 100 yards apart, whose eruptions take place alternately, one beginning to play the moment the other ceases, and continuing in full action for about ten minutes, when its neighbour's watch begins again. Into one of these, named the Whacanapa, some years ago there fell two little children, who were boiled alive and the spot has been *"tapu"* ever since.

Every part of the valley not occupied by the lake and rushes is covered with a hard, half-crystallized crust, as white as snow, and strewn with various objects similarly encrusted, so as to resemble a lake over whose frozen surface had swept a snow-storm. The brittleness of this crust and of the caking of baked clay makes it necessary to step very gingerly, and in some parts to place layers of brushwood to walk upon. Some of the waters have the power of fossilizing wood and similar substances. We found a good-sized fossil tree prostrate in the valley. Others merely cover the objects over which they flow with a hard, white crust. So rapidly does this incrustation proceed, that, not very long ago a duck was found completely imbedded in a half-crystallized crust, which had preserved the flesh perfectly sweet.

Crystallized leaves and other objects of beautiful and fantastic shapes lay scattered about in profusion, and we felt that the day had been far too short when the lengthening shadows warned us to return: we could gladly have spent a week or more in exploring the many and ever-varied phenomena which almost every step disclosed.

Our return route to the canoe led us again across the Te Tarata, just below the crater, when we were greeted with a sight which defies description, but will never be effaced from our memories.

The sun was just setting behind the sombre western hills. Above us were clouds, orange, golden, and purple, of unusually warm and brilliant tints, even for an Australasian sky; before us, acres and acres of water-terraces, such as might belong to some giant's palace in Fairyland; every ray of the sinking sun caught and broken into a thousand prismatic hues by the countless crystals that hung like lustres round the margins of the successive basins, or mingling in the blue waters within them with the gorgeous reflexions of the glowing clouds above.

Lower still, as a foil to this glorious picture, lay the dark waters of the calm lake, buried in the deep shade which the mountains cast eastward, and motionless save where the still surface was ruffled by the teeming flocks of wildfowl. Beyond the lake, towering dark and sharp against the warm western sky, rose the grim mountain "Te Rangi Pakaru," with its great crater vomiting dense clouds of sulphurous vapour.

The feelings which this spectacle brought forth may perhaps be imagined, but the sight itself was one which no pen could well describe — no brush portray. The veriest clod or most blasé and cynical of scenery-hunters must have been touched by such a sight.

During our return the clouds thickened, and a few flashes of lightning were seen over a pass between two distant hills. Lightning is much less common in New Zealand than in most countries, and the natives attach great importance to its appearance, as a good or evil omen. We were accordingly told that the flashes between those hills foreboded dire disaster and defeat to the tribe of Arawa and no amount of argument or of ridicule which we could throw on their fears had any effect in allaying them.

Before re-embarking for the western end of Tarawera, we stopped for supper at a pretty little village on the. shore of the lake, completely hemmed in by lofty cliffs. But neither the scalding tea and smoking potatoes, nor the cheerful light of the blazing fires could drive the confounded lightning out of their heads and, instead of the uproarious mirth of the previous evening, they ate their suppers in solemn silence, seated in a motionless circle round the fire.

We had a beautiful night, calm and starry, though moonless, and the lake was like glass. We were on the water again by nine, and long before midnight even half-way across Tarawera.

As a touching piece of music that has struck some hidden chord will ring in the ear long after the sound itself has ceased, so the impression of that sunset scene remained pleasingly present to our minds, while the Maories plied their paddles in the dark smooth waters to the time of their wild and uncouth songs.

No more lightning having been seen for a couple of hours, the natives recovered their spirits, and one learned linguist even volunteered to sing an English song, in which the others were to join as best they could. But their alphabet is a deal shorter than their creed; and they had hardly got through the first verse somewhat after this fashion,

"Oh teah! Wha can te matta pe?

Jonnie so rong at te pair!"

When a flash of lightning in the ominous quarter stopped their chirruping as suddenly as the report of a gamekeeper's gun amongst a flock of jackdaws, and they relapsed into untuneful laziness for the remainder of the voyage. It was three in the morning before we got back.

December 31st. — Shifted our quarters this morning to the mainland, after a bath in the lake at which the whole available population assisted (as spectators), the ladies replying to Mair's remonstrances on the impropriety of their conduct, that a white skin was so rare a sight as to render the temptation of a peep quite irresistible.

Not at all sorry to give our friends at Motutawa a wider berth, for they were rather a dirty lot. Our new abode is named Ephesus, a large clean *whare* on the shore of the lake, roomy and carefully finished. It was built for the late native magistrate, who was killed last June while fighting on our side.

Mair and Poihipi went to a *"korero"* at the Wairoa (Kepa's place, where we lunched yesterday), where Poihipi was to propound some patent plan of his own for "bringing in" the Kingites; but the day being very wet, Brenchley and I preferred remaining behind to "put the house in order." There was nothing but the bare walls, though they were prettily ornamented, being lined with *kakaho* stalks and flaxen sinnet, worked into various designs; but with a couple of tomahawks, some planks, and raw flax lashings, we rigged up a shelf, bedstead, table, and benches, besides affecting sundry other reforms, such as doubling the size of the windows, laying down fresh couches of fern, &c., which made the place look like a palace compared to the little *whares* we have slept in since leaving Tauranga.

Hotpools on the edge of Lake Rotorua

Soon after proceedings had commenced at the Wairoa, a small body of armed horsemen, with a red flag flying, was seen winding down the side of a neighbouring hill. The cry was immediately raised that the Ngatiporos were coming, so every man shouted to his neighbour to bring out his gun, and nearly every neighbour replied with equal truth and modesty that he had no gun. "Never fear," cried a vigorous old lady, "you have four or five guns among you bring them out, and shoot a few. That will be better than a bloodless defeat."

Fired to martial ardour by this patriotic speech, the worthy Kepa ran indoors, and speedily reappeared, armed with his gun, and in full fighting costume, having put on his belt and cartridge case, and divested himself of his inexpressibles.

Meanwhile Mair, who did not believe that the newcomers were a war party, was devoting his attention to a basket of fruit; and the natives, who have always a keen sense of the ludicrous, became unwilling to lay their fears open to the ridicule of the Pakeha (foreigner or white man), who was so coolly munching his cherries, so one of their number volunteered to go forward as a herald, to meet the strangers, and learn their mission. He started, and when within earshot, hailed them: "Are you for the Queen, or for the King?" They replied, "For the Queen," and the flag having turned out to be the red ensign, the herald returned with the good news that the strangers, instead of being the vanguard of the invading Ngatiporos, were a party of loyal natives who belonged to the hostile tribe of Ngatirangiwehiwehi, but had slipped through their lines to join the Arawas, of whom their tribe was originally an offshoot. As soon as this was known, the greeting with which they were received became one of the most remarkable that Mair had ever witnessed in New Zealand. They brought news of very warlike intentions on the part of the Kingites; but it is difficult to sift the truth from the exaggerations of a native's story.

Poihipi and the other Maories were very anxious for us to spend the night at the island, on account of the proximity of Ngatiporos, but the change of quarters would have been so much for the worse, that, seeing we were obstinate, they departed, affably observing that if the Kingites should come, our throats would certainly be cut before morning.

Mair and the natives who had gone to the *"korero"* did not return till midnight, but meanwhile Brenchley and I had beguiled the time, after our exertions in the general furniture line of business, by holding open levée to all the belles of Motutawa, who paddled themselves across in their light canoes to sing and "haka" to us.

January 1st, 1865, Sunday. — Many Roman Catholics have gone to attend mass in Father Boibeaux's little *"raupo"* church, though the journey there and back makes it a whole day's work.

Visited again today by many maidens musically inclined, but we are beginning to view these entertainments in the light of crafty contrivances for the extraction from the too susceptible "Pakeha" of tobacco, wherewith the fair serenaders may satisfy the cravings of their Maori sweethearts.

While we were at supper this evening, in marched two natives in full fighting costume, i.e. as little as possible, armed with muskets, and having each on his belt two cartridge cases cram-full of ammunition. They entered silently, and halted with ordered arms in front of us.

Our visitors were obviously on the war path, but by this time our education was too far advanced for us to commit such a solecism as to ask what they were after, so we continued our meal in silence, till our visitors informed us that they had been sent over from the island to keep guard over us during the night, as "the Maories' hearts were dark lest evil should befell us." But having great doubts as to the value of the protection offered, in the actual event of an improbable danger, we dismissed our guards with many thanks, and thought we had seen the last of our friends from the island; but this was not quite the case, for among the troops of girls who had flocked over during the previous two days to satisfy their own curiosity and amuse us with dance and song, one had been a specially frequent visitor, and had been much joked at by her companions on a supposed fancy for one of the travellers.

Not half a bad specimen of a wild young savage girl was she; of middle height, with well-shaped hands and feet, lithe limbs and rounded arms (one of them not much improved by the initials of her name tattooed on the swell of it), strong, abundant, glossy black hair rising and falling in all directions at once, and sometimes almost hiding the wild black eyes; nose a little too broad, but suiting well the ever-laughing face, and a pair of full red lips, showing as glorious a set of teeth as ever bit a potato — a comparison not poetical perhaps, but appropriate, for it is to their simple diet that savage races owe the wholesome beauty of their masticators.

She tried hard to soften the heart of the burly chief to let her follow the fortunes of the travellers, of his Pakehas — "she was young, she was strong, she could cook, she could wash, she would carry, or do anything, if they would only let her come." But the chief was inexorable. They were going to a land which knew her not, to tribes where she had neither kith nor kin and, moreover, the rest of the natives of our party, whose voracious appetites had already made great progress with the Government provisions drawn at Maketū, looked with small favour on the prospect of an addition to their number. (We did not hear of this till a day or two after we had left the place.)

Late that evening a canoe gently grounded on the strand a short distance from the house where the white men were staying; the native having watched his opportunity through the unglazed casement, beckoned out one of the party sitting "crooning" over their pipes, and, with some little trouble, explained to him that his presence was wished for over the water; but the course of true love never did or will run smooth, and the unaccustomed ear of the white man mistook in the reply of the native the name "Karolina" for that of the damsel described above, which it much resembled.

Now Karolina was a worthy, but by no means attractive old female, who had charge of the dwelling of the deceased assessor.

So, the Pakeha taking it but as a joke, or at most as a scheme for the extraction of tobacco, told the messenger that his friend was a "kuia" (a not very complimentary term for an old woman), and returned to the house. He had not been there long before the real name of the sender of the message flashed across him, and sent him swiftly to the shore in the hope that he might, at least, be in time to send a more courteous answer. But he was too late; for an instant, he saw the canoe shooting out from the dark shadows of the steep and fern-clad shore, silently cross the bright path of the moon on the still waters of the lake; but again the vigorous arms of the Maori had sped him across the narrow stream of light, and plunged into the distant darkness; so he paddled him back to the watching girl in her island home without the wished-for passenger.

CHAPTER III.

January 2nd. — Made an early start and picked up the remainder of our party at the neighbouring settlement of Kaiteriria, whence, after the eternal Tangi business, we got away soon after nine. After crossing a belt of forest, we had to traverse the same melancholy sort of country as on Thursday — pumice-stone hills and valleys covered with stunted fern.

Hove-to at midday in the fern for lunch, cooked by the natives in a neat and ingenious little fireplace, which they cut out of a bank.

After this the road led along the base of a remarkable ridge, rising about 1000 feet above the plain and 35 miles in length, running in a south-western direction, and named the Pairoa Range.

We struck it first after crossing a swamp, at the hot spring Au-Tawa-Kokori, the source of a stream of very respectable dimensions.

The brook retains its heat for a great distance, and the many-hued rocks decomposing under the influence of sulphurous gases, with the countless steam-jets stretched along the hill sides as far as the eye could reach, showed that the whole range is but one link in the chain of volcanic action extending from Tongariro to White Island.

We bivouacked for the night in the tea-tree scrub near a cluster of boiling mud craters and solfataras named Kopiha, distant about a third from the end of the range. There is here also a *"Soufrière,"* resembling those found in some of the West Indian Islands, but more noisy; the sound apparently caused by large volumes of gas bursting through some heavy and superincumbent weight. These noises were frequent immediately under the open ground where they lay, and had rather a startling effect, when they roused us from our slumbers — sometimes with a loud explosion, or a sound like the passing of subterranean railway trains; at others, dying away in distant rumbling, like thunder among the hills.

Here, as at Rotorua and other places where we have camped, all the boiling necessary for our meals was performed by Dame Nature.

From the foot of the range extends a broad plain intersected by deep gorges through which the water from the hot springs escapes; here grow great quantities of native flax, perhaps the most useful plant in New Zealand, and to be found in profusion all over the country. It is a handsome plant, with lily-shaped flowers growing on stalks 10 or 12 feet high, and long rush-like leaves, which, from the length and toughness of their fibre, afford the traveller an excellent substitute for leather or cord.

The natives scrape the fibre with sea-shells, and make large fishing-nets and mats of fine texture; but the difficulty of cleansing the fibre from its gummy sap has hitherto excluded it from the European markets. There are ten or twenty orange-red flowers on every stalk, and each contains a drop of honey the size of a pea, which repays the trouble of gathering.

New Zealand is *par excellence* the land of honey, and though the bees have only been introduced for, I believe, about twenty-five years, the woods are already full of wild honey. A friend assured me that he had taken as much as 70 lbs. from a single tree, and known others to get 200 and 300 lbs. at one haul; another man collected a ton and a half in a few weeks.

The greatest enemies to the bees here are the dragonflies, which grow to an enormous size. They waylay the luckless bees when homeward bound and laden with honey, and after nipping off the part containing the sting, devour the remainder with the honey at leisure.

We found one today, nearly five inches long, seated on a saddle, devouring one of its own species; there was a savageness in the manner in which it nipped and tore its victim which could not have been surpassed by a tiger.

When it had finished its repast off its brother dragon-fly we tried in vain to glut its insatiable voracity with various kinds of flies and bees, ending with a spider with a body the size of a pigeon's egg, which he instantly crunched with his cruel jaws, as if he had been famishing for a week.

Just before dark two natives, travelling in the opposite direction, arrived in camp, with an account of having passed a war party of Uriweras, probably the wildest and most savage tribe in New Zealand, whom they asserted to be coming along the path before us; but a short cross-examination having convinced Mair that there was more fiction than fact in their story, we devoted our attention to the preparation of sweet-smelling couches of tea-tree and fern, whereon we soon were dreaming under a cloudless, starry sky.

January 3rd. — In our saddles by seven, we resumed our journey along the foot of the range. Slow travelling, for our foot people delay us, and the horses have contracted a bad habit of getting bogged, or coming to grief in some way or other.

We luckily had a fine night for our bivouac, but it came on to rain heavily soon after we had started. Hot springs and steam-jets at short intervals. In the course of the forenoon we rounded the southern end of the Pairoa Range, and in another hour obtained our first view of the river Waikato.

And a very pretty view it was, for the river rushes over a succession of foaming rapids, alternated by deep and whirling pools of the darkest blue, and winds between high and partially-wooded mountains, which are further adorned by a number of waterfalls, whose white stalagmite deposits on the rocks over which they fall resemble the boiling cataracts which cause them, and multiply their apparent size.

We crossed in canoes, swimming the horses, which, from the steepness of the banks, the strength of the current, and the proximity of the rapids, was neither a short nor an easy task.

Before noon we had all got safe across, and arrived at a *kainga*, named Orakei-Korako, where we stopped the night in a *whare* not much bigger than a dog-kennel.

This village is strongly situated on the crest of a hill commanding a fine view of the rapids and of a cluster of beautiful cascades of boiling water on the opposite side of the river into which they fall almost perpendicularly. The chemical substances held in solution by these hot cascades have coloured with every hue of the rainbow the rocks over which they flow, leaving a broad margin of pure white, which causes each waterfall to appear three or four times its natural size.

The village takes its name from a great geyser at the foot of the hill, which raises a column of boiling water to the height of about 40 feet. Unfortunately, this is not its season for playing, so we had to content ourselves with the descriptions given by the natives, and so estimate its height from their comparisons with surrounding objects.

The funnel from which it rises is close to the bank of the river, in the midst of a place which looked like a great frozen snowdrift, and surrounded by a number of very deep holes, in whose dark profundities water in violent action could be heard, though not seen.

There is also here a large natural warm swimming bath with a bottom like glazed porcelain, and the natives of the village, which is within two minutes' walk, spend half their day in it.

There was another geyser — now defunct — farther up the river, which used to throw the water to so great a height, that its downfall is said to have swamped canoes on the opposite bank of the river, nearly 100 yards wide. The whole of the hills and woods visible from the crest where the *kainga* is built, are completely dotted with thousands of steam-jets, whose little wreaths and clouds of steam keep curling upward from amongst the branches of the trees, giving a very singular character to a very beautiful landscape, especially at early morning, when the steam-jets are most clear and well defined.

The village is often called Paul's Settlement, from the name of the chief, instead of by the rather long name Orakeikorako. He joined us last night at our bivouac, and came on with us this morning.

January 4th. — The Queenites here are both willing and anxious for the advantages of English law, and a rather amusing case came before Mair this morning. Two natives living near here owned some turkeys (*"rarae aves"* about here — we never saw one), one of which they kept as a great favourite, and named after a celebrated ancestor. During their absence, a man and his wife, travelling, stopped at the *whare* of the owners of the turkeys, and being hungry, killed and ate one of them, which unluckily happened to be the honoured favourite. When the owners returned, the man had died, and finding that the widow had few effects wherewith to make payment, seized on a horse which she had previously disposed of to a third person. And he it was who appealed to Mair. The widow had offered in restitution a large piece of the precious greenstone, though the latter was an heirloom of value. But this the proprietors of the defunct turkey refused, saying that it was not the bird's value that they cared for so much as the insult they had received *in having their great ancestor eaten!* The decision was that the horse must be immediately restored to the neutral third party, and that if they chose to give honoured names to their poultry, they must stand the consequences; so, they should therefore have the greenstone (which was worth many turkeys) or nothing. To this they at last consented, with the proviso that they should be allowed to throw the greenstone into the river immediately afterwards.

One of the chiefs to whom we carried letters from the Governor was Porokaia, Chief of the Wairoa. He was much puzzled as to how best he might show his good-will, and at last he sent a messenger to Motutawa with £1 to buy provisions of meat, or some such rare delicacy, to present to us. But there were none to be had, so the old man has followed us on here, and with many apologies for the poverty of the country, begged our acceptance of the sovereign in cash.

Mair accepted it on our behalf with many thanks, but afterwards returned it with some tobacco added, with which I think the old man was very well pleased.

Started again this morning after a leisurely breakfast; the land much richer and more wooded than what we have passed through lately. Halted for lunch at a settlement of a few huts by the edge of a great wood, and later at Punu, a settlement belonging to a chief named Reweti, where we were regaled with cherries, while Mair heard all that the chief had to say on affairs in general.

We were much struck with the well-cut and handsome features of two of the young women of the place, more especially the fair Anipeka, who brought us the cherries, the bride of one of our party. She accompanies us to Taupō. From Punu we pushed on to Puke Tarata, one of the settlements which owns Poihipi as chief.

I had lagged behind to gather some rare ferns, when I met a native of rather striking appearance, also mounted, who turned off the narrow path and *"tena-koe"*-ed (how d'ye do-ed) with great cordiality; this proved to be old Ngaperi, a rabidly Kingite chief of high rank.

Slept in a large *whare* at Puke Tarata — the Maories on one side and we on the other, with a blazing fire in the middle, but which went out and left us miserably cold.

January 5th. — We gave up today to rest the pack-horses and footmen but during the course of the morning guns were fired in our honour at the Oruanui *pah*, under the impression that we were already on the way thither. Soon afterwards we received a visit from Dr. Hooper, the Government surgeon for the natives, who has lived in this district for the last two years, all through the troublous times, physicking friends and foes alike. And he says that during the whole of this period we are the first Europeans who have come up here, which agrees with what the Governor said. The post is not an enviable one — for, besides the isolation, the difficulty of procuring even the barest necessaries of life is great.

The natives about here keep neither pigs, poultry, nor live-stock of any kind, and the difficulty of transport from the coast is so great, that with the exception of an occasional pigeon, he does not taste meat more than two or three times a year.

We gladly accepted his invitation to put up at his *whare* at Oruanui, and after lunch rode on to the *pah* at that place, about 4 miles distant. We were received with discharges of musketry on our approach, and shouts and songs of welcome as we entered the gate of the *pah*, and cordially entertained by the chief, Hohepa (Joseph) Tamamutu, at his house — one of the largest we have seen since leaving Maketū, and having within it many little signs of civilization, such as a standing bedstead, glass windows, neatly-matted floors, and on the table in his bedroom two glass tumblers full of fresh-plucked flowers. The chief himself, a tall, rather stern-looking man, with a strong black beard and moustache, and decently dressed in partly European clothes.

We dined with him luxuriously off fresh pork and potatoes, coffee and milk — a rare luxury indeed; he offered to give up to us his house and bed during our stay, but we preferred the comparative privacy of the doctor's *whare* outside the *pah*.

The *pah* is strongly situated on the crest of a small hill, surrounded by a high stockade consisting of a double row of slab-stake fencing, with flanking angles; and lined with a chain of open and covered rifle-pits.

There being no *raupo* to be had here, or at Puke-Tarata, the *whares* are built of wood, and roofed with the bark of the Totara tree. It is difficult to keep these wooden *whares* warm, as we found to our cost last night.

At Puke-Tarata and in the *pah* the inhabitants have consequently built most of their dwellings in the style of a *"whare-puni"* described before, the whole of the house below ground except the roof, and even that plastered over with earth to the thickness of a foot or more; and having no communication with the open air save through the narrow door, which fits quite closely. Hot, stifling, and abominably unwholesome.

The hills surrounding the Oruanui *pah* are covered with forest. There is plenty of open land in the valley, which is watered by a small stream, but the natives plant all their potatoes in the woods, where the soil is much richer.

January 6th. — A brace of "kuku," or "kukupa," had been snared for our breakfast this morning; the kuku is the name of the New Zealand pigeon, a bird which in size surpasses every other known species, with the exception I believe of one found in the Nicobar Islands. They are now out of season and consequently in bad condition, yet these two were much larger than English partridges.

After an early dinner, we got our little cavalcade under way again, and pushed on for Tapuae-haruru,[27] Poihipi's home, by the shores of Lake Taupō.

We passed the remains of two recent landslips, caused by the decomposition of the rocks by the fumes of sulphur, and the perpetual undermining of the hills by the hot springs and steam-pits. We saw one of these of great size, at a short distance from the path, discharging its steam in a rapid succession of puffs like some huge high-pressure engine. Our road led mostly through a district of deep and branching gorges, bounded on the right by distant mountains, and on the left by the river Waikato, quite hidden from sight in its winding bed while ahead of us, towering high above the nearer hills, rose Tauhara, a lofty and very remarkable mountain, rising sheer out of the vast unbroken Kaingaroa plain, on the far

---

27 The modern town of Taupō.

side of the river. This plain of pumice stretches to the eastward far beyond the horizon, but is perfectly level with the exception of the narrow fissures which form the beds of the streams and rivers that traverse it, and so broad and blue in the distance as to seem more like sea than land.

A great part of the country that we have lately passed through presents the appearance of having been swept by a flood in geologically recent times, the subsiding waters in some places wearing deep channels, and leaving high ridges of singular shape, with very sharp extremities.

It was whilst passing through one of these most dismal valleys, that Poihipi pointed out a cairn of earth and stones which marks the death-place of his last and favourite wife, who died last year whilst on a journey with him to the coast.

The monument had rather a grotesque appearance, in spite of the melancholy nature of the place itself and of the event which caused its erection for the large stone which had been set up endways to crown the summit of the cairn, was decorated by the defunct lady's bag, which had been inverted and drawn over the top like a stocking, while the lower part was clothed in her European shawl, and surrounded by the teapot, pannikins, and other articles which she had used before her death.

We have at different times passed many of these monuments, often marking a battle-scene where some warrior chief had fallen in savage strife in the good old days of spear and mere.

Some of them were surmounted by a grim-looking head, carved out of wood or stone; others had merely a post and flax-mat. They serve only however to "" the actual death-place of the deceased — the graves themselves are neatly fenced in on the top of a hill near a settlement.

It was at five this evening that we first saw the waters of the Great Lake. And the sight was a pleasant one as we rested on the crest of a lofty ridge, and recollected how few before our departure had believed that we should ever be permitted to get thus far: so, little was the true state of the interior of the country known in Auckland.

In another hour, we had dismounted at Tapuae-haruru, a *kainga* built on the banks of the Waikato where the river flows out of the lake, and directly opposite Mount Tauhara.

At the actual point of exit the river is not 70 yards wide, but is extremely deep, and the current of waters converging from the surface of the great lake rushes through these narrow portals with tremendous speed and power, expending its surplus energy in a variety of small whirlpools a little farther down the river, where the channel expands to a breadth of 200 or 300 yards, retaining however depth more than enough to float a line-of-battle ship.

The lake itself is very clear, and deep, and cold. Its size has been variously estimated by Dieffenbach and Hochstetter at from 25 to 36 miles from the northern to the southern extremity, and from 20 to 25 miles from east to west. It appeared to us that the lesser of these two estimates was the nearer to the mark.

On the crest of a cliff overhanging the lake, and close to the *kainga* where we are stopping, Poihipi's people are building a *pah* of ambitious dimensions, and the stockade is already nearly finished, but when the whole structure is completed, it will probably be found too large for defence by any force which Poihipi is likely to be able to muster at Taupō.

With the exception of this settlement, and Hiruharama (Jerusalem), a small and almost entirely deserted *kainga*, three or four miles to the southward, the whole of the settlements round Taupō are Kingite.

For a short distance, eastward of the Waikato and Mount Tauhara, the northern shore is rather tame and flat, as there the lake is bounded by the Kaugaroa plain and the lava from Mount Tauhara with its endless pumice-stone levels, varied only by some spare groves of stunted Manuka, a tree resembling evergreen heather. But to the southward the *coup d'œil* presented by the lake is as imposing as a traveller could wish to see, having for background the beautiful Kaimanawha ranges, amongst which towers high above the clouds the great active volcano Tongariro, and beside it, clad in perpetual snow, the still higher mountain Ruapehu — the loftiest in the island.

A large portion of the lake is surrounded by perpendicular cliffs of basalt, rising straight out of the water to the height in some places of over 700 feet, at whose base even a cat could find no footing, and over whose frowning crests many a mountain torrent falls in a single cascade into the dark waters below. In bad weather, an awkward chopping sea rises in Taupō suddenly and without warning, and the natives very rarely venture to cross it, knowing that from the inaccessible character of the banks, canoe accidents in Taupō are almost invariably fatal. From the appearance of these cliffs and of the surrounding mountains, Hochstetter opines that the whole lake is formed out of one vast crater, but to men as unskilled in geology as ourselves, it has rather the appearance of having filled and overflowed many craters.

The supply of water from the very numerous streams which feed the lake, especially from the southern side, is far greater than the discharge by the Waikato, and the difference being greater than can be accounted for by evaporation, the idea suggests itself of a subterranean passage, supplying probably the chain of geysers, hot springs, and steam-jets, between the lake and the sea-coast.

Not far from the centre of the lake there is an island named Motutaiko, which, strictly *"tapu"* from time immemorial, is still held in awe and fear by the Maories of the present day, who will neither approach it themselves nor allow strangers to do so, for — though they no longer believe in the old legend of heathen times, that asserted the island to be the dwelling place of a monstrous and most malevolent *"Taniwha,"* or dragon, ever lying in wait to devour any canoes with their luckless crews who might venture too near his dominions — they found their objections on the more reasonable fear of a dreadful whirlpool, which they say is always gyrating near the island, and is strong enough to suck down and engulf for ever any canoe which has the misfortune to come within reach of its attraction. Should this whirlpool be an existing fact, it would account both for the old legend and in some degree, supplement my wild theory of a subterranean passage from the lake, by indicating the spot where the waters disappear.

A large portion of the river Waikato itself, at a place not very far below Taupō, plunges suddenly underground through a cave-like opening, rising again to daylight a little farther down.

At the opposite end of the lake is the Pukawa *pah*, which with the neighbouring settlements, including Tokanu where there is a very powerful geyser, own the sway of a great hostile chief named Te Heu-heu, to whom we carry a letter from the Governor, but whose character for hostility to the Pakeha, as shown in his more recent behaviour, makes it doubtful whether we shall ever have the opportunity of presenting our credentials. A messenger has however already been dispatched to ascertain what sort of reception the Pakehas from the Governor are likely to receive at his hands.

There was formerly a Church Mission station at Pukawa, with a native school, &c., under the Rev. Mr. Grace; but when the war broke out a feeling of hostility developed itself towards him. He stayed as long as he dared, till one day, finding his congregation holding a "korero" as to the advisability of removing his head as a reprisal for some murders in Waikato of which they accused us, he deemed it prudent to depart until the storm should have passed away, which he did in a considerable hurry. For a long time after he had left them, the Maories of Pukawa appeared to regret their conduct which had led to his departure, and to lament his absence, showing their sincerity by keeping inviolate the house which he had left containing all his property, and the live-stock which surrounded it. But then came the last bitter winter, made harder by the war, with its attendant miseries of hunger and cold, and one by one the sheep of their late Pastor found their way to the roasting or the oven; yet still the house with its contents remained untouched. At last another change, and a worse, came over the spirit of the late Christians of Pukawa: the emissaries of the new fanaticism came to the settlement, and found a soil fit for the seed they had to sow, manured by all the evil feelings which the bitterness of strife in the war against the Pakeha together with famine and suffering could engender; and in a very short time, now scarcely three weeks past, a host of perverts were chanting Pai Marire hymns round a Hau-hau post of worship, erected close to the late Christian church.

With the abolition (for the time at least) of the old religion, went all respect for the eighth commandment, without apparently being replaced even by the old rough notions of honesty which certainly distinguished the race in bygone heathen times — the mission-house was broken into and gradually sacked.

They are still, however, rather ashamed of this last performance, and in the very little intercourse which they have held with the Queenite natives, have endeavoured to make out that they have only distributed the property for safe keeping, ready for restitution to the owner on his return; but some doubt is thrown on this explanation from the circumstance of the chief Te Heu-heu having been recently observed enjoying the morning breeze and his pipe, arrayed in two pairs of the rev. gentleman's small-clothes.

On the opposite side of the Waikato are two ponderous millstones, which, with part of the machinery necessary for a water-mill, have been transported on sledges or drays from the east coast and across the plain, with infinite labour and perseverance, by Poihipi and his people; but the works are now at a standstill, for the fund for the erection of flour-mills and looms, which, in peaceable times had been subscribed by both Queenites and Kingites, was committed to the care of the missionary, and has now with the rest of his property fallen into the hands of the Kingites.

January 8th. — Walked down the river to the *"Te Huka"* ("the foam") waterfall, passing by the way through some very pretty scenery of winding river, rapids, and islands. Te Huka is grand in a style of its own, though not remarkable for great height or breadth. About 300 yards above the fall the river contracts into a chasm, or "cannons" as the Americans would call it, scarcely 30 feet wide but tremendously deep, between whose perpendicular walls the whole body of the river in one foaming torrent rushes with deafening violence, till it dashes over the rocky brink into the deep basin beneath. The great pressure from the compressed volume of water in the chasm behind, forces the waterfall to shoot out horizontally farther than any other that I have yet seen elsewhere. The banks of the river below the falls are nearly perpendicular, but covered with foliage to the height of 50 or 70 feet, and crowned with barren sugar-loaf hills.

Judging by the configuration of these banks, the wall of rock over which the river falls, and the time that elapses before any object, however large and light, thrown in above the falls reappears at the surface, the depth of this basin must be enormous.

I narrowly escaped testing this question in a disagreeably practical manner, for whilst climbing the cliff to find a better place whence to sketch the falls, the branch to which I trusted gave way, and I fell bounding through the foliage that clothed the face of the bank, till my downward course was luckily arrested by a stump only a few feet above the surface of the seething whirling waters.

Meanwhile one of our natives had procured us half-a-dozen wild ducks in the very simplest manner: he paddled quietly along the bank in a little dugout canoe, with his dog on board, till he came to a duck between himself and the shore, under the overhanging foliage. The bird, apparently too tame or too lazy to rise, would then land and scuttle up into the narrow belt of bush under the cliff, where he would be speedily caught by the dog.

According to the account of the natives, the ducks repair at certain seasons to the neighbourhood of Roto-Kawa (bitter lake) (whose waters are highly impregnated with sulphur and other mineral substances), not far from here, where they moult their wing feathers, and are thus for the time unable to fly. At this lake are held periodical grand battues, the ducks being hunted with dogs only and sticks.

Unfortunately, the ducks were all wholly or partly plucked when we heard this rather tough story on re-joining our natives who had gone to procure a canoe, and there was no time left to catch a fresh duck; but the appearance of the bird which still retained part of its plumage, and an examination of the feathers strewn about, rather corroborated the native account.

We returned by water, starting in the canoe from just above the rapids, and stopping to lunch at the Tewakaturou geyser. This geyser, which in the days of its vigorous youth used to eject a column of water across the river, here some 130 yards wide, is now nearly defunct. The orifice is a funnel of silica and stalagmite about 6 feet in height and diameter, curiously lined like some gigantic, bird's-nest with boughs and sticks encrusted with variously-shaped crystals.

The procuring of them for specimens was rendered inconvenient by the behaviour of the effete old geyser, which spouts up every few minutes, with great noise and splash, enough boiling water to scald anyone who does not jump off quick enough.

The ducks and some potatoes were rapidly cooked in a boiling spring hard by, and still more rapidly devoured. Here, as elsewhere, are rare and beautiful ferns close around the hot springs, and all the vegetation which grows in an atmosphere of perpetual steam attains a green, singularly delicate and brilliant.

January 9th. — Mr. Grace with his son arrived today; they have followed us up here to see if there is any hope of re-establishing the mission at Taupō. He anticipates a bad effect being made amongst the Kingite natives (who are always well posted as to anything concerning them published in Auckland) by a stupid paragraph in one of the newspapers, which accounted for the dispatch of the little 'Sandfly,' by saying that she conveyed "Mr. Mair and an officer from the '*Curaçoa*,' who have been sent to find out what the Kingites are doing;" in plain English, or still plainer Maori, that we are spies. Mr. Grace expects to be able to establish himself again, for a time at least, at Pukawa, and invites us to come and stay at the mission-house when we visit that place but I do not think that we will tax his hospitality, as he conceives that our presence under his roof may endanger the present close connection between his head and shoulders, and he expresses his very reasonable fears of the consequences to himself which might be caused by a report, even after our departure, that he had been harbouring spies.

January 10th. — Started at eight this morning for Waihaha, Perenara's home on the south-western shore of the lake. We travelled in a large canoe propelled by twenty paddles, and accompanied by a rather smaller one containing the rest of our native companions. We hugged the shore nearly all the way, crossing only two or three deep bays, for a nasty sea rises quickly on this lake with very little provocation, and the short deep lop would soon swamp a canoe.

The shores we passed were mainly formed by lofty, dark, and perpendicular rocks, grand in their gloom, but relieved by an occasional cascade. Waihaha is a village built on a small alluvial flat at the mouth of a river of the same name, and completely shut in, except on the side of the lake, by lofty columnar cliffs of basalt. It belongs nominally to a Queenite tribe, the Ngatiterakaiaki, but is mainly peopled by the men who escaped from Ōrākau and refugees from other' places in the Waikato country now occupied by our troops.

On approaching the shore, we found a white flag flying over the settlement, in token of a peaceful reception, and the men drawn up under arms in front of the village, and stripped to their fighting costume. They shouted something which our people answered with a corresponding yell, and springing out of the canoes the moment they grounded, formed on the beach, some with muskets and others with only their paddles in their hands, and then, with the red ensign flying, advanced at a run until within 100 yards of the Waihaha natives, when they halted and formed a double line. We, meanwhile, stood off a little, and watched the proceedings. The moment our people stopped, the Waikatos, who had been crouching as though in ambush, sprang to their feet, and went through the war-dance with great spirit and apparent ferocity.

This extraordinary dance is not easily described but it is well calculated both to strike terror into the heart of the foe and to work up those who join in it to a state of excitement and combativeness far exceeding that produced by grog or martial music. Admirable time is kept by one of the chiefs who acts as fugleman, the whole of the warriors in serried ranks springing from the ground together, and giving the ferocious war yell in perfect chorus — brandishing their muskets and stamping as one man, and throwing their bodies into every sort of position indicative of the slaughter of their foes.

After this our people did the same, taking time from Poihipi; the Waikatos then fired a salute, which was returned on our behalf, and the two parties having joined, a long *"Tangi"* commenced, the effect in this instance being rather pleasing than otherwise, from the number of voices composing it, the echoes of the rocks, and the striking nature of the surrounding scenery.

The Tangi concluded, we joined the natives, and the usual hand-shaking business having been gone through, we all squatted on the ground in two adjacent groups for a korero on Maori politics, led off by our friend Poihipi with a solo on his own trumpet, descriptive of his own loyalty ever since the day he signed the Treaty of Waitangi, and advocating generally loyalty to the Queen.

One of the most permanent difficulties in the way of a complete pacification of New Zealand is the Maories' innate love of fighting, for mere fighting's sake. Centuries of intertribal warfare have left traditions of feats of arms inviting the young men to go and do likewise, and bellicose tastes which are not to be eradicated in one generation. Amongst the refugees here we found Takiuira, a fine young fellow, tall and well made, with a very pleasing countenance; he was one of those who made a dash out of Ōrākau *pah*, and escaped through the besieging troops by the skin of his teeth. He then joined the Arawas, and fought on our side against the Ngatiporos; and when twitted by Mair with his inconsistency, characteristically replied, "Oh! as to that, fighting is fighting, and we young men don't care much whom it is against."

We hear that Te Heu-heu has gone to a great war meeting of the Kingites held near the Waikato, so we cannot find out till his return whether he is willing to receive us, which is, however, daily expected.

Karamoa and Reihana, the two of our party who are most highly connected amongst the Kingites, go to ascertain whether we are likely to be allowed to pass through the hostile settlements lying between Taupō and our military posts on the Waikato, which we hope to make our return route.

Meanwhile the few provisions we brought with us being nearly exhausted, Hohepa, the Chief of Oruanui, rides on to Napier, which he can reach in three days, and is to buy us some more.

We rather expected that we might have had the ill-luck to stumble up against William. Thompson (Tamihana), the Maori Earl of Warwick, who was to have left Taranaki with a war party for the eastward the same week that we left Auckland, and so would cross our path; but we have seen nothing of him, and he has probably stayed to attend the great war meeting to which Te Heu-heu and others have gone.

January 11th. — Found too many fleas going about loose in the *whare,* so I slept on the beach most luxuriously, having made myself a fern bed on the sand. The sand is composed of obsidian and clear crystallized olivine and silica, so that by moonlight the strand seems to be literally strewn with diamonds. It was very pleasant being lulled to sleep by the gentle rippling of the tiny waves, and to find a bath ready beside one's couch when roused by the warm rays of the morning sun.

There is here among the refugees from Ōrākau a young woman named Ahumai, possessing no little influence, a well-made, rather good-looking person, but strong-minded and imperious. Her husband was killed in the *pah*, and she herself in escaping received from the soldiers three bayonet and gunshot wounds in the breast, arm, and hand, which have, however, now healed, leaving only the scars.

The height of the volcano Tongariro has been variously estimated at from 6500 feet and upwards to an absurd figure. The heat of its volcanic fires keeps its black cinder cone bare to the summit far above the line of perpetual snow, which by the contrast only makes Mount Ruapehu with its three snowy peaks look all the more beautiful. The latter mountain is estimated at from 9000 to 10,200 feet high.

We have long determined on the ascent of Tongariro, should we be allowed to reach the valleys from whence it rises; but it seems now very doubtful whether we shall be able to accomplish our purpose, for this mountain has always been held strictly *"tapu,"* and even in the most peaceful times the natives would never allow anyone to attempt to scale it. A Mr. Bidwell in 1839, and a Mr. Dyson in 1851, claim to have eluded the vigilance of the natives and made the ascent, and Mr. Dyson wrote an account of it: but the natives assert that neither of them ever reached the summit. The Maories say that they tracked his footsteps, and punished him by enforcing on his house and goods the "Muru," a sort of organized confiscation or distraint.

January 12th. — Slept out on the beach again, and on waking this morning found Tongariro in full blast; great volumes of steam and smoke issuing from the upper crater; after which the steam collects round the summit of the cone in a glistening cloud of dense whiteness, whilst the smoke, spreading far and wide, stained the clear morning air for miles.

The natives assure us that showers of light ashes are even now falling as far as the south-eastern end of the lake, and that the unusual vigour of the volcano points to the probability of an early eruption. They are but ill pleased at these signs and changes, regarding the volcano as an oracle whose manifestations betoken the coming death of a great chief, or too surely the harbinger of some other impending evil to their race.

They have a legend that Tongariro was but an empty crater until the arrival in New Zealand of the progenitors of their race, which is supposed to have taken place early in the fifteenth century, when the ancestor of the great tribe of Arawa, after landing on the east coast, started with a single slave to explore the new country, and left his wife at White Island to tend the sacred fire which they had brought from Hawaii (Sandwich Islands).

Having ascended Tongariro to survey the promised land, his slave fell ill from cold; so, being a man apparently blessed with very powerful lungs, he hailed his wife, then somewhere about 150 miles distant, to bring him some of the sacred fire. The faithful spouse started forthwith by a subterranean passage, and wherever by the way fell any of the holy sparks, the springs began to boil, geysers burst forth through the fissures in the earth, and subterranean fires, never more to be quenched, produced the present fumaroles and solfataras.[28]

She arrived, however, too late to save the life of the slave, so her lord threw the sacred embers down the crater of the volcano, where they have blazed or smouldered ever since; and the principal crater, which is said to have been the tomb, still bears the name of the slave — Ngauruhoe.

Another legend is to the effect that Ruapehu, Mount Egmont, and Tongariro were once three giant brothers living near Taupō; but some lady fair having caused strife and rivalry, the elder and younger made common cause, and ousted their brother Mount Egmont, who retired into Taranaki, where he still remains; but the ultimate disposal of the lady was not much simplified by the ejection of one only out of three candidates; for all the three brothers were punished by being transformed into stone and earth, for a perpetual warning against family discord.

The volcano appears to have been much less active at the time of Hochstetter's visit, and its appearance led him to believe that nothing but steam issued from the crater — in fact that its career as an active volcano was closed.

No later, however, than the summer before last, during the campaign on the Waikato, several eruptions of fire and ashes were observed, the flames being plainly visible during the brightest days, and lighting up the skies by night as far as Rotorua and the hot lakes.

---

28 A shallow volcanic crater.

Today we ascended the ravine through which the river finds its way to Waihaha, till we came to the Patutiki cascade, where the stream, after passing through a narrow cleft in the mountains, falls in a series of cascades, the lowest of which is about 25 feet high. The falls are well set off by the dark pools which receive them, the wide-spreading foliage which shades them, and the dark, beetling cliffs round them. The natives say that under these falls there once lived a terrible *"Taniwha,"* a fabulous monster whose description answers in every point to that of our own dragon, excepting that he was unprovided with wings.

We were assured that not many years ago one of the monster's teeth was found lying in the stream, but has since been lost. This is a pity, as there seems no reason to doubt that a fossil of some interest was actually found.

As soon as the fiercest heat and glare of the day were past, we launched the canoes and started on the return voyage to Tapuae-haruru.

We passed many of the beautiful cascades mentioned above as falling directly into the lake from the summit of cliffs 700 or 800 feet high.

Towards dusk a smart breeze sprang up, forcing us to take refuge for a short time in a little bay, the Maories paddling as hard as they could to reach shelter in time; they have a clever way of warding off with their broad paddles the little waves when just about to break over the gunwale of the canoe. We then landed for half an hour on a narrow strip of shingle of 100-lb. pebbles, under overhanging rocks, where a fire was lit to dry the clothes of those who had got wet during the squall. In truth, the Maories were glad of any excuse for a halt; they would put on a spurt, racing as hard as they could with songs and shouts for ten minutes, but then *"spellho"* for twenty to chaff and smoke.

A glorious night with a bright moon on one side, and on the other, miles and miles of hills crowned and girt by blazing lines of bush fires, lighting up both land and water the occasional mingling on the lake of the red and silver-blue reflexions of the fire and moonlight producing a curious effect.

It was nearly two in the morning before we reached Tapuae-haruru, though we had only landed once more for a few minutes to drop some natives at a place named Whakaipo, on the western margin of the lake, where there is said to be excellent duck-shooting. On arrival, we found Mr. Grace and his son encamped close to our *whare*.

CHAPTER IV.

Mr. Grace driven away — Change in the people — More warm springs — Lava and pumice blocks — Warlike rumours — Native cookery — Grand duck-hunt — River scenery — A wild pig — Ascent of Mount Tauhara — The comet — Long delay and difficulty of returning — Hostility of Te Heu-heu — Choice of routes — Reasons for separation from the rest of the party — Determination of the Kingites to fight — Difficulty in procuring a guide — Dark prospects — A clairvoyant cook — Departure with Hemipo — Fear of darkness — Forest scenery.

January 13th. — Mr. Grace's report is not encouraging. He had started for the old mission station at Pukáwa after our departure for Waihaha; but in the villages which he passed on the way his reception was so different to what he had been accustomed — sullen silence and lowering looks taking the place of outstretched hands and cries of welcome, that his suspicions were aroused, and further confirmed by an old man, once a teacher in his school, who warned him that his life would be in great danger in Pukáwa. He then reluctantly decided to return.

Late last night, sometime after he had pitched his camp, a messenger arrived from Pukáwa, bearing a request that he would return to his house and congregation, but adding that *he was not to bring his boy with him.*

This proposal savoured strongly of treachery, and was declined accordingly.

We were by the same authority peremptorily forbidden from approaching Pukáwa, or from making our way at all along the eastern or Kingite side of the lake.

The house and property at the mission station are a heavy loss to Mr. Grace, for he goes to a fresh appointment in the north and the home which he had made after ten years' labour in a savage land is gone for ever. He leaves tomorrow for Tauranga, and proposes to visit another scene of his former labours, on the east coast, before proceeding to his new post.

He gave us a glowing picture of what the Taupō Maories were five years ago, whilst under missionary rule; of their docility and industry; how they cultivate large tracts of land, sending great quantities of grain for sale at the distant settlements; and then, having gathered in their own crops, travelled away to help at the white man's harvest; — of the well-attended schools, and daily and weekly services how universal was the ceremony of marriage, how rigidly adhered to; how all these good things, and many more, were and flourished in the days when he had the power of sending an offender against morality to rusticate (quite literally) for a month or two in the bush.

Yet it did occur to us that possibly the very power of exercising this sort of authority had indirectly tended to weaken his influence, and lessen his hold on the affections of his people; that the severity with which habits of at least such doubtful wrongfulness, as, for instance, that of smoking tobacco — the one solitary luxury of this simple people — were repressed, produced in the native mind a feeling of impatience of a rule which in other respects had conferred on them great and lasting benefits, and was almost always in the hands of earnest and disinterested men.

This spirit of intolerance in trifling matters — of governing the people *too much* in the minutiae of life, seems to have been the bane of all successful missions, and is even now slowly but surely working towards the same end in more than one of the South Sea Islands.

We were to have started today for Pukáwa and Tokanu; but after Mr. Grace's reception and the prohibition addressed to ourselves, it would now be mere folly so we wait the return of Hohepa with provisions from Napier, and of our avant-couriers who have gone to smooth the way before us by the Waikato route; or of Te Heu-heu himself, to try the effect of the Governor's letter.

January 17th. — Crossed the river and walked to the Waipahihi, described by Hochstetter as "a warm-water river, which, rising in the extinct volcanic cone of Tauhara, falls in a vapour-crowned cascade into Taupō." *Now* however, we found only a little brook of hot shallow water which a child might jump over, pouring over a ledge about six or seven feet high.

This brook, which has evidently frequently changed its course, retains its heat till it reaches the lake, and possesses remarkable connective powers, rapidly converting the sand and shingle into a hard and smooth conglomerate. There is a hot swamp and many more hot springs in the vicinity, and on a rocky promontory jutting out into the lake, there is a small geyser, with an orifice scarcely two inches in diameter; but it did not happen to be playing while we were present, though we tried to irritate it into action by stopping up its mouth.

A considerable portion of this shore of the lake is composed solely of long smooth sheets of lava, which, after issuing from Tauhara, have apparently reached the water in a fluid state. On the way back we examined a group of huge blocks of pumice-stone of a different grain to any in the neighbourhood or elsewhere, and remarkable from their shape and position, having apparently been forced upward through the smooth tea-tree plain by some subterranean upheaval; in shape, they bring to mind the Runic stones of Orkney.

January 19th. — Reports have reached us that hostile war parties from the Uriwera and two other tribes are now on the Napier road, travelling in this direction from the southward and eastward to join the Kingites on the Waikato, and great fears are expressed lest Hohepa and the two natives who accompanied him to Napier to get provisions for us, should have fallen into their hands, as they ought to have been back a week ago. In the meanwhile our own provisions have become exhausted, and we have been living for some time on potatoes and tea without sugar or milk, together with a very little musty ship's biscuit, which latter, however, will only last a few days longer; rather a monotonous diet for breakfast, dinner, and supper but we soon get accustomed to swallow our meals in a mechanical sort of manner, and enjoyed the luxury of the smoke which followed all the more keenly, for luckily we never were short of tobacco. There are no eels, generally so plentiful in New Zealand, to be found in this neighbourhood; but occasionally a successful day with the nets, at a settlement on the western side of the lake, rewards us with a dish of tiny fish. There are two sorts in the lake, both very good eating if you can only get enough of them; for the larger kind, the *"kokopu,"* rarely attain the length of five inches, and the smaller, named *"Inanga,"* much resemble whitebait in appearance and flavour.

The Maories are very cleanly and careful in preparing food, and their mode of cooking is excellent. They first dig a hole two or three feet deep, in which a blazing wood fire is lighted, and heaps of stones thrown on the flames. Before the wood is burnt up, the stones are all red hot. The embers are then swept out, leaving the hot stones at the bottom of the hole, where they are covered with wet mats, on which the food to be cooked is placed between layers of fresh fern leaves, and more mats or fern placed over all. A quantity of water is then poured on the fern, and earth or clay quickly shovelled over, so as to cover everything completely, the slightest escape of steam being immediately stopped by plastering with clay. By this process potatoes are cooked in about an hour.

Today we had resolved to recruit our larder by a grand duck-hunt, and started on foot, with horses to carry our blankets, &c., for Roto-Kawa (bitter lake), a small sheet of water about 12 miles from here, at the back of Mount Tauhara.

Besides the natives of our settlement, we were accompanied by Rewiti, the chief whom we met at Punu, and in whose "mana," or right of preserve, the lake and the ducks are held.

The lake is very strictly preserved, the ducks being only allowed to be killed twice or thrice a year, at stated times; and a very heavy bag is expected for tomorrow, when the battue is to come off. This evening, for fear of disturbing the ducks, we bivouac about half a mile from the lake in the midst of the tea-tree scrub, and a very jolly little camp too, as we lie on sweet-smelling beds of tea-tree blossom, gathered round a bright blazing fire of the dry wood which lies all around in profusion, the fitful glare playing round the stems of the "Manuka" till it looks like a forest of heather in Giant-land. All hands, Pakeha and Maori, smoking, chaffing, singing, or talking, till a wild young native rushing about with a firebrand for a pipe-light, nearly put out one of Brenchley's eyes with the end of it. Fortunately, the injury is not permanent, and we are soon all snoring under the moonlight. Rewiti very indignant at finding fresh tracks — where tracks should not be — leading towards the lake.

January 20th — On approaching the preserve early this morning it became clear that poachers had forestalled us, and spoilt the battue. In one clearing in the bush, where they had plucked the stolen birds, not an inch of the ground could be seen, for though the feathers had mostly blown away, the down had become matted with the grass, and covered a large extent of ground to the depth of many inches. Imprecations loud and deep were heard on all sides against a neighbouring tribe of Kingites accused of being the authors of the mischief.

This is the lake to which the ducks, such as those that were caught for our dinner at the Te Huka waterfall last Sunday week, resort annually and molt their wing feathers. No guns are allowed to be used within sound of the lake, to avoid unnecessarily disturbing more than what are killed. One party in a canoe drove ashore all the ducks whose loss of feathers prevented them from taking wing, and they formed about five-sixths of the flock. They landed, however, only to find half-a-dozen men, armed with sticks, and dogs in leash, ready to hunt them down among the bushes.

But the birds had been scared from their usual haunts by the raid of the freebooters, and in the course of half an hour, only ten having been bagged, the battue was discontinued for fear of permanently depopulating the lake. A miserable failure, for the poachers must evidently have killed several hundreds, Rewiti vowing every sort of vengeance against the said poachers — when he can catch them.

The ducks were soon cooked in a *"hangi"* or native oven, and still more speedily devoured for breakfast by the whole company of hungry "vegetarians;" after which we returned to our old quarters at Lake Taupō, Brenchley and I, with Poihipi and Moe, taking a new route, while Mair and the rest of the natives returned by the old one. Our line was about five miles longer, but we were rewarded with some exquisite scenery on the Waikato — the prettiest part of the river that we have yet seen a succession of waterfalls and foaming rapids "cannoning" between lofty cliffs, partly formed of bare grey rocky steeps and rugged boulders, partly clothed with pendent verdure. In some places the river, or part of it, flows completely underground for short distances, vanishing mysteriously under the rocks; in others, the whirlpools from the rapids have formed beautiful little circular bays, in one of which we saw the fragments of a canoe, ceaselessly gyrating, as they have done by day and night ever since the canoe of which they once formed part was dashed to pieces months ago in the rapids above, and its inmates drowned or torn to shreds against the rocks.

The lake we have just left is ugly enough in point of scenery, its shores being flat, and either barren or covered with stunted manuka, its waters of an opaque dull-green hue, and sour to the taste (whence its name, Roto-*"Kawa"*); but its other natural peculiarities repay the traveller for the want of landscape beauties, for, besides the eccentric habits of its myriads of winged inhabitants, the shores offer an interesting study, being covered in most places with either sulphur or crystallized alum, the latter encrusting great quantities of the driftwood and pebbles, while most of the phenomena to be found in the country, resulting from the effect of subterranean heat on minerals and on water, find some representation on the shores of the lake.

We ascended the right bank of the river for two or three miles, till, finding that Moe had for some reason lagged behind and out of sight, we tethered our horses where they could get a feed off the poor native grass, and crawled up to the brink of the cliff, where we lay, enjoying the glorious view, until it should seem good unto Moe to make his appearance.

With such a panorama spread before us, little did we grudge delay, for nowhere could the pleasures of idleness *in excelsis* be more luxuriously enjoyed. The day was warm and bright, and the clear summer air rendered every part of the landscape brilliant and distinct; the broad rolling plain vanishing into the horizon; the heaving woodlands and distant mountains; the winding stream with its hissing, foaming rapids leaping over the rocky ledges; and farther yet, the Te Huka Falls, the roar of whose waters made itself heard in the distance like thunder amongst the hills while directly beneath us the whole body of the river flowed deep in its cliff-bound bed calmly, intensely, gloriously blue. We had not lain here long before another object more interesting to men in our situation than even the most beautiful scenery diverted our attention from the landscape; it was Moe, followed by his dog, and dragging after him some dark and ponderous body: a few minutes made it clear that they had killed a wild hog, and thoughts of the savoury stew made our mouths water: so hurrah for that porker fat! Hurrah for the broil so rare!

We crossed the river in a canoe far below the falls, and reached home by nightfall.

January 22nd. — Brenchley, Mair, and I, with Poihipi and a wiry young native named Hori, this day made the ascent of Mount Tauhara; we being, at all events, the first white men who have ever done so.

We started early, rode as far as we could, and. then left our horses tethered by a spring in the mountain side. It appeared to Brenchley and myself, when we were examining the mountain a few days before from Hiruharama (Jerusalem), that it could be scaled most easily by following a wavy ridge which leads up the south-eastern side of the mountain, but Poihipi decided on ascending by a spur on the flank which faces the Waikato.

Tauhara is an extinct volcano, and the northern and southern walls of its now silent crater have fallen in. The lower part of the

71

mountain as well as the whole of the interior of the crater are thickly wooded, and the difficulty of the ascent consisted not so much in the steepness of the rocks as in the network of supplejack and other creepers, which, interlacing the trees in all directions, required the frequent use of the tomahawk or bowie-knife.

The natives expected to find water somewhere up the mountain, but in this we were disappointed, and found nothing wherewith to moisten our parched throats till we returned to the spring where we had left our steeds. We reached the summit about 2 p.m., and of course enjoyed a magnificent view, embracing a large portion of the course of the Waikato, diminishing in the distance to a mere thread of silver and blue; the whole of Lake Taupō and the Kaimanawha ranges; the broad Kaingaroa plain, stretching away eastward to the sea, and looking terribly barren and thirsty, though in fact watered by many rivers; the hills which surround Rotorua and the rest of the hot lake district; and the comparatively fertile province of Napier, with its rich and mellow-tinted woods.

After having rested awhile, and taken a bird's eye-view sketch of the surrounding country, together with the compass-bearings of most of the principal mountains of the northern island, we returned in our own footsteps; our downward path being facilitated by the use we had made of our knives in the morning, and reached the foot of the mountain by nightfall.

We made the result of our day's work known to the surrounding country by setting fire to the fern and bush near the top of the mountain, which burnt brilliantly for three days and nights, and on returning to our *whare* further celebrated the occasion by devouring a pot of beef which we had reserved till now — the solitary remnant of the provisions we had brought with us.

A comet which has been visible for several nights past is the object of no little speculation amongst our Maori friends. From this part of the country it appears to hang directly over Taranaki, the hotbed of Kingism and rebellion, and its presence is interpreted by the Maories in very different modes, according to their own proclivities. Thus, while the Kingites triumphantly point to the protecting finger of God indicating the new Zion of His chosen people, the Queenites retort that it is the avenging sword of the angel Gabriel hanging over the devoted heads of the misguided men who have presumed to use His name in blasphemy of the Christian religion.

Meanwhile the suggestion which we ventured to hazard to the effect that the self-same comet, seen from Taranaki, would appear to be far away over the sea, is treated as downright heresy.

Tonight, the comet seemed on setting to fall into the very centre of Tongariro's historic crater — most celebrated in Maori traditions — the burial-place of many a generation of Taupō chiefs.

It was a pretty as well as a curious sight, and we joined the little group of Maories who stood without the *whares* watching the comet's trail of light slowly sinking into the clouds of smoke that curled out of the sombre crater, and asking each other with bated breath what meaning should be attached to these new signs in the heavens. It was no use asking the Pakehas, for it is well known that white men are pitifully ignorant of the meaning of omens.

January 25th. — Three weeks have we now spent by the shores of Taupō, and there is nothing to indicate that three months will find us any opportunities for pursuing our journey, and getting back to Auckland, less risky than those before us at present. We have already considerably exceeded the limit of time within which I individually had promised, if possible, to return to my duty afloat; and reports now reach us almost daily of hostilities already commenced on the plain of the Waikato, and of the blue-jackets having landed — reports whose accuracy we have no means of testing, but still sufficiently probable to form additional motives for me to make a move from here at all hazards. Te Heu-heu has returned to Pukawa, but in a spirit of even greater hostility than before he is said to be actively engaged in making converts to the new fanaticism, and raising recruits for the Maori king, and moreover flatly refuses to have anything to do with us. Under these circumstances, to visit him, or attempt to pass under his "mana" through the hostile country which lies between Taupō and our military posts on the route to Auckland, *viā* the Waikato — the old mail-track, or to forward to him the Governor's letter, would be only to expose both its writer and ourselves to useless insult. Now this man, Te Heu-heu, is the one in whom, of all the hostile chiefs, His Excellency placed the greatest confidence, and it is clear that all hopes of returning openly by the direct route are now at an end. There are two other routes: the one by which we came, returning to Tauranga, where we should have to wait an indefinite time for a passage to Auckland by sea that is, supposing that we could now retrace our footsteps, which is doubtful, seeing that two Kingites have recently arrived at Rotorua, which lies on the road to Tauranga, announcing themselves as the avant-couriers of William Thompson, who they say is quickly following with from 400 to 600 men, to clear the way for the Ngatiporos to join the tribes opposed to us on the Waikato; and this the loyal Arawas are determined to resist. Should there be any truth in this story we should probably find the road to Tauranga closed, for other men say that any Pakehas found on their territory will be made the first sacrifice to their new *"karakia,"* and that any Queenite Maories found with them will meet with the same fate.

Lastly, there is the road to Napier, a seaport on the south-eastern coast of the island, whence we could return by sea to Auckland.

But Poihipi will not hear of our going by this route, as nearly the whole of the four days' journey would lie through settlements inhabited by men who are determined Kingites, though not yet supposed to have had their heads turned by the Pai Marire fanaticism and it is on this road that there is too much reason to fear that the three men have come to grief who went to Napier to get provisions for us; for though they ought to have been with us again a fortnight ago, they have not been heard of since their departure.

Moreover, Poihipi has learnt that war parties from three hostile tribes, the Ngatiporos, Ngatikahungunus, and Uriweras on their way to join the Waikatos, are already slowly travelling along this road.

Under these circumstances, I decided to endeavour to cut through the hostile country, and reach one of our outposts in the plain of the Waikato — a distance of about 80 or 90 miles — by riding hard by night and lying close in the bush by day. But for this a guide will of course be necessary, and herein lay the first difficulty.

My two companions, being masters of their own time and movements, have no object in incurring any special risk for the sake of returning, and therefore remain here till some tidings are received of Hohepa and his two companions, showing that the Napier road is practicable, or till some better opportunity presents itself.

I have hitherto utterly failed in my endeavours to persuade any of the natives of this place to act as guide, though I commenced with upset offers of £10, a large sum for a Maori, and which they knew would have been increased had any of them been willing to strike a bargain with me; but they said that not a man of them would go for a hundred. My good friend Poihipi tries to dissuade me from going, saying that the Governor confided the safe conduct of the whole party to his charge; but the force of his arguments is somewhat weakened by his utter inability to understand what possible difference a month or two could make to me — the value of time is one of the last things that a savage race can learn.

Rode over alone to Oruanui today to see if I could there find a native game to go through with me. There is no time to lose, for day by day the increasing spread of the Hau-hau doctrines renders all prospects of travelling through the territory or among its votaries more and more hopeless.

We had heard that a party of these fanatics were already on their way hither, but it was not known how far off they might be; however, I saw nothing of them, though I kept a precious sharp look-out ahead all the way.

At Oruanui, Dr. Hooper and a Pakeha-Maori named Frank, who lives near him, accompanied me to the *pah* to endeavour to get a guide. Frank is a first cousin by marriage of Rewi, the principal fighting chief of the Maories.

Perenara, lately our host at Waihaha, had just arrived from Te Papa with the latest news of the great meeting of Kingites. His account confirmed what we had already heard, *viz.* that the Kingites to a man are bent on war, and at present purpose making a simultaneous attack on as many of our posts on the Waikato as possible.

It appears that Rewi counselled the immediate execution of this plan, but the King, Potatau II. (Matutaera), or rather those whose puppet he is, decided on waiting for a few weeks or a month, till all the Kingites shall have joined the new faith. And for this purpose, large bands of propagandists have been dispatched in various directions. One of these bands of fanatics is now on its way hither to convert the tribes on the east coast; and the question as to the expediency or possibility of preventing them from passing through the loyal districts is the subject of no little anxiety to the inhabitants of this *pah*.

The canoes at the crossing of the Waikato above our posts have been destroyed; and it is reported that the Prophet, whoever that mystical personage may be (*not* Te Ua), has given orders that all Pakehas and Queenite Maories are to be killed "at sight." And the Pai Marire worshipping-pole has been raised in every *pah* and *kainga* lying between this and the British lines — rather a dark look-out ahead! Here, as at Tapuae-haruru, I found the natives very unwilling to trust themselves anywhere within reach of the professors of this new and sanguinary creed, which seems to have thoroughly "funked" even those who have no belief in it. After two or three hours of fruitless negotiations I returned to Frank's *whare,* weary and dispirited at my failure, and the prospect of being detained an indefinite time, which, judging from the rapidity with which the fanaticism is even now closing around us, might result in our having to remain cooped up at one of these friendly *pahs* till the war itself was over.

January 26th. — Late last evening Frank's wife came in from the *pah* with the good news that she had succeeded in procuring a guide for me, a good-looking, well-dressed young fellow, named Hemipo, with the great advantage of possessing by far the best horses in the country-side. He is himself a stanch Queenite, and trustworthy, though the son of an influential Kingite chief — old Ngaperi, the same that we chanced to meet after leaving Punu on our way to Oruanui and Taupō. Hemipo provides me with a capital horse, and we soon came to terms about payment.

All details having been arranged at an intolerably long korero at the *pah*, I returned to Dr. Hooper's *whare*, where I soon was sleeping soundly on a heap of fern, after the usual meal of potatoes, salt, and tea. About ten o'clock, whilst at supper, we were startled by a succession of piercing screams, evidently the voice of some woman in the *pah*. It turned out to be Takiara, a Maori clairvoyant, who, when these fits seize her, runs away into the forest, as she did last night, and there details to those who follow her the events which she fancies or pretends to see going on at the seat of war, and other distant parts of the country. When not under the influence of this nonsense she is not an unpleasing-looking woman, but dreadfully "strong-minded," and leads her husband a life of it with a vengeance.

Until recently she was *chef de cuisine* and quarter-master-general on our private staff, till one day she roused all the dormant jealousy of her female helpmates by reporting us to have said that she alone knew how to cook and dish np in true Pakeha fashion.

The Maories as a race are not addicted to "Billings-gate," and a slighting gesture, or such trifling words as these, have frequently caused a fierce war between two powerful tribes, and will always produce a deeper and more lasting effect than would result from a torrent of abuse amongst the lower classes of other nations.

The case in point was the only one in which it has happened to me to witness any really angry quarrel amongst the natives, during the whole time we have been with them. As it was, the wordy war waged fiercely between the weaker vessels, till a few words from Mr. Grace, who happened to be present (it was the day after he had followed us to Taupō), stilled the tempest of their wrath but the fair Takiara had to leave the settlement on finding that her companions had detected the false note she had played on her own trumpet.

Returned to Tapuae-haruru in company with Hemipo this morning to pack what few traps I have with me, which, together with my watch and journal, Brenchley takes charge of till we meet again in Auckland.

Poihipi, who is very jealous at my having secured a guide from his rival Hohepa's place, expatiates on the dangers of the direct route which I have chosen, and now talks of sending Brenchley on to Napier after all, with some of his own tribe. But I hardly believe that he will do this, some excuse being found for delay at the last moment; and if Brenchley should get into a scrape, Poihipi has not a horse which could carry him out of it, or stand the fatigue of a forced march, such as would be necessary should the natives on the road to Napier prove as hostile as they are reported to be.

We — Hemipo and I — leave in a few hours for Oruanui, and push on the next morning for Auckland. We propose passing rapidly, but openly through the first hostile settlement — Tataroa — where no danger is anticipated, the men being all away at the seat of war, and the place only inhabited by a few old women and children; we then cross the Waikato at a place called Waimahana (warm waters), the residence of some Kingite relations of Hemipo's; but thenceforward till we reach one of our own outposts, we shall have to make the best of our way by night, hiding by day in the thickest part of the bush, or in some well-sheltered gully.

Hemipo takes charge of the only provisions that we carry with us — a bag of unleavened biscuits, baked tonight by Frank, who has luckily discovered a native possessing a long-hoarded store of a few pounds of flour. As to meat, there is none to be had for love or money, and potatoes would be too bulky and heavy in proportion to their nutritive qualities to be borne by horses who must be ready at a moment's notice to gallop for their riders' lives;

neither should we dare to light a fire on our journey, whether for cooking food or making tea. And besides the consideration of its unavoidable necessity, a bread-and-water diet for three or four days is but the shade of a hardship, even had not the monotonous fare of potatoes and sugarless tea on which we have been living for the last few weeks accustomed us to regard our meals merely as part of the necessary routine of the day, like sleeping and dressing, or at most as giving a greater zest for the enjoyment of the luxury of the pipe which followed.

We both ride as light as possible, I, for instance, having nothing but my blanket, brace of revolvers, a long bowie, and a waterproof sheet. Our route, after crossing the Waikato the first time (we must do so twice), will depend a good deal on what Hemipo learns from his relatives at Waimahana: we shall either push on for the crossing near Mangore, avoiding Waiotu and Whakamaru (very hostile settlements) by a circuit, swim the Waikato at the tails of our horses on the third night, make a dash through Aratitaha at full gallop under cover of the darkness, and reach our redoubt at Kihi-kihi in the morning; or cutting into the longer but less frequented Tokoroa road, after crossing the river the first time at Waimahana, avoid all settlements by riding through the bush or fern land, which is there comparatively level and open, and, if all goes well, swim the Waikato below Maungatautari at daybreak on the third morning; we should then be within a short distance of our redoubt at Cambridge, as it is now called, where we should find ourselves within twenty-four hours of Auckland, if we have the luck to catch a steamer; if not, it is only a matter of two or three days' riding. But at Maungatautari the river is broad and the stream runs fast, with countless thirsty whirlpools; and many a fine fellow, in attempting to cross it, has found a grave beneath its waters.

January 27th. — Left Oruanui this morning with Hemipo, amidst many expressions of good-will and hopes for our safety from our late hosts and the natives in the *pah*; and the fresh morning breeze seemed full of life and hope, as we cantered over the swelling plains and woodlands. I had been somewhat concerned to learn, just before leaving, that my guide has a failing common amongst even the best of Maori warriors — a childish fear of darkness and solitude — a misfortune that might easily prove very mischievous in an expedition like the present. Though few in numbers, the Maories are an eminently sociable and gregarious race. They are never found living alone; they could not stand the isolation which constitutes the life of thousands of white squatters, shepherds, and trappers; their superstitious fears, barely scotched — not killed — by the teaching of the missionaries, would people each overhanging rock or lonely cave with some fresh horror to be feared, some malignant spirit of evil.

Until we left the settlement I had been assured that my guide could neither speak nor understand a single word of English, and all our communications previous to starting were carried on through Hooper or Frank; but as soon as we found ourselves alone in the bush he plucked up courage, and showed that he had picked up a certain number of English words and even sentences, which, together with a few words of Maori which I had learnt during our journey, enabled us to understand each other on most necessary subjects. The process of exchanging ideas on things in general was however too laborious to tempt us into much conversation, and the stillness of surrounding nature impressed me to a greater degree than it ever had before.

The woods we traversed were not nearly so grand or gloomy as in many other parts which we had visited, but there is a silence peculiar to the New Zealand forest which must be felt to be understood. I cannot call to mind any tropical forests which excel those of New Zealand in beauty, for here there is magnificent timber, without the jungle of undergrowth which obstructs the view in more torrid climes.

Brilliant parasites and creepers hang from the uppermost boughs of the loftiest trees, straight as cathedral bell-ropes, or, winding from stem to stem with fantastic curves, interlace distant trees, in the very extravagance of their luxuriant beauty. The lofty Tótara, and the Rimu with its delicate and gently weeping foliage, and the shade-loving tree fern, the most graceful of all forest trees. Wild flowers are few and rare, but the ferns are more numerous and varied than in any other country.

It is the absence of all living things which renders the silence and solitude of the woods so oppressive. Occasionally a pair of Kaka parrots may be seen wheeling high above the hill tops with harsh discordant cries, or the melancholy note of the great New Zealand pigeon comes booming through the woods; but except at early morning the traveller may often wander for hours, I had almost said for days together, through the gloom of these woods where the sun's rays can scarcely penetrate, and the breeze passing over the tree-tops through the uppermost whispering boughs may be seen and heard, but cannot be felt. Not a sparrow — not a mouse to be seen it seems; the silence of death, or more properly the stillness of the yet unborn; the gigantic Moa and one or two other extinct species of birds which, even in historic times had their home in New Zealand, used to shun the gloomy shades of the forest and cleave to the flat marshy lands.

CHAPTER V.

Ihaka's mission — A dangerous meeting — Tataroa — Captured by the Kingites — Pai Marire worship — Ihaka's narrative — Impossibility of escape — Debate on the prisoner's fate — Hemipos defence — Appearance of Ahumai — Release and alarm of treachery — A ride for life — Reach the friendly *pah* of Oruanui — Arrival and report of Ihaka — Rejoin Messrs. Mair and Brenchley — Pai Marire tenets — Mr. Mair's escape — Mr. Völkner's murder and escape of Mr. Grace — Murder of Mr. Fulloon — Mr. Mair s expedition against the murderers — Capture of Teko *pah*.

It was known before we started that a large party of Pai Marire fanatics, dispatched from the great meeting of Kingites which has just been held, were to pass this way on their road to spread their new faith amongst the tribes lying between Taupō and the south-eastern coast. The loyal natives of Oruanui accordingly sent them word by letter, that if they purposed endeavouring to proselytize the Queenites, or if they were journeying with hostile intentions against either loyal Maories or white men, they could not be permitted to pass that way. The bearer of this letter was a "sergeant of police," named Ihaka.

(In nearly all the loyal tribes there are a certain number of natives receiving a small stipend in the Government service, the chief being styled "Assessor," or "Native Magistrate," and having under his orders a proportion of Sergeants and privates of police.)

He had left the *pah* long before daybreak, and had thus a good start of us. We were to meet this man on his way back, and learn from him what amount of danger we should be likely to incur at the hands of these men, who were about to enter the territory of our allies, and what would be our best route to avoid them.

No danger whatever to Ihaka himself was apprehended by those at the *pah*, his person being rendered sacred in his character of herald or ambassador by Maori laws and customs immemorial.

The day wore on, and I was beginning to think the non-appearance of Ihaka rather suspicious, when suddenly Hemipo, pointing to some little wreaths of smoke curling up from some freshly-lighted fires just within the bush, which was then several hundred yards from our road, exclaimed that there were a quantity of bad Kingite Maories; and he was right, for in another instant we discerned many figures moving about amongst the trunks of trees, around their cooking fires. But we spurred on our horses, and passed them safely, and apparently unobserved. We concluded that this was the party of propagandists against whom we had been warned, who had turned off the path to cook their mid-day meal; and we congratulated ourselves on having kept clear of them so easily.

Unfortunately for us, they were only the advanced guard.

Soon afterwards a very sharp turning in the road brought us opposite the village of Tataroa. It could hardly be called a *pah*, there being no stockade or continuous earthworks, but it could easily be turned into one, being built on the crest of a small hill or spur.

We met a Maori in the path, leading his horse to water, and he greeted us with the Pai Marire salutation, which we had often heard lately. He stopped in front of each of us in turn, and pronounced some formula, which apparently consisted in repeating the words "Pai Marire" and some other gibberish as rapidly as possible, accompanied by a succession of gestures, commencing like the Roman Catholic sign of the cross, and ending like a military salute. We listened in silence, with difficulty repressing a smile at the somewhat grotesque ceremony, and replied with the usual "Tena-koe" and shaking of hands. We could see two men, of whom Ihaka was one, standing on the edge of the embankment.

To pass, or attempt to pass a settlement openly, without stopping to exchange greetings, smoke a pipe, or partake of food, would have been a great breach of etiquette, sufficient in itself to draw down on the perpetrators very unpleasant attentions from the inhabitants but perceiving a red flag (the emblem of war) flying from a staff in the midst of the village, I suggested caution to Hemipo. He replied that as Ihaka was there, it would be sure to be all safe, and we cantered up the hill, over the crest or opening in the embankment, into the *pah*.

Instead of seeing only three or four old women and children, as we had been led to expect, we found ourselves in the presence of about 150 armed men, assembled in the open space in the midst of the *whares*; and a more villainous-looking crew I have never set eyes on in New Zealand.

Many of them wore English arms and accoutrements which had fallen into their hands during the war — marines' caps, men-of-war's-mens frocks and swords, and soldiers' rifles, water-bottles, &c., double-barrelled guns, and tomahawks.

Instead of the chorus of "Naumai!" and other cries of welcome which usually greet the traveller's ear on arriving at a Maori *pah*, a single voice bade us "Haere mai" (come hither) and dismount, and a single glance round the lowering countenances before us and the anxious expression on the face of my guide were sufficient to show that we had indeed fallen in evil case.

I was very unwilling to unsaddle my horse as Hemipo was doing, but finding that a Kingite had already approached and cast off my girth, I complied with what I could not prevent. Luckily, however, I had succeeded, when we first dismounted, in passing over unobserved to Hemipo one of my revolvers, which he adroitly concealed under his coat; the other was already safe out of sight in my pocket.

While this was going on, an excited discussion took place amongst a knot of Kingites; and I had hardly got my saddle off when one of them came striding towards me, followed by two or three others with guns in their hands. He was armed with one of our cutlass-hilted naval sword-bayonets, which he flourished in a decidedly unpleasant manner. I learnt afterwards that he owned to his intention of killing the Pakeha there and then.

There was mischief in his every look and gesture, and I was in the very act of drawing my revolver from its hiding-place, to sell my life as dearly as possible, when, while the would-be murderers were yet some three paces from us, a big ugly-looking fellow sprung forward and drove them back into the crowd. He then called out something in a very powerful voice — the whole assembly were marshalled into two sides of a square, of which the flagstaff was the centre, and forthwith commenced the Pai Marire "Karakia" (worship). I was much surprised at their commencing these rites immediately after my arrival, having heard that no white man had yet been permitted to witness them; but I was not then aware that they were being performed solely on my own account. The man who had just come to my assistance was named Te Aokatoa (which means "All the World"), a great burly ruffian, very much tattooed — a fellow who would have made the fortune of any country manager as the melodramatic villain. He was the principal or high priest present, and therefore M.C. of their religious antics. He no more wanted to save my life than did any of his comrades, and was afterwards one of the most violent against me; but he had no notion of permitting so important an event as the sacrifice of the first Pakeha to be consummated except under his direct auspices, and in a manner which should contribute to his own importance and influence over his dupes.

He therefore announced, when he stopped Karouria and his companions who wanted to kill me straight off, that there must first be a great "Karakia," or ceremony of worship, to induce the Great Atua (spirit) to inspire them rightly as to what was to be done with the Pakeha. He, Te Aokatoa, having long ago made up his own mind on the subject in a manner which would have saved anyone the trouble of reading these lines.

I must now go back a little, to give Ihaka's version of the circumstances which prevented him from giving us warning of our danger. He says that, on reaching Tataroa in the forenoon, he found that the fanatics whom he had been sent to meet had only just arrived and purposed stopping until the evening; that they had heard that I was coming, in spite of the precautions which were taken at Oruanui to prevent its being known in improper quarters; and, connecting my advent with that of Ihaka, they violently upbraided him for "bringing a Pakeha among them, to spy out their doings;" that one of them kept threatening him with a club, and that, being in fear of his life, he could not get away to return and give us warning; but that later a chief named Paora Toki made a speech recommending them not to molest me, on the grounds of not offending the people whose country they wished to pass through. He had scarcely finished speaking, when the cry was raised that the Pakeha was in sight, and immediately afterwards we rode into the *pah*.

There was no attempt to rob or search us, either because that ceremony was deferred until after the Karakia and the meeting, which was to follow, should have decided as to our disposal, or because there was nothing in our appearance, or the rough clothes we wore, to tempt their cupidity: we were not likely-looking characters to have much money about us, and I need hardly say that our carrying arms was never suspected — had they had the least inkling of this *our* fate would have been sealed, and that of a few of their number as well. But this part of our little secret was safe enough so long as it was not in danger of discovery by other means than eyesight; for no one would be likely to suspect a Maori of having a revolver, and the other one hung ready to hand, and full-cocked, from two loops within my inner breast-pocket, so contrived that, though the jacket itself remained ostentatiously thrown open, no one could detect that it contained anything so solid.

Escape was, from the moment we entered the *kainga*, utterly out of the question: before we could have got twenty yards we should have been riddled. Hemipo and I were seated on some wood, with our backs to a *whare*, forming as it were the third side of the square, under charge of a sentry with a sword, and another with a gun, with Ihaka close to us. The "Prophet's staff," which had been set up in the middle of the open space, was a stout spar, some 30 feet high, from which floated first the *"Riki,"* or war-flag, a long red pendant with a white cross. Beneath it, a large handsome flag, very carefully made — black, with a white cross next the staff, and a blue fly, the whole surrounded by a narrow scarlet border; and beneath that again another red pendant, much broader than the upper one, with a St. Andrew's cross and some other design which I forget. The priest stood near the staff, which was further "supported," as they say in Heraldry, by three little children who stood with their backs against it, while two men with drawn cutlasses walked up and down the inner sides of the square to prevent anyone approaching too close to the sacred staff, or the high priest, whilst he was under the influence of divine inspiration.

As soon as silence and order were established, Te Aokatoa commenced gabbling away at a tremendous rate, varying the performance with occasional yells he then being supposed to be the favoured mouthpiece of the Deity, and to have the gift of divers tongues. Thus, I was told at one time that he was speaking English, at another French, and then Hebrew — I need hardly say that it was all gibberish. At intervals, he would stop to make obeisance to the staff and to the four points of the compass, with the usual Pai Marire salutation, but accompanied by genuflexions. When he had apparently come to the end of his wind and his Hebrew, he paused a little to take breath, and then chanted a hymn in Maori, followed by something which appeared to imitate the style of our Litany, to which the people gave responses in their own language.

Then, at a signal from the priest, the whole of the assembled tribes (there were delegates from many) sprang to their feet, men, women, and children, and having formed round the flagstaff in a circular column, eight or ten deep, began slowly marching round the staff, pointing to the skies above them with swords or guns or spears, and chanting the responses after the priest in excellent time and powerful voices. It was the first time that I had heard Maories singing in tune. It appeared to resemble some of our own church music, from whence it doubtless took its source, though with many wild variations.

The striking character of the surrounding scenery — the scarlet, black, and blue of the flags, with their white crosses waving forth in strong relief against the dark woods beyond, — the varied and many-coloured drosses — the throng of eager upturned faces, fervent with fanaticism — little children, young girls, swarthy warriors, with upraised hands and weapons pointing heavenward — and the swelling chorus rising through the stillness of the primeval forest — all combined to produce a very remarkable effect.

This was the end of the *"Karakia;"* and after they had all made obeisance to the staff as described above, the congregation resolved itself into a *"Runanga"* to decide on my fate.

Of the first two speakers who addressed the meeting, the first urged the immediate execution of myself, the second that of my guide as well; both on grounds furnished by their fanaticism, and the presumption that I was a spy; and after each had concluded, as well as when they paused — for they spoke slowly and deliberately — the bulk of their hearers signified their approval with cries of "Let the pig be stuck!" "Let the calf *(te kuao)* be killed!"

Then uprose Hemipo and addressed the Runanga on my behalf and his own. He had been well primed by the Pakeha-Maori Frank before starting with some good stiff lies. I had thought it better to trust to their knowledge of their countryman's character for the concoction of a plausible account of myself, which should satisfy any Kingites whom by ill-luck we might chance to meet with, than to any story which I could evolve from my own comparative ignorance of the people whose lands we wanted to traverse, by fair means or by foul. He accordingly explained to his audience that I was a civilian Pakeha, who had never had anything to do with either army or navy, or heen connected in any way with the war; that I had only recently come out in a merchant vessel for my own pleasure to see the country; that I was going to return to England almost immediately, and that my only reason for wishing to pass through their territory was to avoid missing my passage in the ship, which was to sail next week, &c., &c.; and then a good deal more on his own account, addressing himself more particularly to the Ngāti Raukawa present, a tribe to which his father, old Ngaperi, is related.

But though his own life was nearly as much at stake as mine, I could not help admiring the cool, almost careless way in which he spoke, playing with his riding-whip, as though he were speaking to his own people at home; behaving, in fact, as became a *"rangatira"* in difficulties.

After Hemipo had finished, Te Aokatoa rose, and advocated my death in a very violent speech of a quarter of an hour's duration. "How dares he," said he; "how dares he come amongst us while our blood is still flowing?" (This was rather a strained metaphor, for it is now many months since last our people tapped their claret — they must have a large supply!)

"Mate rawa! Mate rawa! — let him die! let him die!"

Hemipo or Ihaka translated to me at intervals what the various speakers said, Ihaka being able to speak quite enough English for the purpose; but no knowledge of the language was necessary to distinguish the excited words of the savages who wanted my life from the calm delivery of those who were for letting me go in peace.

I had with me His Excellency's letter to Te Heu-heu, which I had brought to be used as a last resource, in case of our falling in with any of his tribe but the animus displayed against the Governor by more than one of the speakers was so bitter, that any allusion to him, or the production of his letter, would only have left us in worse case than before.

The speakers sometimes addressed me personally, *'E Pakeha!'* (stranger!), but more often spoke of or at me by a term of abuse. I could, of course, take no part in the discussion, in which my ignorance of the language would only have exposed me to ridicule; so I had nothing for it but to light my pipe, and endeavour to look as if I thought that the bare idea of their killing such a swell as the late honoured guest of the Arawas was really too preposterous to be entertained for a moment.

This, however, was not quite so easy as it may seem, for various small boys would come and squat themselves right in front of me, grinning in a way which plainly showed what sport they expected to have with the Pakeha; and at one period of the debate, so confident were the bloody-minded ones of carrying their point, that they went into the *whares* for their guns, and loaded them.

The next speaker of any note was Karouria, and he not only recommended that I should be killed, but offered in the most handsome manner to do the job himself, emphasizing his remarks by sundry little preliminary flourishes of the aforesaid cutlass so close to my face as to be exceedingly disagreeable.

It was evident from the tenor of his speech and that of others that they expected the immolation of the Pakeha to be literally as simple a matter as the killing of a calf. But Hemipo was evidently game to the backbone, and ready for action; and it was comforting to think that, by running amuck in the crowd which surrounded us, the moment death should be decided on, we could, having the advantage of surprise with eleven barrels and the bowie-knife, send a good many of the vagabonds to precede us to the world of shades. Hemipo had stipulated before starting that he should be allowed the use of one of my revolvers in the event of any fighting being imminent, and had been duly instructed in its use. I learnt afterwards that the display of loading guns was mere wanton braggadocio, or at most but a precaution in case either of us should try to bolt, and that the tomahawk would have been the instrument. The man who was to have used it stood close at my left side during the latter part of the Runanga; a tall man, with no hair on his face, and rather a humorous expression of countenance he wore his blanket like most Maories, toga fashion, and twitched it at intervals as if to keep his right arm clear and free, for he carried a small bone-handled tomahawk, which he took small pains to conceal.

But he was so close that I could easily have shot him through the side of my coat before he could have swung his arm, for, by smoking with folded arms, I could keep my finger close to the trigger without exciting suspicion.

At the time when things looked blackest — when the chances of seeing the sun go down that evening seemed small indeed, — a young woman left her place amongst the Kingites, walked slowly across the open space, and sat down by my feet. This was Ahumai, the same whose three bayonet and shot wounds, inflicted by British troops at Ōrākau, were shown to us at Waihaha. My acquaintance with her had been of the very slightest, and she had no motive for the demonstration she made in my favour other than a kindly wish to save the life of a comparative stranger. We learnt afterwards that she did us no small service, both at this critical time and while they were expecting our arrival. She is, as I have said before, a woman possessing no small influence with her associates of both sexes, being rather feared by the one and liked by the other — &, good-looking, self-willed sort of Amazon. Her husband was killed at the same place where she was wounded. It so happened that Mair, who was present, was desired to communicate with the garrison of the *pah*, for which purpose he went to the end of the sap, which was then close to the native entrenchment, and having called for a cessation of firing, stood up on a little ledge or banquette within the sap, and held a korero with the besieged. But he had scarcely finished the ultimatum which he had to deliver, when one of the men within the *pah* fired at him. Simultaneously with the shot, the loose soil of the ledge he stood on gave way, and he disappeared into the sap. The Maories concluded that he had been killed, and vehemently condemned the treachery of the man who had fired. This was Ahumai's husband; he was killed a few hours afterwards, and in the words of his fair widow, when relating the circumstance to us at Waihaha, "served him right."

From this time forward our prospects began to mend, and in spite of a hostile speech from an influential old savage, named Paku, the majority of the speakers were of opinion that it would be bad policy to risk provoking an attack from the Arawas, whose territory they wanted to pass through unmolested, by murdering their late guest. But even those best disposed towards us said that had they supposed me to have had any connection with the fighting tribe of Pakehas, or had we met them on the march, we should have been settled with, without any Runanga at all. We were aware of the extra danger of meeting them on the march, and would have taken good care to give them a wide berth. They also said that had not Hemipo been the son of a chief related to the Ngāti Raukawa, he would have suffered the same fate.

One chief only was in favour of letting us proceed on our journey.

At last we were told that we might go, returning by the way we came. Finding ourselves at liberty, we walked down the slope to saddle our horses; avoiding, as well as we could, all appearance of hurry, which might have been likely to provoke an attack, in the same way that snatching one's hand away from a parrot induces it to bite.

But we were not yet at the end of our difficulties, for before we had finished saddling, an Uriwera native came running down from the *pah*, and called Hemipo on one side. This was to me the most unpleasant moment of all, for I made sure that he was called aside to allow the natives to shoot me comfortably from the *pah* above, not fifty yards distant. To have been finished after a good scrimmage, and having emptied our pistols into the crowd (who could hardly have used firearms against us without shooting one another), would have been bad enough; but to be shot here like a rabbit, and get no change for the coin of life would have been dismal indeed.

Luckily, I was wrong: the man had called Hemipo out of sight of the *pah* to warn him that a reaction was taking place among the Kingites, and that a strong party were still bent on our destruction. Hemipo exclaimed, in the wonderful jargon — the medium of communication between us, — each apparently cherishing the pleasing illusion that he was speaking the language of the other, "Nga kakino Maori Kingi wantee makee kiri koe!" *i.e.* The blackguard Maori Kingites want to kill you!"

No second hint was needed — we sprang into our saddles and rode for our lives; for whilst the Uriwera was speaking to Hemipo, I had observed four or five vagabonds leaving the *pah* in the same direction; and from the sneaking way that they were sloping along, in a stooping posture, it was plain that they were after mischief. The fern and bush were thick, so there were probably more whom I could not see. They were doubtless making for a place which commanded the road, and whence, had they got there before us, they would have had some very pretty shooting. As it was, we preceded them, and, avoiding the place where we had seen the Kingites camping in the bush that morning, scarcely drew rein till we had placed some eight or ten miles between ourselves and the enemy. Then perceiving no signs of a pursuit, though we had left some twenty or thirty horses tethered round Tataroa, and being close to friendly territory, we planted ourselves and horses at the bottom of a gully, well out of sight, and regaled ourselves with biscuit and watercress, which we found growing in profusion.

We reached the friendly *pah* of Oruanui, between 9 and 10 p.m., without further adventure.

The writer was the first white man who fell into the hands of these fanatics. The second was a most excellent missionary — him they hanged, and ate his eyes and brains.

January 28th. — The history of our adventure, detailed and retailed by Hemipo again and again, caused no little excitement at the *pah*, and the chiefs large *whare* was crowded with Maories who sat round the fire far into the night, discussing the conduct of the fanatics and the kindred question as to the mode in which they should be received on passing through Oruanui.

Ihaka made his appearance some hours after our return, bearing the written answer from the Hau-haus to the demands of the Queenites. In this document, they promised they would not endeavour to proselytize any of the inhabitants of the loyal districts, and asserted that, far from intending to attack the Queenites, or the white settlers of Napier or elsewhere, they only wished to carry peaceably their revelations of the new faith to the Kingite tribes southward and eastward. They concluded by asking to be allowed to pass unmolested, and in a postscript pointed to the fact that the *"Runanga"* had permitted me to return safely, as an additional reason for their request (or demand, for such it was) being granted. They conveniently omitted all allusion to the attempt that was undoubtedly made to cut us off after we had started; perhaps thinking that we knew nothing of it; but there can be little doubt as to the necessity of the friendly warning which was given to Hemipo, or of the intentions of those whom I at the same time saw creeping away from the *pah* through the bush; for it is not long since a small party of Queenites, who had fallen into the clutches of similar fanatics, were permitted to depart, and then treacherously followed up and tomahawked or shot — all but one, who escaped to tell the fate of his companions.

Having been baffled on this route I proposed to Hemipo to endeavour to gain our outposts by a road which we had had under discussion before — to re-cross the Waikato at Orakei-korako, and by following a certain unfrequented track from that place, strike into the Tokoroa road, and thence on to the plain of the Waikato. But he had apparently had enough of the Hau-haus, and assured me that he had learnt from Ahumai and Ihaka that the track in question, as well as all others leading to the military posts to the northward, are carefully watched, and that there would be no chance of getting through. It would have been no use pressing the matter any further, so I concluded a fresh agreement with him to take me on to Napier instead.

Moreover, Ihaka brings word that the Hau-haus whom we met at Tataroa are followed by another band of armed fanatics, seventy-five in number, who have just arrived at Waimahana, where they remain for a day; they are of the Ngatimaniapoto (Rewi's tribe), and are bound on a similar mission.

We left again for Tapuae-haruru as soon as a fresh horse could be caught for me, the sturdy black being rather "cooked" from the effects of the previous day's gallop.

A wet morning, and bitterly cold evening. Found Mair alone. News had been received that the two natives who were sent with Hohepa to bring back the provisions are coolly amusing themselves at Napier instead of returning immediately, as they were ordered; and the road is said to be clear.

Under these circumstances Poihipi consented to Brenchley's immediate departure for Napier, and has himself accompanied him part of the way, to judge of his reception at the first two or three Kingite settlements, after which he was to leave him to pursue the rest of the journey with three natives and two pack-horses.

Before Brenchley left all the natives of the settlement assembled in front of the *whare* that we had been living in, and laid before him various presents, mostly heirlooms of the tribe. With Mair's advice he selected a handsome *"taiaha"* (a sort of spear, or sword-shaped club, of dark red wood, carved and polished, with plume of white dog's hair and small scarlet feathers, and more as a mark of the bearer's rank as chief than as a weapon), and a small eardrop of the precious green-stone, together with a photograph of Poihipi, which the worthy chief had sat for in Auckland.

Mair returns shortly to Maketū and Tauranga, with Hooper. He described to me the stir amongst the natives on hearing, late last night, of the adventure with the Hau-haus; a messenger had been dispatched from Oruanui, who arrived after most of the inhabitants had lain down for the night, but they all turned out at once, and having obtained Mair's leave to assemble the tribe at his *whare,* the Oruanui man got on his legs, and remained there for a good hour or more, treating his audience to a "full and particular account," with many embellishments. We learnt a good many additional details of the affair at Tataroa from Eruera, who had seen one of the Kingites; amongst others the correctness of my conjecture as to the tall man with the little tomahawk being the intended executioner. And in many ways the conviction of how near a thing it had been came home to me far more vividly than at the time of the occurrence.

"You wouldn't have smiled like that if this had been explained to you yesterday," said Mair, when Eruera, to show the place where the *coup de grace* would have been struck, gently laid his cold forefinger on my temple. — Possibly not.

Sunday, 29th. — Made an early start this morning, after sleeping for the last time at the old *whare,* and parted with sincere regret from my good friends at the village by the lake. I determined to make my "Sabbath day's journey" a long one, for the double purpose of overtaking Brenchley and of putting a wholesome distance between ourselves and those of the Hau-hau party who are to follow on the Napier road.

The latter, who have reverted to the observance of the Jewish Sabbath instead of the Christian Sunday, remained all yesterday at Tataroa, thereby giving us a clear day's start.

I may as well pause here for a while to glance at a few of the particulars which we learnt at the time concerning the Pai Marire religion, as well as to mention what I have heard, since writing the above last year, from those we left behind us — friends and foes. The information furnished to us bore out most of what Father Boibeaux had told us, but as the new religion has no recognized head capable of controlling its followers, its tenets and ceremonies are constantly changing.

The original germ sprang from Te Ua, a comparatively well-meaning and harmless old idiot on the west coast, who lost the very few senses that he had ever been troubled with, from vexation at the obstinacy of his tribe in refusing to comply with his exhortations in favour of peace and honesty at the time of the wreck of the 'Lord Worsely;' and it was he who initiated the peaceful greeting, "Pai Marire!" which has since become the watchword of a sanguinary fanaticism. But the leading agitators soon perceived the advantage to the war party which would accrue from the banding together of the whole Maori race in the ties of a common religion, different from that professed by the Pakeha; and while presenting their followers with a brand new religion of their own, they took care to hash up the Protestant, Roman Catholic, and Jewish creeds into such a parody on all three, as to allay any sectarian jealousy which existed among those who had previously been members of the Protestant or Romish Churches.

Some one — one can hardly help fancying that it must have been some mischievous white man — has put into their heads that the Maories are the remnant of the lost tribes of Israel; and their observance of the seventh day, their stories of recent miracles at Taranaki, and of the personal appearance of the Almighty on earth in that province, as in the days of the patriarchs, and a great deal more, are all taken from Jewish history. They told us that as soon as all the Maories, or at least all the Kingites, shall have been converted, a certain number of warriors from every tribe are to assemble at some place on the Waikato, whence, after a grand praying-match, a certain holy Seventy will be selected by Divine inspiration, and march down to the sacred river Puniu (a tributary of the Waikato), where they will perform the *"karakia"* by the banks of the stream, and forthwith the troops will be impelled to advance against them when a misty veil will descend from heaven, rendering the faithful Seventy invisible to the soldiers, who will be divided by the miraculous cloud, and cut to pieces with impunity by the remainder of the warriors. Then the Maori race shall do unto the Pakeha as the Jews did to the Gentiles, whose cities they went in to possess.

It was obvious that delusions such as these could not long survive the success of our arms, and even now (1866) the Pai Marire faith is on the ebb, and the latest reports say that on the east coast, where the mental disease broke out in the most virulent form, the natives are returning to the Christian religion, and rebuilding their churches.

Two other superstitious delusions have obtained for a while amongst the natives, in times gone by, since their first conversion to Christianity, but neither of them so dangerous, so widespread, or so lasting as the present. Curiously enough, the prophet or leader of the last fanaticism, who foretold a millennium, and season of miraculous abundance of food and good things of all sorts, so close at hand and so bountiful that it was both useless and impious to go on planting or rearing stock, himself died of starvation in the woods whilst on a short journey.

The Queenites of Taupō and Oruanui decided to let the Hauhaus pass in peace, for various reasons: the principal of which was that they could not stop them. They reconciled their loyalty to the Queen and aversion to the fanatics with the duty and custom immemorial of showing hospitality to all strangers journeying through their land in any other than hostile array, by placing raw food with fuel for cooking, in heaps outside the settlements, while they themselves remained within the *whares* with their arms in their hands. At Oruanui, finding how short-handed were the Queenites, the Hau-haus became very bumptious, and having raised their staff, went through their mummeries before the faces of the inmates of the *pah*. They pushed on to Taupō sooner than was expected, and Mair nearly came to grief in consequence. It appears that the vagabonds wanted to get hold of him, because they believed that it was he who had guided the troops to Ōrākau, at which place he acted as interpreter. He was on his way to the *pah* at Oruanui, but luckily turned off the road to examine a large steam-jet. Whilst he was doing so, the greater part of the band came streaming along the path in a long straggling line, without either seeing or being seen by him. A few minutes more, and Mair, having satisfied his curiosity, cantered back to the path. A sudden turning brought him face to face with a small number of Hau-haus who had lagged behind the rest. They looked at him very hard, but not knowing that he had avoided the others, took for granted that Paku and Te Aokatoa and the other leading chiefs had some good reason for letting him pass, so they, being moreover on Queenite territory, let him go unmolested. At Taupō, they were received in the same manner as at Oruanui; not one of Poihipi's people stirring outside his doors, till the Hau-haus, having got hold of a weak-minded old woman belonging to the place, and having made a circle round her, proceeded to subject her to mesmerism, or whatever their mode of influence may be — one at all events well calculated to obfuscate the mind of the individual operated on. An opinion gained ground in the *whares* that the old lady was rapidly becoming a Hau-hau, when two young men — native police — very gallantly rushed out of a *whare,* broke through the circle, and dragged her off; at the same time reproaching the fanatics for breach of their written promise. Somehow the latter were ashamed of themselves, and offered no resistance, though they had vastly the advantage in numbers.

After crossing the Waikato at the Taupō ferry, they appear to have broken up into two or more parties, some going eastward and some to the south. Judging by the account in the newspapers of the arrival in the province of Napier of a portion of this band,

I must have considerably underrated their numbers. In every direction, the new religion spread like wildfire, and a month had barely passed before the effects were shown in the abominable murder of the Rev. Mr. Völkner, one of the best and most zealous missionaries in all New Zealand. The leading facts of the martyr's death are well known to the public the details are unfit for publication.

Mr. Grace remained, though a sort of prisoner at large, in great danger for many days, the Hau-haus occasionally disputing as to whether it would be better to put him to death at once, or to take him with them alive across country to Taranaki, making use of their living prisoner, and of the baked heads of Mr. Völkner and that of a soldier which they had brought with them, to excite the tribes on their road.

On the 16th of March, a fortnight after Mr. Völkner's murder, the natives went to a great meeting a few miles away, to consecrate a new staff, leaving Mr. Grace but slightly guarded; the next day H.M. dispatch gun-vessel 'Eclipse,' sent by the Commodore from Auckland, arrived off the bar, having Bishop Selwyn on board. An opportunity offered, Mr. Grace having been left with only an old woman to guard him, his sentries, thinking there was no chance of an escape, having gone off to the meeting; Mr. Levy, the master of the schooner 'Eclipse,' who, being a Jew, was allowed to go where he liked, pulled him on board the man-of-war, the namesake of the schooner.

This man published part of his journal in the daily papers, and was soon the hero of the hour; a public meeting being convened to do him honour. But he made a variety of misstatements, all tending to his own glorification and the abuse of Mr. Grace, which were afterwards refuted by the evidence of his own crew and of the other traders living at Ōpōtiki but not, however, till they had been most recklessly repeated, and sent home for publication in an English Magazine, by one who, though writing only under initials, took small pains to conceal an animus against the minister of a rival creed.

The same day H.M.S. '*Eclipse*'s' boats, under Lieut. Belson, cut out the schooner, and on the 19th they arrived at Auckland, where Mr. Grace had long been considered a dead man by almost everyone excepting his own wife, who never lost hope and faith. Mair afterwards ascertained that amongst the murderers of Völkner were several of those who had voted for my death at Tataroa.

When the news was first received, the deed was execrated on all hands; even our old and inveterate foes, the Ngatiporos, hastened to assure us that the murder of innocent missionaries was not their mode of making war, and offered to co-operate with us by raising the country to rescue the prisoners and capture the murderers; and the Poverty Bay chiefs came up by sea to make a similar offer, but stipulated for a reward in the event of success. Unfortunately, the colonial politicians were busy squabbling as to the seat of government, and consequently where the headquarters of the troops with the fat commissariat contracts should be; so that there was no one in Auckland with authority to take the immediate steps which might have secured success.

Four months later came the murder of Mr. Fulloon, Government interpreter, and the crew of the 'Kate,' by the Hau-haus at Whakatane, both on the east coast. By this time, the whole country-side from Taupō to the East Cape was one seething hotbed of fanaticism, encouraged by the impunity which followed the murder of Völkner. The Government had avowed their inability to assist the plucky little band of loyal natives who yet remained at Taupō, and advised them to fall back on Rotorua, which they did with heavy hearts; and the Queen's flag floats no longer by the waters of the Great Lake.

When Fulloon was killed, Mair was at Rotorua, and as soon as he heard of it, he took measures to avenge his death. In about a week he collected and equipped a sufficient force, and at the end of that time he started from the lower end of Lake Tarawera with 200 Arawas, having sent about 150 more to march down the coast from Maketū.

On the 16th of August, the coast party attacked the Pai Marire *pah* at the confluence of the Awa-o-te-Atua (River of the Spirit) and the Rangitaiki without success, having no boats or canoes. On the same day Mair's party attacked Parawai, a very strong position on the above-named river, about seven miles from Mount Edgcumbe, but met with no better luck, and for the same reason. He then effected a junction with the coast party, which the enemy tried to prevent, but failed, losing a chief in the attempt. There were three *pahs* near the sea, but all too strong to be taken without artillery and boats. Several days were spent in skirmishing, usually picking off one or two Hau-haus, and waiting in hopes of assistance from the Ōpōtiki expedition (English troops, which landed Sept. 8) in this, however, they were disappointed. They then detached a party, who seized all the canoes at Whakatane (the scene of the murder), and got them by fresh water to the rear of the enemy, while the remainder dragged others overland into the lake behind the *pahs*, and thus cut off their supplies. The Hau-haus evacuated all the *pahs* during the night of the 10th of October, and retreated in canoes up the intricate channels of the Delta, leaving no traces of their route. But on the 15th, Mair learnt that they had thrown themselves into the Teko *pah*, and following them up, captured all their canoes, with eleven barrels of powder, and lead for bullets. On the 17th, travelling by land and water with nearly 500 Arawas, he reached the *pah*.

The place was very strong, having in its rear on one side the Rangitaiki — swift, broad, and deep; and on the other three sides nearly 300 yards of smooth glacis. Three lines of palisading with flanking angles, and three rows of rifle-pits and breastworks. The *pah* itself was 90 yards long by 45 broad, and every hut within it was separately fortified. There was, moreover, a covered way communicating with the landing-place on the river.

Sapping was the only way to take such a place. Mair, though a civilian, was present at Ōrākau, when that place was sapped under the direction of Captain Hurst, R.E., and seems to have made good use of his eyes. Three saps were accordingly started, under cover of a slight undulation of the ground, and, in spite of a

heavy fire, made such good progress that on the 19th the Hau-
haus craved a truce to arrange terms. Firing was suspended for
twenty-four hours, but the saps were kept driving, and the only
terms were unconditional surrender. Meanwhile Hemipo, whose
father Ngaperi (the old chief whom we met in the wood at Taupō)
was one of the leading men in the *pah*, improved the occasion
by lecturing his papa to such good effect, that he came over to
the Queenites, bringing with him twenty-five Taupō warriors, the
flower of the garrison; and as none of them were implicated in
the murders, they were allowed to change sides, and fight in the
trenches of the Queenites.

By 2 A.M. on the 20th the Arawas had cut off the covered
way, and got close up to the southern angle. Mair then for the last
time summoned Te Hura to surrender, assuring him that if forced
to carry the place by assault, no quarter would be given.

They saw that the case was hopeless, and at sunrise the whole
garrison marched out, and laid down their arms.

As they came out, each *hapu* of the Arawa sprang from their
trenches with a yell, and immediately had as fine a war-dance as
ever was seen — dear old Poihipi and three or four other hoary
old sinners giving the time. It must indeed have been a stirring
sight: the long column of prisoners standing with drooping heads,
while their captors danced the wild war-dance with all the fury of
excitement and success — the war-cry of the Arawa echoing from
hilltop to hilltop, while the earth trembled under the stamp of a
thousand feet.

And well might they exult, for besides having captured a
number of the murderers who had brought such disgrace on the
Maori name, there were among their prisoners many of the men
who had carried so high a hand at Tataroa, at Oruanui, and at
Taupō.

Mair placed the murderers, thirty-one in number, under the
special charge of the native police, and the remainder became
prisoners of war to the tribe of Arawa. The murderers were first
tried by court martial, and mostly convicted, but the court being
afterwards deemed informal, they were tried again by civil law in

Auckland, and the sentences were recently carried into effect; five have been hung, and others sentenced to hard labour for life, or shorter periods.

On the other hand, more than one of our late fellow-travellers have died or been killed.

Poor Wharetini, the "Southern Planter" as we nicknamed him, the handsomest, the merriest, the most impudent of all — foremost in the war-dance, foremost in the fight — has found that consumption is more deadly than the bullets of the Hau-hau.

William Thompson, Te Heu-heu, and Te Ua have recently consented to meet the Governor; Te Ua has given up the religion which he originated, and is now as well as Te Heu-heu at Wellington with the Governor. The two former, by the advice and example of Sir George, have taken "The Pledge."

CHAPTER VI.

Cross the Waikato — Meeting with Poihipi — Party of Uriweras — Overtake Mr. Brenchley's party — Camp out — Mountain terraces — New Zealand pigeon — Mohaka — Evening prayers — Pohuhe — Between the sheets — Arrival at Napier — Auckland Club — Points of Maori character — Immorality — Infanticide — Hospitality — Administration of justice — Capacity for work — Christianity — Prospects of the race.

To return to our journey: —

We crossed the Waikato by the ferry on Sunday morning, and soon afterwards entering the tea-tree scrub, the last glimpse of Poihipi's *pah*, with the Queen's flag waving over it, was shut out from our view.

For the greater part of the day we were traversing the south-western extremity of the Kaingaroa plain. Its surface is as even as a pavement, diversified only by a few shallow basins whose sides and bottoms are also perfectly smooth. Though watered by many streams it is altogether barren, nothing but small pumice-stones with widely-scattered tufts of worthless native grass and tea tree stunted to the dimensions of heather.

After fording two rivers, the Waipunga and Rangitaiki, we passed a tremendous chasm, terminating at the edge of the path. It was here that in days of yore prisoners of war were thrown down alive.

We stopped a few minutes at the Kingite village of Opepe, for to have passed by without doing so would have been an insult; but we declined their offer of hospitality and kept pretty close to our horses. There was, however, no cause for alarm, as these people had not then become Hau-haus. After this we came to a belt of wood, a mile or two in breadth, where we halted for our simple dinner of hard biscuit and water, and met Poihipi on his return from Brenchley. He was of course much surprised at seeing us at all, but in an instant I saw by the expression of his face that he thought I had merely pretended to go by Waikato to get rid of him and secure the services of the more lively Hemipo and his well-conditioned horses, which would have been very ungrateful after all the trouble he had had with us. Hemipo was too proud to make the necessary explanation, and Poihipi apparently would not understand what had happened by any combination of English, Maori, and signs which I could affect. I know I looked dreadfully guilty, and the old man rode away with a melancholy look of reproach which quite spoilt my dinner.

Soon afterwards, leaving the woods on our right, we passed over more plain, with a little swampy lagoon, and then found ourselves among the hills and mountains which extend thenceforward all the way to Napier, and which include two distinct and lofty ranges.

In the midst of a vast flat-bottomed valley, we met a long train of Kingites, Uriweras, with numbers of heavily-laden packhorses, wending their way from Napier, where they had been making their purchases, to Taupō and the Waikato. Could we have seen the contents of those packs, there is little doubt that many a parcel of gunpowder and lead would we have found. According to custom on these occasions, as Hemipo explained, we diverged from the path a hundred yards or more, and halted with a salutation while they passed, which they did in peace.

Immediately afterwards we descried Brenchley and party in the distance at the end of the valley, and spurring on our horses, overtook them at a gallop. It appears that B________'s natives, not expecting to see us, mistook us for some of the Kingites whom we had just passed, and cried out that the Uriwera were galloping back to attack them. We accordingly found Brenchley "cleared away for action," with revolver in hand, ready to defend both life and luggage.

With pack and bad horses and dilatory companions, he had not of course been able to travel as fast as we, who had ridden hard, this being his third day out.

When about abreast of Runanga, a Kingite settlement a little off the road, Takiuira (our handsome friend who fought for "love" like an Irishman) and some of the Waihaha people joined our party: the more the merrier.

January 30th. — We bivouacked last night in a beautiful ravine, or fissure, in the side of a lofty mountain, whence, looking between the trees on either side, as through a picture-frame, we enjoyed a right glorious view of vistas of thickly-timbered mountains, with curiously well-defined terraces and deep gorges, and here and there a silvery bit of winding river, almost hidden in the foliage of the valleys.

We had a glorious fire, some 30 feet in diameter, round which the natives busied themselves in cutting for us the most luxurious beds, and then laughed and sang till long past midnight.

We left the camp at early dawn; for though there was enough rain to wet us through and chill us to the bones, there was no water for washing or breakfast; so, after fording the Aratotara, a stream too deep and rapid to be crossed, even now, dry-seated, in any acrobatic position, and therefore I fancy quite impassable in winter, we reached Tarawera, a village perched on a high and steep terrace overlooking the river Waipunga.

Terraces such as that on which this village is built form the distinctive feature of the scenery throughout the greater part of the Northern Island, though they differ much from one another in shape, extent, and height. They occur in single, double, and treble rows, one above another. In the country, we are now passing through, there is generally a single row of terraces, suspended, as it were, midway between the summits of the mountains and the streams at their feet, with upper surfaces perfectly level and divided by clean-cut edges from their steep and lofty sides, which are far more heavily timbered than the flats above them. The effect is to give the scenery an appearance of singular massiveness and grandeur.

The chief, a silver-haired old man named Paora Motutawa, welcomed us with great cordiality, and producing his little stock of flour for our breakfast, we feasted sumptuously on damper and tea.

Then came a plunge in the cool running river, and after some delay, caused by the unwillingness of our natives to leave such pleasant quarters, we got our little cavalcade clear of the village before noon.

The forest was very beautiful; quantities of graceful tree fern; lofty timber with weeping foliage; and pendent creepers in great variety and luxuriance. We met with a very few small birds, which made up for the want of numbers by the beauty and clearness of their notes. Later in the day we saw several specimens of the kukupa, or great New Zealand pigeon, sitting sometimes on the lowest branches of trees which overhung the path. I fired at two or three with a revolver, as they sat dreamily gazing at the men with the strangely-coloured skins, but missed them all, in spite of their size and their tameness.

We had some heart-breaking mountain ridges to cross during this and the following day, more especially one just before arriving at Te Haroto, — miles of steep and slippery ascent without a single break. We found Te Haroto nearly deserted, but there were a few scattered groups of *whares* in the neighbourhood, whose inhabitants mounted their horses on seeing our approach, and accompanied us on to Mohaka, where we passed the night.

This settlement is curiously situated on the banks of a river traversing an apparently oval piece of table-land surrounded by mountains, suggesting the very unromantic idea of a deep and gigantic dish, divided by a crack, through which flows the river Waiaoao. We found here a great concourse of natives, who lodged us royally in a tent carpeted with new mats on fern, and regaled us with beef.

The bullock had only just been killed, and the flesh of the veteran made our teeth ache; again but meat of any sort is a great luxury after living so long on potatoes alone. There has been recently a great sale of land here to the Crown, which accounts for the beef, as well as for the unusual number of natives. Some of the men have very Jewish features: some of the women pretty faces, though of pure Maori blood. At sunset, this evening the little bell of the chapel, or "*whare-karakia*," checked for a time the eating and smoking and boisterous merriment around us; while from every side, old men and young ones, girls, and mothers with their children in their arms, came streaming in to attend the usual evening prayers read by a Maori deacon.

January 31st. — A cold night, with a sharp, white frost. Prayers again — well attended — at seven this morning. Left at nine, and crossed the river. The track between Taupō and Napier may occasionally be dignified by the name of a road, some part of it being passable to a cart. For the last two days Brenchley and I have been riding on with Hemipo, leaving the other natives to follow with our baggage more leisurely. It took us several hours to cross the next range of mountains, Brenchley comparing the scenery to that of the Pyrenees; after which we passed two Pakeha-Maories' houses, near the native village of Titiokura, and at two reached Mr. P_______'s station at Te Pohue, about a mile off the road.

He has only been out about two years, and has at present but 3000 sheep and a small quantity of cattle. His daughters look after the house, while he with his four sons and two servants do the remainder — burning off the fern, sowing English grasses, fencing in the paddocks, and building bridges. There are everywhere signs of cleanliness, of contentment, and of the cheerful hard work which is daily improving and civilizing the little home in this desert of fern.

Our host soon made us free of the house, and set before us a savoury stew of smoking steaks, with draughts of rich sweet milk. Our table had not had such grazing grounds as these for many a long day, and the trim little damsel who so kindly ministered to our wants could hardly conceal her surprise at the voracity with which, after emptying the ample dishes before us, we hungrily craved for more.

But even eating cannot last forever, so after declining our host's pressing invitation to pass the night under his roof, we saddled our steeds, which had been enjoying themselves as much as their riders, in a paddock of soft English grass, and started again at four, hoping to reach Napier the same night. In another two hours, we reached the river Petane, whose course we had to follow nearly all the rest of the journey, fording it just nineteen times during the evening. The moon set early behind the hills, and we had to ask our way at the only house we saw.

We reached Irin before 11 p.m., but finding that there yet remain some five miles of heavy shingle and a ferry to cross between this and Napier, and our horses having been nearly twelve hours on the road, we stay here the night, revelling in the unwonted luxury of beds.

February 1st. — In the course of the afternoon the rest of our party came up with the traps, and we all went into Napier the same evening.

Their powers of digestion proved even greater than ours, and kept the kitchen of the little inn in full operation for several hours before they were satisfied. But remembering our own appetites, I shall in future think more charitably of the excesses of savages who, after long months of abstinence gorge themselves when they suddenly obtain possession of an abundance of meat.

February 9th. — Arrived at Auckland, after a two days passage from Napier, where we were made welcome during our short stay at the club, having been introduced by the superintendent of the province, with whom we had to communicate touching the provisioning of the natives of our party by Government until their departure on their return journey. The gentlemen who form the majority of the members of the club are mostly holders of sheep-runs, and amongst them a more kindly spirit is shown towards the Maories than is to be found among the politicians and speculators of one or two of the larger towns.

Several settlers told me of the faithfulness with which the natives have held to their land contracts, permitting the lessees to retain the land for the whole term of years agreed upon at the original rent, although not bound by law, when they might, from the increased value of land and the competition among the whites, have easily obtained two or three times the amount of rent. Others have told me that they prefer the neighbourhood of Maories on their stations to that of the lower class of whites, on account of the greater security of property.

On the whole I prefer the Maories to any uncivilized race with which I have yet come in contact. We have now been living for the greater part of two months with the Maories, under circumstances of intimacy which have afforded us better opportunities of judging their character than years spent in town or camp. But, of course, I can only speak of those amongst whom we have been, for the natives on the east coast, north of Auckland, and in other parts, differ much in habits and character.

I will endeavour to mention the more prominent points in their character which strike the newcomer most forcibly.

The first is their great and undoubted valour: that, at least, is allowed by their bitterest detractors, and they have many.

As a race, they are honest. There are thieves among them, but they are few and despised.

During the whole time that I was up the country, living often in the same *whares* with the natives of our party or our hosts, my baggage was never locked, and often left open in my absence, yet I never missed anything, though it contained many things which they covet.

They are a very good-tempered people, easily pleased, but keenly alive to a slight, not quarrelling much among themselves individually, and still more rarely coming to blows.

Much has been said of the immorality of the Maories — rather too much, I venture to think; certainly, at some of the garrisoned seaports they are bad enough, but in the interior, with the exception of Ohinemutu, where the mingling of sexes bathing nightly in the warm lake leads to a singular state of affairs, the standard of morality is not lower, if so low, as in many parts of Scotland and Wales.

Infidelity in the marriage state is rare on the part of the men, but the daughters of Eve are not quite so immaculate. Almost promiscuous free-love follows in the wake of Hau-hauism.

The Church marriage-service has rather fallen into disuse lately, it having been found that it has not the effect of making the married ladies more circumspect in their behaviour. The natives can recover damages before a bench of English and native magistrates for *crim. con.*,[29] but they have no means of obtaining divorce, so that women, knowing that their husbands cannot get rid of them for any cause and be free to marry again, are less careful.

Infanticide was in days gone by a very common crime; now it has succumbed to the influence of Christianity, together with the fear of national extinction whilst the viler crimes so common amongst the natives of southern Europe and elsewhere are almost unknown. The ancient hospitality of the Maories is rapidly degenerating, and after a few more years of contact with white men will become a thing of the past.

There was an old chief — one of the old school — who scorned to take payment for feasting his guests but he too in time caught the thirst for money which at one time became a sort of *"quinte"* with the natives. One day a friend of mine, who had known him from childhood, stopped at his house, where he slept and left again the next day, never thinking of such an insult as offering payment for his board and lodging. He had not gone far when he heard the old chief running after him and calling him back, crying, "You have murdered me," in a very doleful manner. He stopped, and found that his host meant that he had never offered him payment, and therefore forced him to *ask* for it; he

---

29 "Criminal conversation" — a common law mechanism for a husband (generally) to get compensation from an unfaithful wife, or her lover. Essentially it viewed adultery as a breach of contract.

wanted money, but being ignorant of the value of it, laid his *"utu"* at 6*d.*

These mercenary ideas are very much on the increase, especially among the "friendly" natives, who see more of us civilized people, and are losing their old feelings of independence and habits of self-support, mainly from the quantity of money they receive from Government in the shape of salaries as native magistrates, assessors, or policemen.

The Arawas, with some of their offshoots between Rotorua and Taupō, are the only loyal tribe which we came near during our journey, and at some settlements from the half to two-thirds of the able-bodied men are receiving pay from Government in one of the above capacities.

As far as the administration of justice is concerned, the present system seems to work quite as well as can be expected amongst tribes where European resident magistrates are only appointed at the request of the natives, and cannot act with vigour unless supported by Maori public, or rather local, opinion. And it is to the credit of the magistrates of both races that Europeans, when they have a civil complaint against a Maori, prefer to bring their case before a native magistrate, and *vice versa.*

This sort of indirect bribery by paying such a large proportion of the faithful for nominal services is no longer necessary to keep them on our side, as the enmity between them and the Kingites, whom they have fought successfully on several occasions has become too deep for any fear of reconciliation; indeed, the Kingites have ceased to make overtures to them. But it will now be very difficult to alter this system of Government officials without creating profound dissatisfaction. Another bad effect of this system is the encouragement, if not the creation, of idleness. The Queenite natives are certainly the laziest race I have ever seen. During the whole time that I was with them I never saw one man doing a hand's turn of work, with the exception of occasionally fishing in the lake, which can hardly be called work. There is no doubt that they can work, as is shown by the wonderful rapidity with which they throw up rifle-pits and construct *pahs:* but they require excitement to keep them up to the mark, and I fear do not understand properly the "dignity of labour," about which we hear so much in England, and are not at all proud of being seen hard at work.

While we were at Taupō the natives began building a *whare*, in which they hoped Mair would come and live in peaceable times; now though this house rose about as fast as it would have under the hands of the same number of dockyard "maties" *working by the day* yet I never succeeded in detecting one of the Maories with adze in hand, though I came out surreptitiously at all hours. As travelling companions or servants their dilatoriness is irritating beyond measure.

They are very intelligent and reflective; they learn what is taught them in the schools much more rapidly than Europeans, and he who wants to "weather" a Maori in a bargain will have to get up very early in the morning. At the same time, they are very superstitious, having a childish fear of darkness and solitude, ascribing omens to the commonest occurrences, and often cherishing a doubting, hidden terror of their Tohungas and the objects of their old deserted heathen worship.

Amongst the latter is the green tree lizard, from which, whether alive or dead, men, women, and children are said to fly in real terror, and even take refuge in the water.

They do not fear the ordinary ground lizard (at least not where we have been), but merely experience the same sort of loathing that one of us would if required to go to bed with half-dozen eels.

Nearly all the chiefs are as proud as Lucifer — pride of race, of influence, and of broad lands. And their mutual jealousy is proportionate; this has always been one of the principal causes of numbers joining our side against their own countrymen.

The residence of a Pakeha is a very frequent cause of bitter jealousy. They look on a Pakeha as a most useful animal causing all sorts of good things to fall in the way of those amongst whom he lives, and speak of him to one another as their "property."

Thus, Hohepa, chief of Oruanui, solemnly and three times over cursed Poihipi: taking a piece of flax, he said, "Here is his body" and then cut it into three pieces, merely because, from our protracted stay at Taupō, he thought Mair was going to take up his abode with Poihipi instead of himself.

What sort of a hold religion has on the Maories it is difficult for me to say when the missionaries themselves disagree. They are certainly not the angels on earth which you read of at home, yet in many places we stopped at where a missionary does not show for months or years together, the good seed sown in former days still bears some fruit in the shape of well-attended daily prayers, both morning and evening. I think that many of them are at least as good Christians as the average run of Europeans, save in the one particular of licentious conversation; and more cannot well be expected when it is remembered that a few years ago these people were all heathen cannibals (many of whom are alive now), and that the Christian religion is the faith of a nation against whom the Maories have fought long and fiercely.

The Maories are an undeniably well-made race, especially about the lower limbs; but in spite of the size of their calves, which would make the fortune of any London footman, they are not so fleet-footed as Europeans neither in trials of strength can they lift such heavy weights.

The principal causes of the diminishing population are said to be the barrenness of women when married to their own countrymen, intermarrying, which still prevails to a great extent in some places; scrofula, which taints more or less nearly every *hapu* in the kingdom; the early abuse of tobacco; living in *whare* pens — hot, unhealthy, half-sunken houses, without ventilation and eating a favourite mess made of half rotten fermenting maize and lastly — to those who live near towns — drink.

The rotten-corn luxury is now nearly out of fashion, and from the day that we left Auckland till the day we returned, I never saw a Maori drunk, though I can't say as much for the white men.

The possession of horses and the increasing rareness of wars have allowed the Maories to seek wives amongst other tribes, and the Arawas between Taupō and Maketū are now decidedly on the increase, their settlements swarming with children.

The "Half-castes" are one of the finest races I have ever seen, and the Maories are very proud of them, and always endeavour to get hold of the children and bring them up amongst them. Nearly all natives have great individuality of character and countenance. In many places, we were struck with the strongly-marked Jewish features of both men and women, especially the former.

They would be a much handsomer race were it not for the custom — now, however, fast falling into disuse — of forcibly flattening by pressure the noses of the children.

The Half-caste race seem well fitted, both by their size and comeliness, their vigorous intelligence and the fecundity of the race, to form in days to come no inconsiderable portion of the inhabitants of this country.

How long the pure native race may be preserved in times of peace it is difficult to say. At present, they seem bent on war — a war not for the redress of grievances, or for revenge, nor for the conservation of their lands, but simply for the sovereignty of New Zealand.

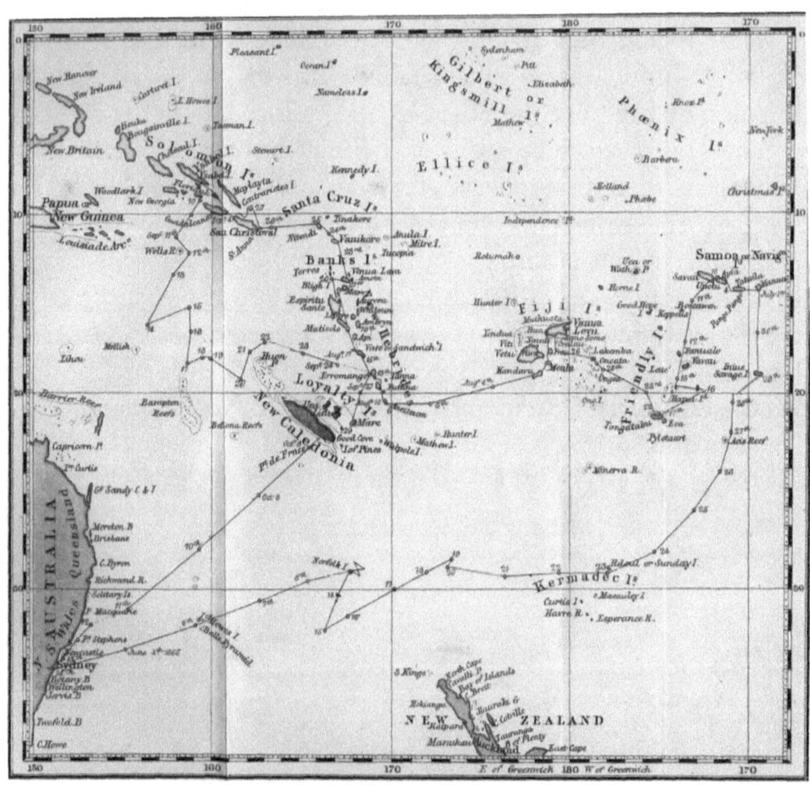

The Voyage of the HMS *Curaçoa* in 1865

CHAPTER VII.

Norfolk Island — Sydney Bay — Singing and dancing — Confirmation and the Bishop's sermon — Savage Island — Mr. Lawes and the Samoan teachers — Dress and character of the islanders — Tutuila — Pango Pango Harbour — Beautiful tropical scenery — Native houses — Maunga the chief — Visit to the great waterfall — Native dance on board — Population and religion — A proselytizing captain and a trader's trick — Crime, climate, and government — Upolu — Apian morals — Dinner at the consul's — The didunculus — A christening on board — Waterfall — Religion, government, and produce.

NORFOLK ISLAND.

June 9th, 1865. — Made the land at daylight this morning, Norfolk Island some thirty miles distant. About half-past ten we anchored in Sydney Bay, and had not been there long before a whale-boat came off to us, containing George Adams (1st generation), his son John Adams,[30] Quintal, Christian, Evans, Nobbs, jun., and others. After hearing their account of the surf at this landing-place, the Commodore[31] decided to weigh at one, and proceed to Cascade Bay, an anchorage on the other side of the island. John Adams soon found me out, and asked me whether I was not related to the captain of the *Tribune,*' which had recently visited Pitcairn's Island,[32] to which some of their people not long

---

30 Foljambe says, "John Adams (son of John Adams of the Bounty), and his son." (p.135) There is thus confusion over who was who. Brenchley however agrees with Meade: "One of them was George Adams the son of a mutineer of the *'Bounty,'* a man sixty-one years of age, accompanied by his son about forty years old." (Brenchley, p.4)

31 Sir William S. Wiseman.

32 "Of course every one has read of the Pitcairn Islanders having removed to Norfolk Island, where there are now about 200 of them; the remainder

ago returned. I was at first surprised at this, as he had never seen either my brother or myself before, but afterwards found that he knew half the Navy List by heart. John Adams dined with us on our passage round to Cascade, to which place we towed the islander's whaleboat; he wore no coat or waistcoat, collar or cravat, yet his manners were those of a gentleman, and betrayed no awkwardness at table. We landed at four at Cascade Bay, where we found horses awaiting us (miserable brutes, but better than none), which some of us rode across the island to Sydney Bay. Bishop Patterson,[33] Mr. Nobbs, and many others welcomed us on landing. The Bishop, who arrived here yesterday in the mission yacht *'Southern Cross,'* has called in on his way to the mission stations already established, and to those of the South Sea Islands, where he hopes to start others in course of time. T________, Master R.N., is skipper of the schooner. The grass-grown road to Sydney Bay, or Kingstown, some three miles, showed us as fair a little island as any man could wish to see; undulating hills and valleys, covered with an exceedingly rich soil, and dotted with the handsome Norfolk Island pine tree, fern, and wild lemon tree, both singly and in groves, in a style which reminds me of some large park laid out by a well-skilled landscape gardener. These pines grow to a great height and circumference; one has just been cut down over 220 feet high.

It was nearly dusk when we reached the settlement, but we had not been there five minutes before we were dispersed over the different houses in the town, which the owners had placed at our disposal. There were sixteen of us, besides the Bishop's party, S________, P________, T________, and I were entertained at John Adams', who did all in his power to make us comfortable, in which he was ably assisted by his wife, a cheery little matron of somewhat under forty summers, who did the honours of her own

---

(sixty in number) returned to Pitcairn's Island." (Foljambe, p.136)
33 Murdered 1871 in the Solomon Islands. Some confusion over whether locals mistook him for a slave trader (common at the time), or whether it was some other motive.

table with a quiet "aplomb" and good grace which many a smart lady might envy, but not imitate.

The Pitcairners all live in the Government buildings, which had been used for the officials connected with the convict establishment. Most of these: buildings are falling into disrepair, partly from the circumstance of there being no person on the island who understands plastering or masonry, and partly from the inbred indolence of a race who, for three generations, have seen their food grow ready to their hands in a soil and climate which require no sweating brow and aching back to make it bring forth abundantly.

After supper, we adjourned to the singing-room, where we found nearly every grown-up person in the island. Singing and dancing are their principal amusements, and they certainly go in for both *con amore*.[34] The chanting and glee singing, which was led by Driver Christian, and unaccompanied by any instrument, was pronounced to be really very good by the Bishop and those of our party who understood music.

This lasted for about two hours, after which the seats were cleared away, most of the girls slipped off for a minute to make some little alteration in their simple dress, — a fiddle wielded by a most muscular musician soon followed, and a rattling dance was kept up with hardly a moment's interval from 9 till nearly 3 a.m. What fun we had! We all agreed next day that it was worth half-a-dozen regular balls lashed together, and that we had never seen so many pretty girls in one room before. Most of their complexions are a shade of olive, some have skins as fair and transparent as any European, but the majority are rather sunburnt, and a few a little freckled, which makes them look best by candle-light.

Their principal attraction lies in their eyes and teeth, which are perfect; their plump, healthy, well-shaped forms, which have never yet been deformed by stays, and to which crinolines are as yet a rare novelty and, lastly, to the free gait and elastic step which they inherit from their Tahitian ancestresses. Besides the advantage of feeling that you really have hold of your partner's waist, instead

---

34 With love.

of a bundle of whalebone and steel springs, the girls have a jolly, free, unaffected sort of way about them, which is very pleasant, but to which I will only say that the grossest of mankind could impute no evil.

At first, they would only dance such dances as the "Triumph," "Sir Roger," and a marvellous test of activity and wind named "Sixteens," but we soon substituted valses, galops, &c., which they danced very fairly, in spite of their protestations that they had never danced them before, and did not know how.

June 10th. — Blowing and raining. Found the ship gone to sea, which did not break our hearts, though the most of our wardrobes were confined to a toothbrush apiece, or less. Called on the Bishop, and Mr. Nobbs, with whom he is stopping. Had a long yarn about the islands with the former, who appears to consider that most of the affrays which take place between the Europeans and the savages are caused by the intemperance or violence of some of the traders, who are mostly a wild and lawless lot.

June 11th, Sunday. — No signs of the ship. I walked over in the afternoon, after church and dinner, with John Adams and S______, to see if the ship was in sight. We all attended morning service in the old convict church. There was a Confirmation and exhortation by Bishop Patterson. The girls looked very well in their white dresses and veils.

This is the Bishop's first visit since a painful affair at Santa Cruz, one of the New Hebrides[35] group. He had taken with him for a missionary cruise in the yacht two of the most promising young men in the island, a son of Mr. Nobbs, and one of the Christians. They landed at Santa Cruz, and there were signs of mischief brewing, but no actual violence until they were shoving off on their return, when some of the natives endeavoured unsuccessfully to detain the boat, which succeeded in putting to sea, only to be followed by a shower of arrows, shooting Nobbs and Christian through the jaw and wrist respectively, and another

---

35 Vanuatu.

of the crew through the chest, — he, strange to say, recovered, but the two former died with symptoms of tetanus, on the passage southward. Christian continued pulling his oar till they reached the schooner, although his wrist was completely pierced by the arrow.

The Bishop is unable to guess at the precise reason of these murders, but believes them to have been committed in retaliation for some act of violence on the part of whoever were the last white men who visited the island.

Of course, the subject was alluded to by the Bishop, as most of those in the church were related to the young men who had been killed there. Before church we went over the prisons; they are in tolerable preservation now, but will not remain so long. The windows are all broken, some of the wooden fittings torn down for firewood, and the courtyards and workshops where the convicts used to be chained to their forges, strewed with leg-irons; the whole dismal ruins, the only relics of crime and misery of days gone by, offering a strong contrast to the peaceful state of affairs in the island now.

Choral singing again this evening, from which we broke up at 9.30. Our dinner party today comprised four generations, *viz.* George Adams (son of the mutineer); his son, John Adams; his granddaughter, Mary Buffitt and his great-granddaughter, a child. John Adams married at fifteen, and begat a child at once. Much interested today dipping into John Adams's Journal, which, however, illustrates the truth of the proverb, that "happy are the people who have no history."

June 12th. — This morning the ship hove in sight, and came to an anchor in Cascade Bay; I cannot say, however, that any of us were very glad to hear it, for we could all have spent another week here very pleasantly, though, of course, it was time to relieve our friends on board, and give them a spell on shore. The surf this morning was too heavy, else we were to have pulled over to Phillip's Island, which is said to be tenanted by fabulous numbers of rabbits, wild goats, and wild fowl, for an hour's shooting at daylight.

It was no easy matter to get our flock together, as everyone found at the last moment some very particular party, to whom a last adieu had not been bidden and my exertions in driving in my wandering messmates account for the circumstance of my being myself the last to leave.

Before leaving, our various hosts pressed our acceptance of pretty well everything they had in their houses which they thought would be worth giving us. John Adams did all he could to persuade me to take the most valuable article he possessed, a desk made by himself and his father of woods brought from Pitcairn's Island — a very fine piece of workmanship, beautifully inlaid with pretty-coloured woods. I took, however, a leaf from Midshipman Young's "day's-work" book, on one side of which is a prayer written by Adams, the mutineer, when teaching himself to write at Pitcairn's Island, and on the other some very wild navigation by Young. I wonder whether punishment incurred for his faulty "day's-work" had anything to do with his joining the mutineers?

Watch and watch on board. Adams and his wife, and two or three others came on board for an hour or two at our invitation, and we sent them back well loaded with various little things of which we supposed them short, and for which they were very grateful. The islanders neither make themselves nor import any kind of fermented liquor; but John Adams had by him a few bottles of ale, which were all produced for our refection during our stay.

The *'Southern Cross'* sailed this evening with the Bishop, who is to meet us again to the northward.

SAVAGE ISLAND[36]

June 29th. — We made the land at daylight this morning, long, low, and well-wooded, though rocky shores. After some

---

36 Niuē – "Niue was first visited by [Captain James] Cook in 1774, who, having attempted a landing, was furiously set upon by the natives, and not being under any necessity of spilling blood, humanely took his leave, satisfied with the innocent revenge of calling it 'Savage Island.'" (Brenchley, p.29) Another story has it that on first encounter the Niueans were covered in what appeared to be blood.

trouble, we found an anchorage about three cables' length from the shore, and abreast of Mr. Lawes' house. He was sent here in 1861 by the London Missionary Society. The population of the island amounted last year to five thousand. They all now profess Christianity, owing, in a great measure, as the missionary told us, to the exertions of the Samoan native teachers, who came here in 1848, and have done great good.

The island, 33 miles long by 9 broad, is entirely formed of coral, and raised above the sea apparently by a subterranean upheaval subsequent to the formation of the upper strata of coral.

One of the results of this disturbance is a great chasm, narrow, dark, and deep, about a mile inland, which we went to explore. The path lay through groves of coconut and banana, springing from a soil of only a few inches in depth.

The island is a mass of vegetation, though the soil is very spare.

Close to the path we found the fissure straight and with perpendicular sides. Stones dropped down the mouth took four seconds to reach the water, the depth of which we had no means of testing. The water in these and other inland caves is said to be affected by the rise and fall of the tide. Here the islanders collect the stalagmites which, when rounded something like a mower's hone, formed, with spears and clubs, their only weapons prior to the introduction of firearms.

The houses were neatly thatched, clean, and divided by partitions into rooms. Many were built with solid outside walls, and furnished with a rough kind of Venetian blind. The natives appeared clean and good-tempered. We could move about everywhere in perfect safety, and I frequently wandered quite alone, finding a welcome in every village.

Sharks abound, and several were shot from the ship today. They are said to be harmless, so far that they will not attack human beings; certainly, the natives appeared to swim about within sight of them without fear.

Mr. Lawes and his family are the only Europeans on the island, but they feel perfectly secure in the good-will of the people. Good paths are to be found all-round the island, built by offenders in payment of fines inflicted as punishment. The crime of most ordinary occurrence is that of theft (chiefly of food), but that is not frequent. During the time that the ship was swarming with natives, they might easily have stolen many articles of great value to themselves without fear of detection, yet I never heard that anything was lost.

They are, however, most pertinacious beggars, importuning one especially for articles of clothing and for the contents of one's pockets.

As a race, they are pleasing, intelligent, and said to have a great aptitude for quick learning.

The men and women indifferently wear cloths round the waist, or sometimes long fringes of a shining fibre drawn from the inner bark of the hibiscus. Some, however, of both sexes presented a somewhat incongruous appearance, having previous to our arrival arrayed the upper portion of their persons in European clothing, and very uncomfortable they seemed to be. Money and all ordinary articles of trade were in great demand. The climate is said to be healthy and equable, the thermometer averaging about 80°. There are no centipedes or venomous reptiles.

Before the introduction of cows, goats, pigs, and fowls, rats were the only indigenous animals. There are perroquets, small birds, and wild pigeons, but not enough to repay the trouble of carrying a gun.

Even these islanders have a history, and not altogether a happy one. In the years 1862-3 more than 100 of their young men were kidnapped, and many shot down by Peruvian slavers, who carried off their captives to work in the Chincha Islands.[37] One of the villages is now full of orphans and widows. The inhabitants formally expressed their desire for the establishment of a British Protectorate. The government is now administered by the heads of families, who rule in the place of the chiefs, who were all killed in a general rising of the people some years ago.

----

37 Around 21km off the coast of Peru.

We sail this evening for Tutuila, one of the Samoan group; the natives jumping overboard at the last moment, and swimming to their canoes as the ship steamed slowly away.

TUTUILA.[38]

July 1st. — Received a pilot this morning (a Sandwich islander now living here) off the mouth of the harbour of Pango Pango,[39] the best in the group.

It is situated on the south side of the island, with a very narrow entrance; perfectly land-locked, and very deep, being formed by an extinct crater, of which the top has partly fallen in on the seaward side.[40]

We found a good anchorage in 22 fathoms off the village of Fango Tongo;[41] the other place from which the harbour takes its name is at the head of the bay.

It would be difficult to conceive a much better specimen of grand tropical scenery than is to be found in this harbour and other parts of the island: —

At sea, the contrast between the brilliant cobalt blue within the reefs which skirt the shores, and the dark olive green of the deeper waters, separated by lines of foaming breakers on the coral walls.

On land, the black lava rocks along the shore, with intervals of white sand, dazzling in the sunlight, and fringed with coconut palms and bananas, bending to the sea breeze and interspersed with the thick thatched domes of the native houses. The whole surmounted by the towering crater, of which the sides are densely clothed with foliage to the very crest, save in one direction, where a single lofty cliff rears its grey walls against the sky as grimly and

---

38 American Samoa.

39 Pago Pago.

40 "Pango Pango Harbour is a very secure and convenient one, its only disadvantage being its great depth. As it is an extinct crater, ships have to go very far up it, to get less than thirty or thirty-five fathoms. We anchored in twenty-two and a half." (Foljambe, p.150)

41 Fagatogo.

as bare as when, years ago, the volcano was in the plenitude of its power.

The Commodore sent me ashore to try and find a place fit for hauling the seine.

This I failed to do, the coral lying too close to the shore in the few places which are not lined with scoria; but the time passed more pleasantly than had I stopped on board in my watch, dancing about amidst buckets, and dodging the brooms and holy stones.

The houses are built in the shape of a dome, or circular pyramid. The eaves of the roof, which is thickly thatched with long fringes of sugar-cane leaves strung on coconut leaf-ribs, are supported by posts, and reach to within four feet of the ground; the centre is supported by three lofty pillars of breadfruit wood, and the whole is erected on a raised platform of fine gravel, banked up by a circle of rockwork. The whole of the framework of the roof is secured with a sort of sinnet lashing, very neatly worked, and stained various colours, producing a very pleasing and cool effect. The inside is carpeted with mats, and clean ones are always laid for a visitor, though his stay may not exceed two minutes.

In one of their houses I made the acquaintance of Maunga, the chief of Pango Pango, who surprised me as I approached with an English "Good morning, sir," and a courteous invitation to enter. He was a quiet dignified middle-aged man, but had not added much to his appearance by the addition of a black frock-coat to his shirt and waist-cloth, donned for the purpose of visiting the Commodore, in company with Mr. Powell, the missionary.

We were informed that no sharks have ever been seen in this harbour, so officers and men bathed morning and evening — a great luxury.

There were great numbers of jellyfish, but no one was stung by them.

All the fish which can be caught here by net or line are said to be good for food, with the exception of one small species a few inches long and of a rounded form, which is said to be very poisonous. We were told that a short time ago a man who professed unbelief in their poisonous nature died in a few minutes after eating two or three of them. They are distinguished by having their fins at the reverse way from all other fish, that is, jutting towards the head instead of towards the tail.

There is another missionary, Mr. Scott, and twelve more Europeans living on the island; one of them, a Yankee known as Sam, came on board today.

None of the women that I have seen can be called pretty, but many have pleasing features; when young they have good figures, but soon deteriorate after marriage, and many are deformed by elephantiasis. They rarely wear anything but the mat or cloth round the waist.

Both men and women wear their hair in a variety of ways: some black and hanging naturally; some cut close and stained a reddish sandy colour; others, and especially among the men, grow their hair to a great length, and gather it in a great bunch by a ring, with the ends only stained sandy, so as to look like something between a huge fox-brush and a grenadier's bearskin.

We saw many girls with their hair covered with a white cosmetic, which had a pleasing though slightly comical effect. They occasionally decorate their hair very tastefully with two or three wild flowers.

July 2nd, Sunday. — Duly observed by the inhabitants. Even yesterday there was hardly a house that I entered without finding a Bible, either lying open or in such a position as to indicate habitual use. A delicious bathe morning and evening. I made a sketch today of the harbour from near Pango Pango. Thermometer, 105 in the gun-room.

July 3rd. — D________ and I were to have started in a canoe this morning at daylight to visit the great waterfall, said to exceed 2000 feet in height; this sounded very like a whale, but we thought it worth exploring, so we engaged two natives, Messrs. Bill and Foa; the latter is a chief at Fango Tongo, and as fair a specimen of a good-looking athletic young savage as you could wish to see. By starting at daylight, we hoped to get inside the reef with the high tide, and land at Nou-oudi,[42] a place on the coast only three or four miles from the waterfall, but it rained so heavily as to detain us till it was too late to cross the reef, and D________ gave up the expedition. The natives objected to go overland from Fango Tongo, saying that though a Kanoka might get there that way, no white man could do so.

However, I assured them that if they carried my gun and haversack I would get over any ground that they could, and with some difficulty persuaded them to start soon after 9 a.m.

I found the height of the cascade and the difficulties of the road much exaggerated.

The former is certainly not 1000 feet high, much less 2000; still it was the highest I have ever seen. There was, I should think, about 400 feet perpendicular fall over a black volcanic cliff.

Yankee Sam called the distance 8 to 10 miles to his house at Nou-oudi, and 3 to 4 more to the fall, and I put the distance there and back at not more than 25 miles, but from the nature of the ground, bush, and rocks, it was about the hardest day's work I have had since I left Mexico; but it was well worth the trouble. The last part of the way was simply wading up the rocky mountain torrents which flow from the cascade. I shot a pigeon and a few other birds by the way.

On my return through Nou-oudi, I found that Sam's wife — the nearest approach to a pretty woman that I have seen amongst the Tutuila islanders — had prepared dinner for me of fowl, stuffed with eggs, as I had refused to allow her to kill a pig for my entertainment.

Reached the ship about 7.30. I had taken my sketching materials with me for the purpose of trying to make a water-colour drawing of the waterfall, but the mist of spray was falling too thickly for any use of the brush, and I was deterred by the danger of resting in so cold and wet a place after toiling for hours in a tropical sun.

----

42 Nu'uuli.

Mr. Powell and the chief Maunga dined on board today with the Commodore. Maunga behaved with great propriety, and nothing disturbed his equanimity till some ices were handed round, when he spat out the first mouthful, under the impression that he had terribly scalded his tongue.

There was to have been a great dance in our honour at the village of Fango Tongo, but by the Commodore's wish it came off on board instead; and when I reached the ship this evening, I found such a Babel as the old ship has never seen since her keel was laid — about seventy natives, male and female, on the port side of the main deck (which was lit up for the occasion with fighting lanterns), dancing and singing; five or six of the finest specimens of the men danced at a time, the remainder keeping time with voice and clapping of hands, led by a small native drum, all in perfect chorus.

Before dancing, the men rubbed themselves all over with coconut oil, and diminished their clothing successively between each dance.

Several of the men looked exceedingly well in their light and airy costumes, being all well-made men, over six feet high. Master Foa amongst them. They wore small aprons of scarlet dracaena leaves fastened round the waist by a garland of similar colour, both of which being likewise oiled, glittered in the light of the suspended lanterns, as the wearers bounded in the air to the time of the clapping hands and sounding drum. Some of their head-dresses are really very handsome, coronets formed of two or three rows of large silvery beads, made of the pearly part of the inside of a nautilus shell, the whole set off by the scarlet flowers of the hibiscus tastefully placed in the hair, and necklaces of shells and berries.

The women, who danced sometimes alone, at others simultaneously with the men, were dressed in much the same way, and looked well, having good figures. The missionary's presence on board acted as a check on the natives, and the dances were conducted with greater propriety than usual. Mr. Powell has nearly succeeded in stopping these night dances altogether, as they lead to immorality, and none are ever held in the village where he resides.

July 4th. — With Sam's assistance one of the natives had been prevailed on to agree to sell me one of these coronets or reflectors of nautilus shells.

They value them very highly, as they are handed down as heirlooms, and take a long time to collect. Each shell provides only one bead, and can only be found uninjured when caught alive floating about at sea, and it is not every day that a canoe can catch even one.

At the last moment, however, the Samoan who had brought the "*fonio,*" as they call it, alongside, altered his mind, and unable to part with his "family jewels," turned his canoe and paddled ashore again as fast as he could, leaving me to jingle my dollars at the gangway.

Weighed at five this evening, and the wind being, as usual, directly up the harbour, went out under steam.

The entire population of this island is nearly 4000, and has remained pretty stationary for many years.

Of this number, some seventy or eighty are Mormons, having been persuaded to join that sect by two Hawaiian Mormons, who have established themselves at a place on the coast called Tula Alas; this creed does not, however, flourish, owing to the opposition of the chiefs, who will not permit polygamy to become the custom of the people.

Christianity was introduced by Messrs. Barff and Williams in 1830. All the population are professedly Christians, that is, there are no pagans, but there are many whose faith is in rather a bad way: Bill, for instance, boasting that he does not believe in any of the missionaries.

I have read that the Samoans subscribe £1200 a-year to the general funds of the mission, which is a large sum to be drawn from so poor a people, whose minister receives only £120 salary; and it appears to me that 9*s.* 6*d.* is a very large price to charge a nearly naked savage for a copy of Holy Writ.

A curious story is told in a neighbouring island that a merchant captain stopped, for a short time, and commenced converting the natives. He prevailed on them to destroy their idols, but had not got much farther when he had to set sail. The islanders were therefore left with little or no religion to supply the place of the paganism which he had destroyed. He told them that he had no Bible to give them, but that they should endeavour to get one by the first opportunity, as without the Word of Grod they could not hope for salvation.

A long time passed before another trader touched at the island, and then their first request was for the holy volume. The trader, seeing an opportunity for what he considered a smart bargain, replied that he fortunately had a "Word of God" on board, but that they were such exceedingly rare and valuable articles that he could not part with his, except for a large quantity of oil, and an agreement was made by which the natives were to pay 120 gallons of oil, value at least £20, for the skipper's New York Society's Bible, marked 3*s.* on the cover. The natives went to work, and having succeeded in collecting the quantity demanded, obtained their Bible, but did not know what to do with their prize when they had got it, for not one of them could read a word of it. So, it was wrapped carefully up in ever so many folds of *tappa*[43] mats and coconut leaves, and hung up in the chief's house, as a sort of Fetish, where it remained for years, till a few months ago, when some native teachers were landed on the island to expound the Gospel to them.

More than a third of the whole population can now read. Sunday is observed here as strictly as in Scotland, and the state of morals is worse.

The men are exceeding jealous, and watch the women very narrowly, especially when a ship is in harbour.

The fair ones are the cause of the present war, and of most of the very few deeds of violence which occur on the island.

---

43 Barkcloth.

Marriage is sometimes solemnized by the missionary, or teachers, and sometimes dispensed with.

Theft here, as in Savage Island, is the principal crime, and is more frequent.

Murder has only taken place once in the last twenty years, and on that occasion the culprit was tried and speared to death.

They are good-tempered, merry, and cleanly, soap being the article they ask for first in payment for anything sold or any little service rendered.

Nothing was stolen from us or our ship during our stay, though the natives had plenty of opportunities for so doing.

At this and other islands a great similarity is observed to the Maori language in many words, the difference being solely caused by the substitution of *f* for *w* and *h*, as *"fafine"* for *"wahine,"* *"fai"* for *"wai,"* *"matia"* for *"matake,"* *"tagata"* for *"tangata,"* &c., &c.

Tutuila is 17 miles long by from 2 to 5 broad. There is an anchorage in Fangasa Bay, at the narrowest part of the island, on the same coast as Pango Pango, and there is another at East Point, Ava; but Pango Pango is the only good harbour in the whole group.

The government is half-patriarchal, half-democratic, and not of the strongest.

Wars appear to be frequent. Maunga's tribe had just concluded a three years' war when visited by the '*Fawn,*' and now they have begun it again; but since the substitution of firearms for hand-to-hand weapons, their battles have not been very bloody affairs.

The climate is healthy, but was extremely damp at the time of our stay, and is said to have a marked tendency to aggravate any disease of the brain, and to foster lunacy. There is also a fever, which ends in elephantiasis, among European residents, as well as natives, many of whom are deformed by this disease, as well as scrofula.

The principal produce is oil. There are many different species of fruit and vegetables, over 150 kinds of ferns and 90 of mosses, some of which are very beautiful.

The only aboriginal animals are black and brown mice, and a very small sleek species of pig, quite different from the imported breeds. Green turtle lay their eggs on the shores.

The inhabitants are very anxious to become part of the British Empire, and Maunga requested the Commodore to sanction his hoisting the English flag, which of course could not be granted.

Fear of slavers and of the fate of Tahiti and New Caledonia, together with a sincere wish for the advantages of a strong government by a race in whose good faith they have confidence, appear to be the main reasons for this wish.

UPOLU.[44]

July 5th. — Arrived off the little town of Apia at 9.30 this morning, and anchored in 5 fathoms within the horns of the reefs. The place looks quite civilized, being composed of a string of little low white houses, under the coconuts, along the beach, and the Catholic church with the regular extinguisher steeple, an ornament of which the Protestant church cannot boast. This place is inhabited by some seventy or eighty whites, who, with a few exceptions, are about as disreputable a lot as you could find in a year's cruise, and have turned the whole settlement into one big brothel.

July 6th. — Mr. Williams, our consul, dined with us this evening. He is the son of the Williams, the Erromango[45] martyr, and seems to be a sensible man.

There is a difficulty about a Hamburgh merchant, named W_______, having taken the law into his own hands in a dispute with a native. I was very glad to hear the Commodore express strong opinions to the effect that all men should be bound by the laws of whatever race they come to live amongst. Naval officers on this station have more than once been made the tools of unscrupulous traders in these islands, sometimes resulting in the sacrifice of life in an unjust cause.

---

44 An island in the Samoan group.
45 An island in the Vanuatu archipelago.

July 7th. — Took away a seining party last night, but got no luck, catching only a dozen or two of wretched little fish. We were away from soon after 8 p.m. till 3 this morning, but the water within the reef was everywhere too shallow for big fish. A turtle once got into the seine, but escaped again. We hauled the seine at the only practicable place, round the western point, where there is a grove of coconuts.

Close to where we are lying there is a wreck of a barque with her mastheads (lower) just showing above the water, at the edge of the reef on which she was wrecked with the loss of all hands but one, though but three or four hundred yards from the shore. She belongs to Mr. McFarland, of this place, and, by his request, two attempts were made this afternoon to blow her up by M________ with our diver, and a fuze led to a breaker of 50*lbs.* of Mr. McFarland's powder. The fuze, however, would not burn all the way down, and the attempt failed.

What I could see of the place, during a short stay ashore, previous to dining with Mr. Williams, went far to confirm all that I had heard of the profligacy of the place; it seems to be another Port Royal.

The dinner was a pleasant one, and cool, being in a sort of outhouse, though there were eighteen of us, including Mr. Williams's wife, son, and mother-in-law, the McFarlands, Mr. Weber, and Mr. Murray the missionary. We were waited on by native girls, who fanned us, when not otherwise employed, very pleasantly, especially one named Mary, as straight as a poplar, who performed her various duties with a sort of coquettish dignity that was rather attractive. Our band came ashore in the consul's garden, attracting a great crowd of natives, and amongst them the most striking-looking person I have yet seen among the islands, a woman with really good features, with good eyes, without the spreading nostril, and with a magnificent head of coal-black hair flowing over her shoulders and down her back.

One of the chief's guard was on sentry at the garden gate, for the purpose of keeping his countrymen outside, which he did effectually, by flourishing a hunting whip about their bare legs. The uniform of these warriors looks like a caricature: scarlet tailcoats, made of woollen shirts, but fitting them like another skin, and with two ridiculous tails behind, the whole well garnished with buttons, and completed by trousers and fancy caps. Yankee muskets and bayonets.

July 8th. — Another unsuccessful attempt at the wreck this time the fuze enclosed in gutta-percha[46] tubing over all, but the sun caused it to open.

We all bathe, here as at Tutuila.

Mr. Williams says that during all the years he has been here, the killing of a dog has been the only harm done by sharks.

Saw a very rare bird, the *"didunculus,"* native name,[47] which is peculiar to this island. It has the feet of a pigeon, the beak of a hawk, with three teeth on each side of the lower mandible, plumage blue-black, body of the shape and size of a partridge.

July 9th, Sunday. — A christening on board today. It appears that Mr. Murray, the Baptist missionary, declined to baptise Mr. McFarland's children, the father being an Episcopalian. The Congregationalist minister having also refused for a similar reason, the children were brought on board. The Commodore and B________[48] stood sponsors, and the ceremony was duly performed and entered in the ship's log, much to the satisfaction of the father and mother.

I have not been inland in this island, owing to the duties of the ship requiring one of us to be on board besides the commanding-officer; two other lieutenants have been away every day in charge of coaling and watering parties. We have coaled in hired boats, our own stokers filling the bags.

---

46 A tree that produces natural latex.
47 A "tooth-billed pigeon, of which I have met but two specimens … it has the feet of a pigeon, short legs, the beak large and strongly hooked at the tip like a bird of prey … the plumage is dark and uniform in colour, the body of the shape and size of a pigeon." (Brenchley, p. 86)
48 Probably Julius Lucius Brenchley.

The watering place is not good, it being difficult to get really fresh water without taking our boats too high up the stream to be able to float out again till next tide.

There is a crater some 12 or 14 miles distant by land and water containing a lake of about 12 acres, which was visited by V________ and F________, who report, though the view was undoubtedly a very fine one, it hardly repaid them for the labour of reaching it.

P________ and D________ say much the same thing of the waterfall of which we heard so much. They compute the height of the perpendicular fall at 200 feet and judging by D________'s sketch, it is certainly smaller than that at Tutuila, though it is visible miles out at sea.

Great numbers of flying foxes.

H________ was ashore yesterday, vaccinating children. I learn that the natives are generally not only willing but anxious to be vaccinated, though small-pox has not yet shown itself in the island. The island is about 130 miles in circumference. Population: European, about 120; native, about 15,000; one or two families still heathen; about 3000 Roman Catholics; the remainder Protestants.

Beef, pork, and vegetables are to be had at Apia. There is also timber on the island fit for ship-building and for small spars.

Greatest elevation, about 4000 feet, if so much.

The government is patriarchal, but not very strong, the ancient seat of which was at Apolina,[49] a small island on the east coast, fortified by nature.

Roads run across and round the island. A few centipedes and small scorpions, but no venomous snakes. Exports, over $200,000 per annum; oil, cotton, *beche-la-mer*,[50] fibre, &c.

Mr. W________'s case was not eventually submitted to the Commodore's decision. It appears that Mr. W________, who is the Hamburgh consul, caught a native, who had broken into, and stolen from his premises; so instead of giving him up to be tried and punished by the natives, as he assuredly would have been, he kept him cruelly tied, hand and foot, and fed on bread and water.

---

49 Apolima.
50 Sea cucumber.

The matter was only prevented from causing an outbreak by the prisoner effecting his escape. It appears that he belongs to one of the other islands.

Mr. Williams, our consul here, has had probably as much experience of the South Sea Islands as any man in Polynesia, and seems anxious to see justice done to all races, for which he is of course abused by that portion of the whites who consider that natives in general are made solely for *their* enrichment and convenience. His idea of the state of morals in this group may be gathered from his statements, that the morality of this island (Apia being only one settlement) is perhaps the highest in the group, "because there are virgins here:" he omitted, however to specify the age of these interesting damsels.

The first cargo of oil was exported by Mr. Williams, in a vessel built by himself (in 1842, I think). The house in which he lives, the largest in the island, and in every way a civilized house, was built entirely by the hands of himself and a single native, as were also several articles of furniture handsomely inlaid with precious woods.

Mr. Murray is exceedingly bitter against the Catholics, whom he regards as children of the devil, one and all. His principal complaint against them, and a serious one if true, is that they affect to ignore all marriages celebrated by the clergy of other persuasions, so that when a native gets tired of his wife, or fancies another, he goes to the priest, who tells him that his former marriage is void, although he may have, perhaps, several children, and on his consenting to turn Catholic marries him to a fresh wife.

CHAPTER VIII.

Tongatabu — Protestant missionaries — Visit to King George and his palace — Taxation and land tenure — Royal dinner on board — Charley Moafu — Lesieli, the Tongan belle — Repulse and death of Captain Croker, of the 'Favourite' — The King's dinner-party — Religion and dress — Lakunba and Ovalau Islands — Viti Levu — Mr. Moore, the missionary — The gathering of the warriors at Bau — King Thacombau — Cannibal cookery — Viwa Island — Expedition to Rewa — Meet Mr. Crulman — The great river — Rewa, the Fijian Venice — King Tui Drakete — Messrs. Carey and Baker — The boat capsized — Purchase of curios — Thacombau's history — Fijian proverb — Charles Savage — Fijian cruelties — Fiji group — Exports and government — Kandavu — Messrs. White and Nettleton on polygamy — Amiteum or Annatom — Homicide on board a trader — Mr. Underwood's whaling station.

TONGATABU.[51]

July 17th. — Anchored off Nukualofa,[52] Tongatabu, at noon today.

The whole island is extremely flat, the most prominent object being the church, a large building on a small hillock.

The Wesleyan missionaries, Messrs. Whewell, Montrose, and Stevenson, came off to call on the Commodore. Some of my messmates landed in their boat, and were rather disgusted with the specimen they saw of the practical teaching of the religion of love and gentleness.

One of the natives had brought down Mr. W________'s horse to meet him, and had ridden rather too fast, I suppose for, the moment he got off, Mr. Whewell ran at him, took the riding-whip out of his hand, and began laying it about his bare back in very

---

51 Tongatapu, Kingdom of Tonga.
52 Nuku'alofa, the capital of Tonga.

vigorous style! The native, who was big enough to have eaten him, took his thrashing without offering to raise his hand.

Canoes came crowding round the ship, as at the other islands, with clubs, fruit, yams, and a few pigs and fowls for sale.

King George of Tonga by Julius Brenchley

July 18th. — Landed for an hour's stroll with M________ this afternoon. The village is divided off into something like streets by reed fences neatly made.

The houses are roomy and thatched, as at the other islands, though of an oblong instead of circular shape, as at Samoa; the walls built of the aforesaid reeds.

There is a law imposing a fine of $5 on any woman seen outside her fence improperly dressed, but this does not appear to be very strictly enforced.

We called on King George at the "Palace," and were presented to his Majesty by the Chief Secretary of State — an Englishman named Moss.

The King is a very tall man, with an intelligent countenance; and, in spite of his colour, looks every inch a statesman. Cigars and champagne were produced for our refection, and a few little compliments passed through Mr. Moss.

The King understands some English, but will not speak it.

The royal residence is a three-roomed cottage, but open above the partitions; built much like the other native houses, only with boarding outside the walls, and some smart European furniture within.

There is, however, a new house being built for his Tongan Majesty alongside the old one, and in a rather more ambitious style.

The roads are broad and good, and a number of offenders are now employed in cutting a boat passage through the reef.

The people are very heavily taxed, and payment is enforced vigorously; the whole property of debtors to the crown being frequently confiscated, and no "change" given. The capitation tax is $4 annually.

It is illegal in Tonga to sell land to aliens; therefore it is impossible even for the missionaries to buy land; but still land can be obtained on very long leases, with a tenure as safe as a freehold.

In this manner a Mr. Payne, who lives here with his family, rents 500 acres of the best land in Tonga, on which he has already a flourishing coffee plantation.

We looked in at the council house whilst Mr. Moss was engaged in paying the salaries of the judges and constables, the former of whom comprise all the principal chiefs of the islands. I think that about £50 was the highest salary, and £18 or £20 the lowest.

July 20th. — Met the King, his secretary Moss, and the three missionaries, at dinner with the Commodore.

His Majesty behaved very well at table, and returned thanks for his health in a neat little speech, saying that it was meet for him to do so, not only on account of the good-will expressed by the Commodore, but also for the good feeling which had always been shown him by the English nation, of which he had always with him the most convincing proof in the bones of Captain Croker and of the other brave Englishmen who fell fighting for the true faith on his side, &c., &c. He was rowed off in a gig manned by natives. His Majesty paid his first visit in state yesterday morning, and was received with a guard of honour, a royal salute, and manned yards. He wore a dress something like a naval uniform, with heavy shoulder-scales instead of epaulets.

The missionaries came on board the same day with their families, and brought a number of natives with them — a very fine-looking set of men: one of them, Charley Moafu, as handsome a man as you would find in any country. It is said here that he will probably be the successor of the present king, but at present he is a very wild youth, a regular Don Juan amongst the ladies, and said to have a sneaking fondness for strong liquors. He is the son of a great chief now settled in the Fijis. He talks English fluently, and seems very intelligent. He wants to take a passage to Fiji in us, but the King has not sufficient confidence in his promises of steadiness to trust him out of sight.

The missionaries also brought on board a very favourable specimen of the fair sex in the person of Lesieli, the belle of the Tongan group. She is shortly to be married to a young native missionary. I got Moafu down first and sketched his portrait, and afterwards, with some difficulty, persuaded Lesieli to come below and sit for her picture as well. She was as demure and precise as the primmest English maiden could have been under the circumstances. She has very regular features and the worst of it is that no one at home will believe the sketch to represent a South Sea Islander.

Landed yesterday with L________ and D________, and walked out to see the "Bea," where Captain Croker and the men of the 'Favourite' were killed. The site of the stockade is about 4 miles from Nukualofa. There remains now only the ditch and bank on which the stockade was built, and the village within it.

It appears that Captain Croker was induced by the missionaries to land his men and attack the pagan enemies of King George in the year 1841. He seems to have been a religious enthusiast, and is said to have preceded his men to the stockade gate with a Bible in one hand and his sword in the other, with which he began cutting the lashings, in spite of their warnings to him to desist; so, finding him obstinate, they fired and wounded him. Still he continued; so, they prodded him with a bayonet lashed to a stick.

Then he retired, and leant against a big tree hard-by, which was shown to us, and here he was shot dead through the heart. The remaining officers and men were repulsed with heavy loss, and the first lieutenant took the ship away.

The greater part of the way we found plantations of bananas, taro, yam, or *tappa*, on either side of the road, which was broad and even, and pleasantly shaded by rows of coconut palms.

The sound of the tappa hammer was not to be heard resounding in every village, as at some other places, but we were informed that this was caused, not by the idleness of the people, but by the recent death of a great chief, in mourning for whom all noise in the settlements is discouraged.

July 21st. — The Commodore, B________,[53] and I dined with the King this evening, where we met the (Governor or Viceroy — an extremely stout man, who could speak a little English (but like most of the Malayan races would not do so for fear of covert ridicule) — and the Chief Justice, a smaller man, with a not unpleasant, though hard, knowing face.

We were in jackets and white waistcoats; the King in the same blue tailcoat and gilt buttons which he wore when dining with the Commodore on board. The Governor wore a frockcoat, something like a naval captain's of 1855. We were waited on by one half-caste and two native girls, while four "Beef-eaters" with white staffs stood at the inner and outer gate. A table was spread in European fashion, and the viands, awaiting their turn, were disposed in dishes on the ground in the next apartment, causing the attendant nymphs, whose duty was to pick them up and hand them in through the door, to present a still stranger appearance, as

---

53 Brenchley.

they stooped in their lava-lavas, than ever was depicted by Leech's pencil.

The preparation of this dinner had occupied the greater part of the day, under the personal superintendence of his most gracious Majesty.

In former days, we were told that two or three cooks, if not more, would probably have lost their lives for spoiling some particular stew, but today there were no ghosts of strangled cooks to haunt the banquet. There was nothing remarkable about the dishes, except the great variety and numbers of fish, birds, &c., which successively loaded the table, together with champagne and other wines, and good bottled beer. The only new dish was a native delicacy, being a sort of baked pudding of coconut and cane-juice, and something else, rather too rich for my taste, and served up in banana leaves.

These people carry their ideas of rank and exclusiveness to as great a degree as the most aristocratic nation in Europe, and it appears that no little offence was given to the Tongan swells by the missionaries in bringing Lesieli, who with all her beauty is not of noble birth, into the Commodore's cabin and the presence of the King. The queen, who is too unwell to receive visitors, as she suffers from elephantiasis and a variety of other diseases, sent a basket fairly woven to the Commodore during dinner as a present, with a polite message, which he answered by an equally flowery one. H________, who visited her in his medical capacity, describes her as the largest woman he had ever seen, and estimates her probable weight at 20 stone. The present king, whose name is George Tubon, and title "Tuikanakubulu," governs with the assistance of a parliament of chiefs, and has reigned for twenty years. There are fifty-four Europeans in this island, who look to the consular agent in the Fijis. After two failures, a mission was established here in 1826.

The native population numbers from 9000 to 10,000, all of whom profess Christianity: of these the Wesleyans claim all but some 1200, which they estimate as the number of the Roman Catholic congregation. Three of the missionaries of the latter religion came on board to ask for the dispatch of a mail, and to pay their respects to the Commodore, but we could not persuade them to stop to dinner. Our missionaries give a bad report of the climate, which they describe as enervating in the extreme.

Crimes of violence are very rare, but immorality prevails to a greater extent here than at any place we have visited yet, except perhaps the village of Apia. But I do not think that the blame is to be laid at the door of the white man here, as at Apia.

Shirts are rather more common here than with the Samoans, and the women *generally* comply with the law which requires them to cover their bosoms when outside their own enclosures or those of their friends; but the covering is the very scantiest pinafore, suspended from the neck, and blowing aside with every breeze. The truth is that dress does not suit the figures of these savage girls, who live in a climate which requires only enough to satisfy decency. Lesieli certainly looked handsome when she came on board, although clad in a dowdy European dress which ill-suited her form; but at home, fettered by nothing but the lava-lava round her waist, she was a picture of grace and symmetry.

LAKUNBA[54] AND OVALAU.

July 22nd. — Sailed for Lakunba, one of the smallest islands in the Fiji group, at 11.30 this morning, at the same time as the 'Falcon,' which goes on to Auckland and carries our homeward-bound mails.

25th. — Off Lakunba today, but there being nothing attractive in the appearance of its steep hillsides, the Commodore stood on his course for Ovalau Island, where we anchored off Levuka on the 26th, at 1.15 A.M., in a natural harbour formed by a vast curving reef, with a very narrow opening, which together with the little white-roofed settlement of Levuka[55] and the mountains and ravines afford a view of singular beauty. The great island of Viti Levu (Great Fiji), which is some 90 miles long by 60 broad,

---

54 Lakeba.
55 A settlement on the east coast of Ovalau.

is plainly visible from this island, and is probably about 15 miles distant.

July 27th. — Landed with F________ and D________ this morning, armed with sketchbooks and towels, determined to spend the day between bathing and sketching.

We first called on the missionary, Mr. Moore, who impressed me very favourably, being free from the bigotry which shows itself in the words and deeds of some of his co-religionists (Wesleyans), and he actually talked to me for half an hour without saying a word against the Roman Catholic missionaries.

He has not been here very long, having before been stationed in Viti Levu. His house is the neatest and prettiest white man's house that we have yet seen in these islands, and commands a beautiful view of the little settlement beneath, the breaker-bound reef with its many tinted waters within and without, and the distant islands beyond.

We found the people uglier, dirtier, more mean looking, and in every way more repulsive than any we have seen during the cruise, and even their pastor assigns them a lower place in the scale of morality than any in the group.

The whites complain much of thefts committed by the natives, for which no redress can be obtained, as the chief, Tui Levuka,[56] is a drunken vagabond, who will not take the trouble to keep his subjects in order. Levuka is tributary to Bau.[57]

Here, as nearly all over the Fijis, the woolly haired, dark Papuan race has mixed with the fairer and straighter-haired Malayans or Tongans, and produced a great number of shades and characters.

There are several streams, with cascades of various heights flowing down the ravines; there is one about two miles from Levuka, where there is a fall of about 40 feet, and two other smaller ones, each with a deep pool at the bottom, so disposed that a bather may jump successively down the whole three of them.

---

56 Paramount chief on the island of Ovalau. It is a title, not a name.
57 One of the smallest islands at the time, but also the most powerful.

S_______ returned this evening from Bau, whither he had been in the whaler to inspect the passage through which the ship will have to pass.

At Bau he had the good luck to witness the gathering of the warriors, some four hundred and thirty in number, who have assembled at the call of King Thacombau[58] from Levuka, Kandavu,[59] and other places, allies or tributaries, to make war on Bau.[60] About one-third only had firearms, the others having clubs or spears, or both.

Thacombau first went through the form of asking them whether they would join in the fight, and then put them through a sort of exercise, in the course of which they performed various antics, indicative of their desperate valour and loyalty.

It appears that the impending war arose on this wise. The inhabitants of Bau invited one of these tribes to a feast, at which arrangements were to be made about planting and similar peaceful matters. Their treacherous hosts fell suddenly upon their unsuspecting guests, and cooked and eat seventy of them.

The favourite Fijian mode of dishing up human flesh is to boil or bake a man alive, for which purpose they use whalers' oil pots. But you must first catch your hare.

July 29th, — The rain came down in torrents the greater part of the morning, but towards noon it cleared up, so we weighed about one o'clock, and very well the little coral-girt island looked as we steamed briskly through the narrow gateway of the reef.[61]

---

58 Known as Seru Epenisa Cakobau. Brenchley used the title 'Tui Viti,' or the paramount chief of Fiji (ie. King). His war of unification ended in 1871 with the formation of the Kingdom of Fiji.
59 Kadavu, the fourth largest Fijian island.
60 A confusing sentence. The gathering was *on* Bau Island, they were not making war *on* Bau. Thacombau wanted to extend Bau's power over all Fiji.
61 On that day: "I [Cecil Foljambe] had heard an explosion in the after ward-room, and this was caused by the bursting of a cask of brandy, which had ignited. The ward-room steward was drawing off some brandy for use, and incautiously held a candle too close to the bung. Lieutenant Meade ran into his cabin, and seizing his blankets, bedding, &c, threw them on the fire

Charles Wise, the half-caste, was on board as pilot, and he, together with S________ and B________,[62] conned the ship clear of the reefs and through the channel from the foretopsail-yard.

Anchored off Viwa Island, and about 3 miles from Bau at 4.30 p.m.

VITI-LEVU

There has been a difficulty in Viti-Levu, a British subject named Crulman[63] having been clubbed by a native; not killed indeed, but still seriously injured; and I am to be sent to explain to the two chiefs of the tribes to whom the offender is supposed to belong, how unfortunately the Commodore cannot stop here long enough for us to deal with them immediately; but what a very particular scrape they will get into, when the '*Esk*' arrives here about a fortnight hence, should they prove on investigation to be in the wrong, and the guilty man remain unpunished. Wise goes with me as pilot and interpreter; one of the culprits is a pagan cannibal, the other a Christian, who should have known better.

July 30th, Sunday. — I started for Rewa at 11.30 p.m. — a dark and rainy night. The cutter was pretty full, for besides the men, their arms, provisions, blankets, and a shift of clothes, and the interpreter, midshipman of the boat, and myself, there were B________,[64] who goes to see the country, and F________,[65] who is sent to sketch for the Commodore.

---

and smothered it. It might have been very serious, for it was close to the after magazine." (Foljambe, p.203)

62 Brenchley.

63 "The day after our arrival the Commodore was appraised by a written deposition and formal complaint, that a white man, of the name of Creel-man [sic], a small cotton planter in the island of Viti-Levu, had been beaten and wrongfully used by some natives on the banks of the Wai-Levu. Being further informed from another source, that the offenders had escaped pun-ishment owing to the protection of two petty chiefs of the interior, the one a heathen, the other a nominal convert to Christianity, Sir William thought propter to despatch an officer to the King of Rewa…" (Brenchley, p.154)

64 Brenchley.

65 Foljambe.

July 31st. — It rained with hardly an instant's cessation till sunrise this morning.

We crossed the reefs with the high tide, and reached the mouth of the river Wai-ni-bocasi about half-past 1 a.m. We got on shore a good many times, but were very lucky in always getting off again at once.

After entering the river our course lay for several hours through thick mangrove swamps, the river only about 100 yards wide, and winding very closely. We laid in the two after-oars so as to have more room for ourselves and the provisions, in the sternsheets, and to give all the men in turn a spell of one hour out of every five. It was not very cheerful work, pulling all night soaked to the very bones, through the utter darkness, the ceaseless rain, the light foul wind, and the miasma of a tropical swamp, but the men kept to their work for eleven hours without a check wonderfully well.

We spliced the mainbrace soon after midnight, served quinine at daybreak, and a nip of raw gin all round somewhat later.

About an hour before daybreak, we met a whaleboat full of white men coming down the river; hailed her to close, and found that she contained a deputation of the white settlers in Viti-Levu, bearing a petition to the Commodore to inquire into the case of Mr. Crulman, who, together with his witnesses, was in the boat.

On hearing that theirs was the very affair which brought me up the river, they proposed to return; but by my advice proceeded, to tell their own story to the Commodore.

Soon after daylight broke, I shot a brace of wild duck and one or two kinds of small heron. After passing the mangrove swamps the banks were lined with wild sugar-cane, occasional cotton plants, and foliage of greater variety than usual. We saw very few natives, not a dozen altogether, though we passed two small villages; those, however, whom we did see cheerfully exchanged salutations with us, in marked contrast to the only white man we saw, a sulky fellow, who, like some of his race in these parts, seemed ashamed to meet civilized men, and stood away from us at his door, though we stopped close by to pick up a hawk which B________[66] had shot.

About nine o'clock we struck the Wai-Levu (great river), a river as broad as the Rhine at Coblentz, and navigable by large boats for 50 or 60 miles above the place where we entered it. We followed the Wai-Levu to Rewa, a large native town, built on a perfect water labyrinth, the river separating into a great number of channels, so that nearly all the communications within the town are carried on by means of canoes in this little Fijian Venice. We found the King, Tui Drakete,[67] on the point of starting in a small schooner to be present at the burial of one of the principal Fiji chieftainesses who had just died, taking with him a splendid turtle as an offering; but whether to the living or the dead, I did not quite make out.

His gracious Majesty expressed great regret at being unable to remain at Rewa, to do us the honours of the place himself, it being impossible for him to be absent from the burial of the "Queen-woman." He complied with everything that I had to request, and placed his "palace" at my disposal.

Our cannibal friend is away at a place too distant to be reached by me and my handful of men, or to be got at at all within the time which will elapse before we sail from Fiji. But the King has sent the Commodore's despatches to the two chiefs by a messenger capable of reading their contents to them; the man was dispatched from my presence in a canoe up the river as fast as he could go.

We reached the house of Mr. Carey, the Wesleyan missionary, about eleven o'clock, and the men, having had ten hours' constant pulling against wind and stream most part of the way, were so tired, that while I stepped out to meet Mr. Carey at the bows of the boat, three of them fell asleep on their thwarts.

We gladly accepted Mr. Carey's hospitality and quartered the men in the King's house, where also the excellent missionary took care that they should want for nothing.

---

66 Brenchley.
67 Tui Dreketi; paramount chief of Rewa, then B. V. Rabici, though little is known about him.

Being anxious to give the men a day's rest, and time to sleep and clean their arms and dry their clothes, I left them at Rewa snoring, under charge of F________, whilst I with O________, having done justice to a good meal at Mr. Carey's, pushed on to Davui in a canoe, taking our guns with us for the chance of duck by the way. But our powder had suffered from the previous drenching night of rain and swamp mist — or else we shot very ill, for we only bagged a brace.

The missionary of Davui-Levu, Mr. Baker, who since our visit has been killed by an inland tribe, and eaten, was away at Vicia, but his wife entertained us. The house, which, with its high peculiar-shaped roof, looked in the distance something like a Chinese building, is beautifully situated on a hill overlooking the river, and commanding a glorious view of the broad stream winding through the rich plains to the southward and eastward, and separating into many branches at Rewa and below; on the other side a panorama of rolling woodlands, rising gently to the lofty mountains of the interior, four ranges of which, each distinctly rising above and separate from the other, and crowned by a handsome row of peaks, are visible from the house.

This place may be said to be at present the utmost limit of Christianity in this island, the house itself overlooking the heathen temple below. Mr. and Mrs. Baker have only been here a few weeks.

On the way down the river, in returning, one of the natives managed to capsize the canoe: the outrigger flying over, knocked us under, and struck the gun out of my hand, which, together with various other articles, went straight to the bottom of the Vai-Levu. But luckily for us we were near the bank, and the river was shallow, so we soon recovered nearly all we had lost, the only thing spoilt being my sketch-book, and the chief inconvenience was that of having to pass part of another night in wet clothes, and cramped up in a canoe: very chilling work.

August 1st. — The natives about here are as ugly as the rest of the Fijians; they stain their hair in the same manner as the other islanders and wear rather less clothes. The Fijians are not, however, so dark skinned as I had been led to expect, though that portion of the inhabitants who obviously, spring from the Papuan race have hair nearly as woolly as a negro's.

Yesterday, Mr. Carey got the chiefs to send out into the villages and make the people bring in whatever curios and samples of native manufacture they had for sale, and B________ with Charles Wise purchased a good deal for the Commodore, not that there was much worth taking — clubs, spears, mats, and pottery being the principal articles. Mr. Carey, however, insisted on my accepting from him a very handsome blackwood spear, some 20 or 25 feet long, carefully grafted over and bound with native sinnet and twine.

We got back to the ship by 4 p.m. today, thanks to a fair wind, having been only eight hours *en route*. At several points, we found the natives wading out into the river to meet us with clubs and spears for sale, in consequence of the order from the chiefs. I got two large clubs and three small ones, all well finished, for 15., and a little tobacco. One of these clubs, of black ironwood, was polished by constant use or rubbing, with a number of teeth, or what were said to be teeth (human), purporting each to represent one man killed by means of the said club.

We noticed on our way a few long-tailed parrots, with very brilliant plumage, circling high above the river. One was shot by B________. My bag was eight duck and three other water birds. We never diverged from our course, but only took what happened to come across us.

We passed several parties of natives wading up the river along the bank, there being no roads in the country, and the rivers taking their place. All those who were travelling carried their clubs with them. I am informed that this is caused by the universal distrust and treachery of the Fijian character.

During our absence Thacombau and his wife, or queen consort, an enormous woman, have visited the ship and were received with royal honours. Thacombau was once a great cannibal, and it is not many years since he walked through an alley of vanquished foes suspended by their feet, and with his club marked off those who were to be "killed for the use of the house." Now, however, he has embraced Christianity, and is determined that it shall be the religion of all Fiji, of which he is undoubtedly the most powerful chief, though not the actual sovereign.

He expressed great friendship for the Commodore, offering him the choice of all the clubs and spears in the island (Bau) which is his capital; and expressed his intentions of forcing the Ovalau natives and others who have robbed white men to give up the thieves. The Commodore gave him his own rifle (a Westley Richards), with which he was of course delighted. He is a much finer looking man than most Fijians, and has some beard he wore a white shirt, and a cloth about his loins. The ship is loaded with savage arms and other curios, which are to be had here very cheap.

There is a small fort at Bau, mounting four guns, from which Thacombau saluted the Commodore on leaving. The town is said to be very dirty. News has arrived that Thacombau's warriors have taken eleven villages or towns, which they wait his orders to burn. The Fijians are arrant cowards, which accounts for the facility with which the Tongans usually thrash them.

Three men killed constitutes with them a very sanguinary battle. A favourite Fijian proverb well illustrates their ideas on fighting.

Q. "Where is the brave man?"

A. "Being dragged" (*i.e.* to the oven).

Q. "And where is the coward?"

A. "Talking of his deeds in the town."

They are very hospitable to all strangers whom it does not suit them to eat. Cannibalism, however, has died out in those parts, and wherever white men live or have familiar access. This vice, however, has not always been confined to the natives, and it is said that up to the present time the palm of having eaten the greatest quantity of human flesh on record has been borne away by a white man appropriately named Charles Savage, who assisted the people of Bau in the wars wherein they obtained their present supremacy. He excelled in all vices peculiar both to savage and civilized life to such a degree as to disgust even his cannibal allies, and it is satisfactory to add that he was eventually eaten himself. We have heard stories of the Fijians which show them to have more innate cruelty in their character than the islanders we have visited in other parts of these seas: launching their war canoes over the prostrate bodies of living captives, which were made to serve as rollers by being lashed to soft trunks of young banana trees; burying men alive round the feet of the posts which support the chiefs' houses; boiling alive and baking alive their prisoners previous to a cannibal feast, &.

The name of Fiji or Viti is given to some thirty islands, of which the two largest average about 3500 square miles apiece; and the entire population of the group is variously estimated at from 100,000 to 300,000. Of these 60,000 are claimed to be professed Christians, and the religion is spreading fast.

Cotton is being planted more and more extensively, and the exports of the group have increased from £13,000 to £20,000 in the last year. Of general government there is none, but a number of petty kings and chiefs exercise absolute power in their own dominions, but they for the most part are tributary in some degree to Bau.

KANDAVU.[68]

August 3rd. — Arrived at Kandavu at 9.30 a.m., having sailed at 10.30 on the previous morning. A pretty little settlement nestling in the heart of a bay both broad and deep, formed by softly wooded rolling hills, and terminating at the southern horn in a huge cliff rising directly and almost perpendicularly out of the sea to the height of nearly 4000 feet.

We made the land soon after midnight and hove to at four till daylight. I was much taken with the two missionaries (Messrs. White and Nettleton) and their flock, whom we prefer to other Fijians as far as any conclusion can be arrived at during so short a visit. The Kandavans profess to be entirely independent of Bau, but within the last few days Thacombau sent a canoe to fetch away the shinnet lashings from off the chiefs own house to repair

---

68 Kadavu Island, in the Fijian group.

his war canoes, a service which he could hardly have obtained through mere intertribal politeness.

Most of the men are also away serving under Thacombau in the present war.

The population is about 11,000. A census is taken every year, and shows an annual diminution of several hundred.

The missionaries claim the whole as professing Christians, and give them a character for a higher state of morality than is to be found elsewhere in Fiji, and all that we could see bore out this statement very fully, notwithstanding the absence of the men.

We got the leg of one of the reverend gentlemen slightly on a stretch on the vexed question of admitting polygamists to baptism, Mr. Nettleton affirming that a heathen never expects to be formally admitted into the Church till he has put away all his wives save one, and married that one, although they will regularly attend service and read their Testament.

Polygamy has the effect of reducing the population, it being very rare for a man with many wives to have three children who reach man's estate.

AMITEUM.[69]

At 4 P.M. this afternoon we sailed for Amiteum, and arrived on Sunday the 6th, anchoring in a snug berth between the bay and Whale Island. We found the *'Esk'* lying here with our mail on board — all my letters from home have miscarried — nothing for me but a dun from the Admiralty.

August 7th. — An A.B., named Craighead, who died on board yesterday, was buried today.

There is a sandalwood trading brig here, whose master, named Robinson, has shot his mate with a revolver loaded with small shot; the mate died eight or ten days afterwards, but I believe there is some slight doubt as to whether he died from the effects of the shot (in the head) or from dysentery. He goes to Sydney a prisoner on board the *'Esk,' via* Fiji.

---

69 Aneityum, in the Vanuatu group.

August 8th. — Mr. Underwood has a whaling establishment on the little island, where he also stores his sandalwood and *beche-de-mer*.

Last week they killed two whales and were fast to four in five days; today and yesterday the boats have not gone out.

I have arranged to start in one of their whaleboats at daylight tomorrow, and, judging by last week's work, we shall have bad luck indeed if we don't get fast to a whale. P________ comes also if room can be found for him.

August 9th. — Blowing too hard for the boats to go out today, so we are disappointed as to the whaling. Our homeward mails went by H.M.S. '*Esk*,' which sailed this forenoon for Fiji and Sydney. I have not landed except for a few minutes on Whale Island, but all the natives who came off to the ship were small, ugly, of stunted growth and woolly-haired. The missionaries give a poor account of their mental faculties, though I believe that they are all Christians, and have been so for the last seven or eight years; the first teachers (Samoan) were placed here in 1841. The last case of cannibalism occurred thirteen years ago. Every person in the island above five years old can read more or less and attends school. Crime is rare, life and property secure. Mr. Inglis, the missionary, states that their standard of morality is at present a high one, but asserts that before Christianity took hold on them they were as bad as any in the group.

Some of the traders and others call the island Annattom.[70] It is about 14 miles long by 8 broad, and bears a population of 2200, which is at present stationary, or very slightly decreasing but in recent years, beginning with 1836, three epidemics have swept the island, each one taking about one in three. The last was measles, the former a sort of cholera. The climate is damp and rather

---

70 While modern name is Aneityum, it has been called Amiteum, Anatom, and Keamu.

unhealthy. No venomous snakes. Cotton grows well. There are about twenty Europeans, traders and others, usually in the island.

The island is volcanic, but reef-bound. Hurricanes frequent and severe.

CHAPTER IX.

Messrs. Gordon and Paton — Their determination and prospects — Nova Scotian Mission Society — Tanna — A chief's dress — Failure of negotiations — Operations of the landing party — The Marum, or dancing ground — Engagement with the savages — Death of Quatangan — A misfire — Submission of the native chiefs — Laws and government — Dillon Bay — Erromango — Mr. Henry, the sandalwood trader — Murder of Fletcher — Messrs. Williams and Harris — Projected expedition against Narai's village — Scouting by night, with its results — Submission of Warris Nangri — Fate of the guide — Vila Harbour — Vate and Deception Islands — Moafu's exploit — The chiefs submit — Leave the New Hebrides and sail for Banks Islands.

August 10th. — Sailed at 5.30 from Amiteum in company with the missionary brig *Dayspring,*' on board which craft there are several Dissenting ministers belonging to this (the Nova Scotian Mission Society), amongst them Mr. Gordon, brother to the Gordon who, together with his wife, was murdered at Erromango,[71] the island we are going to after Tanna,[72] His fixed determination is to renew the task wherein his brother lost his life (as well as Mr. Williams and others before him), and he hopes that the operations which the conduct of the natives who have murdered other white men since have rendered it necessary for us to carry out on our arrival there, will enable him to live amongst them.

There is, however, little chance of a man imbued with his extreme principles — anti-smoking, anti-dancing, teetotal, anti-everything in fact which rejoices the heart of man — succeeding amongst a set of savages. Mr. Paton, late missionary at Tanna,

71 An island in the Vanuatu archipelago.
72 Another island in the Vanuatu archipelago.

is also on board her. He likewise is sanguine of resuming the mission at his island though he has had fever and ague twenty-four times in one year, and has buried his wife there; though he has had his house and church destroyed, his own life several times attempted and only saved by the interposition of a friendly chief, and though he has had to watch gun in hand by his wife's grave for ten consecutive nights until her body was completely decomposed, to prevent the cannibals from exhuming it for food, he still wishes to return and resume his labours.

Still, the impression left on our minds by the missionaries of this Society was not altogether favourable. In recounting their grievances in general, and their sufferings at the hands of these islanders in particular, too much stress was laid, to my thinking, on the loss of private and mission property — of Mr. Paton's piano, and of "upwards of £100 worth of other furniture and stores" — which these ungodly pagans or pseudo-converts had destroyed.

That these men are not the huckstering humbugs that their opponents represent them to be is well attested by the blood of their comrades shed in the New Hebrides,[73] and by the readiness with which they constantly expose themselves to similar risks. But they have courted harsh criticisms by the unctuous language of cant which makes their conversation and writings too often offensive to all sensible men; by their exaggerated accounts of sundry attempts on their lives, when, according to their own evidence, they were so helpless and unresisting that it seems hard to believe that a really serious attempt could have failed; and lastly, by calling in the sword of the naval power for the punishment of their persecutors, thereby causing great scandal to the South Sea missions in general. I believe these men to be in the main honest and well meaning, and the present condition of Amiteum shows that in the long run they are successful, though they may not necessarily be men of education and refinement.

Whatever opinions may be held as to the propriety in a religious point of view of missionaries applying for armed protection, the duty of the naval officer is simply to assure himself that

---

73 Vanuatu.

the applicants are British subjects, and that their complaints of outrage to life or property are well founded, and then to afford them the protection which is their right, without regard to the colour of their neckcloths.

TANNA. [74]

We arrived at Tanna and anchored in Resolution Bay[75] at 1.15 p.m. The entrance is narrow, and I am told that the natives often fire on trading vessels, but they attempted no such impertinence with us, though they clustered down on the beach in considerable numbers armed with guns and spears.

On the northern side of the harbour is a very active volcano, the lowest of a fine range of mountains which traverses the island. During the whole time of our stay at Tanna dense volumes of very white smoke, with fire visible by night, issued from the crater, while eruptions took place of lava-flame and hot stones every six or eight minutes.

The village off which we are lying is really very prettily situated on a white sandy beach, between two rocky points, with well-varied tropical bush, the whole guarded by a curving coral reef from point to point. Some of the chiefs were induced by Mr. Paton to come off to the ship. They were the ugliest, the most indecent, the most grotesque, and the most utterly barbarous both in appearance and actual fact, of any people whom we have yet seen.

There was only one chief who wore any garment save the exaggeration of indecency common to all of these islanders; he wore an old red jacket of the 12th Regiment and a naval officer's sword-belt (probably belonging to one of the officers of the 'Iris' who was killed here). His hair was divided into an infinite number of tails, each about two feet long, composed of half-a-dozen hairs apiece, parcelled or wormed with a blade of white grass, the whole confined by a tight band at the nape of the neck, and then spreading out again over the back. A white cock's

---

74 An island in the Vanuatu archipelago.
75 Named after Captain Cook's *Resolution*, which visited in August 1774.

feather, artificially lengthened to about three feet, was erected in the forepart of his head-dress; each ear was decorated with eight or ten large rings of tortoise-shell, and his face painted red and black. Altogether he was about the queerest-looking specimen of humanity I have ever seen here or elsewhere.

The above description will do for most of the Tannamen,[76] with the exception of the jacket and of the feather, which seem to be the mark of a chief. The Commodore, through Mr. Paton, warned them of the punishment which would befall them and their people if by noon tomorrow they, together with the other offending chiefs, do not make their appearance on board to guarantee better behaviour in future.

August 11th. — Mr. Paton obtained a further respite for the natives until this evening, in hopes that they would yet give in and come on board — which, however, they did not.

The village on the beach between the points is friendly, and the two which it is intended to punish are situated, one in the bush at the head of the bay, the other between the volcano and the northern shore, also in the bush, but in such a position that they can be easily shelled.

This afternoon we shifted our berth command the landing-place and the northern village, and got the boats out ready for landing tomorrow.

This evening Mr. Paton landed to make one more effort to bring matters to a peaceable solution, and was met by a crowd of natives on the beach. Fearing foul play, we kept a forty-pounder, loaded with shell, trained on them during the conference. They allowed him to come away safely, and when he was reporting his failure to the Commodore on the quarterdeck, he very nearly broke down — and he had in fact been sobbing like a child.

August 12th. — Immediately after breakfast a stream anchor was laid out, the ship swung broadside to the landing-place some 700 yards distant, and the landing party was mustered, numbering

---

76 Tanna Islanders.

178 all told. Some little time was spent in arming the boom-boats and rocket-cutters, and at nine we went to general quarters and opened fire with shell and rockets and marine small-arms on the bush above the landing place, and on the two villages, as nearly as we could guess their situation. The bush was so thick that it was almost impossible to see whether the majority of shells burst or not, but the rockets did their work well.

The natives on the northern shore attempted to return our fire with their muskets from the bushy hill which overhangs the ship.

There had undeniably existed a pretty strong undercurrent of opinion that we were likely to get a dusting, as happened to the 'Iris' at this same island, where she lost an officer and several men; and to the 'Favourite,' which was repulsed at Tonga, with the loss of her captain, two other officers, and a heavy proportion of men; but there's luck in odd numbers, and this time we accomplished our task.

Mr. Paton endeavoured, but in vain, to get us a guide from the friendly village, and we were therefore left to find our way through the bush to the hostile village as best we could, by the light of the vague directions which the missionaries were able to give us before landing. Our object was to destroy as much as possible of the villages and plantations, and then try to burn the bush.

We landed about 11 a.m., under cover of a cheerful fire from guns manned by crews composed mainly of officers, cooks and stewards, &c., who remained on board the ship. We also fired two rounds from our boats' guns into the bush before effecting our landing, which was unopposed.

Of the swarms of natives who had been visible before, nothing had been seen since the stern-chasers were run out, previously to opening fire, in the morning. Near the landing-place we found a path leading up the hill. Here we formed: the Commander leading up the path, the first part of marines next, then my company, then the others; the whole extended in skirmishing order. The "Advance" was sounded and then the "Double." Finding in a very few minutes that the bush was in parts quite impenetrable, and that those on the flanks could not under any circumstances keep pace with the centre files in the path, having a quarter of a mile of hill before them, I gave the word "on the centre close," on my own hook, the Commander being out of hail; and on advancing to the head of my company, which was now in Indian file, found that the marines had done the same.

Near the top of the ridge we found a small fenced clearing in the bush, where we had just room to fall in and muster; then the Commander, judging that we must be close to a village and plantations, made us extend in skirmishing order, C________ on the left, supported by H________, and I on the right, directing me to sweep along the top of the ridge in the same order, destroying without burning anything I found on the way, and to look out for the bugle for assembly, which he would sound as soon as he reached the dancing-ground — a clear space under a very large tree on the highest part of the hogback, which had been pointed out to us the previous evening by the missionary — and to be careful not to separate.

I have seen some bad tropical bush, but I think that this was some of the very worst; and though the ground was level and the footing tolerably good, we had not gone far before I found that it was impossible to force a way through it at more than a snail's pace, and that the greater part of my men, instead of cutting a way for themselves, kept following in my footsteps.

It was no use giving the order "on the left close," as the files, already much separated by the unequal obstructions of the bush, would only have lost themselves in the maze of the bush in rear of the left and centre, and I should have had to trust to the direction taken by whoever happened to be on the left; I therefore called in the men to follow me in Indian file, and took the first path leading away on the port bow, in the direction of the line of march proposed by the Commander, and consequently of the rendezvous at the dancing-ground.

Sometimes the bush was a perfect labyrinth of paths, if they can be called paths, through which we frequently had to crawl on hands and knees, though uncertain of what sort of a reception was to be expected before rising to our feet again: paths in fact that a high-spirited Irish pig would have disdained to make use of.

Sometimes the paths all led away, and we were again forced to cut our way through the dense bush, — a process so fatiguing to the leader that I was obliged to make my coverer and right-hand man take turns with me in leading the way.

We passed several small plantations by the way, which we destroyed without wasting any time, it being a beautiful arrangement of Nature that the trees which are the principal sustenance of these savage nations, which occasionally require punishment, are of so soft a wood that a banana, or mummy apple-tree, 6 inches thick, can be hewn down with one blow of a sword.

We heard the bugle, or fancied we did — once and only once — very distant and indistinct, in the direction we were taking (we had then inclined to the left). We occasionally (I or another) ascended the trees to verify the course I was steering. Once, when S________ and I were aloft, the ship still firing guns which we could hear though not see, a shell burst in the woods, right in the line which I had good reason for imagining Captain D________ to have taken. This was rather perplexing; but I concluded to continue my course along the ridge, shells or no shells, and effect a juncture with the main body at all hazards.

The men followed me as closely as possible, but the paths were so tortuous and narrow that I could never see more than five or six at a time. In reply to my oft-repeated question, the answer was always that the men were closing up in the rear; and it was some little time after we had turned to the left that I became aware of the fact that I had only the 1st Section following me, with R________, the P.O.[77] of the 2nd Section, who had lost his men, but never reported the circumstance. Soon afterwards we came across O________, the midshipman of the 2nd Section, who had lost all his men and himself too.

It appeared afterwards that his right-hand man had done the same. Halted for five minutes, and mustered while F________ climbed a tree, and got some coconuts wherewith to quench our

---

77 Petty Officer.

great thirst, for the sun was very hot, and we were somewhat fagged. We passed a place where a corpse had been recently dragged along the ground, but saw no traces of our men.

We reached the *"Marum,"* or "dancing-ground," before one o'clock — a flat bare smooth piece of ground, shaded by an enormous banyan tree, on the highest point of the ridge. We halted the men at the edge of the clearing, and examined the spot. The remainder of the landing party had never been here, though this was the rendezvous. There were two paths leading away from the dancing-place, along one of which were native footprints freshly made by men running, I therefore decided, after making the men cooey in chorus for some time ineffectually, to pursue this path for a quarter of an hour, and if we found no signs of our men, to return and wait at the dancing-ground; and I wrote a notice to that effect across the smooth floor. We found a plantation hard by, which we destroyed. Then, moving on, struck tracks of white men, and immediately after effected a juncture with the remainder of our party.

I was very glad to find that H________ had the whole of the remainder of my company with him. They had all borne down to the left, and had never found the dancing-ground.

It appears that the bugle had been sounded several times, and that messengers were sent by the Commander to communicate with me, though somehow, they all took the wrong direction, and that what we took for the explosion of a shell from the ship was an abortive attempt to fire a rocket to show us the position of the Commander.

The rocket struck a tree before it got above the foliage, and burst in the bush close to the point of departure. I set my twelve men to work cutting down the banana trees, &c., with their swords (without grounding their rifles) in the plantation, where we were divided from the main body similarly employed only by a hedge.

We had not been here many minutes when we were attacked by the natives, coming up at first from our proper rear.

There was a small irregular volley from the edge of the bush ten or twelve yards distant, and then turning, I found poor

Holland lying mortally wounded, with his entrails hanging over the waistband of his trousers; the next instant the devils were yelling all round us.

The yell of these savages is a peculiar one — not extremely loud, but more like the cry of some beast of prey than of human beings. The men dashed off in the direction of the thickest of the yells — where dark forms could be seen glancing through the thick bush — like a pack of hounds thrown off in close cover to the sound of a view-halloo.

A tall native, as naked as the rest of his countrymen, sprang out of the bush with a long musket in his hand. He was, I think, the man who shot Holland, and was looking for a chance of getting hold of the body, but finding that I had left a file of men to guard it, he thought better to make a dash for it.

He passed me at about ten yards, and I covered him with my revolver; but before I could cock and fire it, he was hidden by an intervening bush.

He was making straight for Heathcote, the midshipman of the other company, who was endeavouring to persuade his revolver to go off and discharge its contents at two others beyond him, but it missed fire; so, I shouted, "Native to you, Heathcote!" He went at him like a brick with his sword, cut him down with a blow at the back of the head, and triumphantly held up the captured musket, crying, "I've got him, sir," as I passed him.

The native yells were now apparently, all round, but were succumbing to the English cries from the remainder of the blue-jackets and the marines, who were coming up fast from the neighbouring plantation, where they had been employed when we were attacked.

I heard native voices talking close to me, and the next instant saw four savages, armed with muskets, coming along the path, separated from me by a high and thick live cane-hedge or fence.

I could not have cut a way through in time to meet the savages with my sword, even had I felt inclined to do so at such long odds (which I am not at all clear about), and there were none of our men in sight except H________; so I ran on a little to where the hedge was thinnest and closest to the narrow path, and where a tree in the hedge enabled me to wait with cocked revolver, unseen by the natives, till they were abreast of me, and so close that I could have reached them with a boarding-pike; and the muzzle of my pistol, as I aimed successively for their stomachs, could barely have been eight feet from the object.

Click! click! click! click! every barrel missed fire — never was so sold before.

They had been walking before, but the sound of the hammer on the harmless cap made them turn around, and seeing me aiming, they made tracks in a particular hurry: I suppose that their muskets must have been empty, and to that circumstance and their cowardice I probably owe my life. I gave away the revolver before leaving the shore, determined never to be sold again the same way.

We continued the pursuit for about ten minutes or a quarter of an hour longer, when the Commander enforced a halt; and quite right too, for it was impossible to keep the men together, and the savages would have had an enormous advantage if they had made another stand, for we could not see ten feet on either side from the thickness of the bush, and we knew not where we were going.

As soon as we had mustered the men, as we had done all the mischief we could, having destroyed all the huts and plantations we could find, the Commander desired me to lead the way with my company to the landing-place, wherever that might be, which I did, I think, by a tolerably straight line; but it was very tiring work, leading through that perpetual thicket; and when a halt was sounded for a few minutes to allow the men to slake their thirst with coconut milk, I lay on my back, panting like a fresh-caught fish, and caring for nothing but the hope of long drinks of beer and rest which waited us on board.

We reached the boats about half-past three, having passed through a small gully whose sides we could not occupy, when the Tannese might have attacked us with impunity, Holland died as soon as he got on board.

During our absence, S________ had considerably added to the damage inflicted by destroying all the canoes he could find along the coast — twenty-one in number — a loss they will feel, as the construction of a single canoe occupies many months. Before coming off we endeavoured to set fire to the bush; but failed owing to the drenching rain of the previous evening, which had soaked all the underwood. Very lucky for the Tannese, for if the bush had once fairly caught fire with the wind in that quarter, they would have been pretty well driven into the sea at the other end of the island.

One of the rocket-tubes was lost overboard from the cutter or ship's side.

It turns out that the native whom Heathcote cut down was one of the principal chiefs in the island, named "Quatangan," and that the red-coated chief of the opposite side of the harbour was, if not wounded, at all events knocked over, and frightened out of his wits by a shell which burst in the ground beneath him.

August 13th. — Before we sailed this morning, Mr. Paton went ashore at the friendly village of Samoa (named after the Samoan teachers), and there met several of the principal hostile chiefs. They seemed evidently thoroughly cowed by yesterday's proceedings. One of them, who had never before met Mr. Paton without threatening his life, was friendly and humble in his manner, for the time at least, and promised anything and everything.

The following extract of the message or statement sent by them through Mr. Paton to the Commodore will give an idea of the frame of mind they were in.

I believe him to be an accurate interpreter, and to have the ultimate good of these people at heart: —

"Formerly we had been guilty of so many murders that we feared men-of-war would come and punish us; but when we found they came and did not punish us, we all thought and said they durst not try, and so we delighted in our bad conduct. Then we had no idea of the multitude of fighting men in a man-of-war, and of her awful power to destroy us and our lands; but now we have seen it, and our hearts have failed us. We are all weak and crying for fear.

"The great inland chief Quatangan, who came to help us to fight the man-of-war, was cut down by one of his chiefs (officers), and many more are hurt, and we know not how many are shot and dead.

"Our canoes, our houses, and our lands are laid waste by his fighting men.

"We never saw anything like this before — now we are all weeping for our evil conduct.

"Go and plead with the chief of the man-of-war not to punish us anymore, but to go and leave us, and truly we will obey his word. Tell him to inform your good Queen Victoria that we will kill no more of her people, but in future be good and learn to obey the word of Jehovah."

Yaufanuga, also from the west side of the bay, sent a messenger to say that if we would only "go away and not fight any more, they would obey the word of the good Queen Victoria and of the Commodore."

They also begged the missionary to return and live amongst them, and bring back the Samoan teachers, and promised that if the ship-of-war would return in two or three months she shall find church, mission, and teachers' houses all rebuilt, fenced in, and planted round.

The Commander purposes testing the sincerity of these promises.

In Tanna the island is called "Aipari," and by the Amiturnese "Aipegerouma."

It is about 25 miles long by 12 broad, and the population is between 16,000 and 20,000.

But since the introduction of European diseases and weapons, there has been a steady decrease. In 1861 a third of the people died of the measles.

The state of morals is extremely low; the natives assert that the present excessive licentiousness was introduced by the whites who formerly resided on the island. The chiefs endeavour to get drunk every night on kava. The women do all the work, the men the fighting, which is their constant employment.

The Tannese are proud of successful theft, and are only ashamed of being caught or of failure. Murder is common. The aged and the newly-born are alike frequently destroyed to save trouble to the survivors.

As in some parts of Fiji, widows are strangled at the death of their husbands.

Almost every mentionable and unmentionable crime is constantly practised. Cannibalism is the custom all over the island. Sometimes they eat their own dead, or if very affectionate, sell or exchange them with a neighbouring tribe. While Mr. Paton lived on this island, for one feast ten persons were killed, for another seven; it is common to kill two or three for eating.

All persons killed in war or kidnapped are eaten.

Natives often die from eating poisonous fish, which are many.

Earthquakes are frequent and severe. Before 1862, when the mission was broken up and Mr. Paton and the teachers driven away, there were about 500 professed and fairly practical Christians, who had given up their national crimes. Most of them have been killed by the pagans, and only two chiefs with their people now continue friendly and worship God.

Laws. — Might is right.

Government. — A number of petty chiefs who squabble under the directions of two or three greater chiefs who squabble also, and settle every dispute by fighting; now, with musket and tomahawk; in past times, with bows, clubs, spears, slings, and stones like mowers-hones,[78] used for striking or throwing.

Among different kinds of birds there appears to be one which from the description of its look and habits must be a kind of megapodos. We were told there are some venomous spiders, and a very deadly snake on the other side of the island. Also, a shell-fish, which, when handled, ejects a fluid so poisonous as generally to cause death by mere contact with the unbroken skin.

---

78 [sic] unsure of author's meaning. Perhaps stones like those used for honing scythes back home.

ERROMANGO.[79]

August 13th, Sunday. — Sailed for Erromango at 8 a.m., and arrived at that island about 4 p.m., anchoring in Dillon Bay.

There is here a small river flowing picturesquely through a deep gorge in the high hills, which are flat-topped and terraced; the slopes are covered with bush, but only part of the table-land is timbered.

August 14th. — At the mouth of the river in the bay is a sandalwood establishment[80] belonging to a Mr. Henry, who employs a large number of Sandwich islanders (Vate) and Tannamen, for the double purpose of cutting and bringing in the wood, and of protecting his person and property from the Erromangana, who are perhaps the most savage and treacherous cannibals in these seas.

He and Mrs. Henry came off today: the latter is a very courageous woman, having lately, during her husband's temporary absence, led her people with great spirit in defending the station against an attack made on them by the Erromangans.

The natives very much resemble the Tannamen, but appear to be rather smaller men and have a more sneaking treacherous expression of countenance than any we have yet seen. They are inveterate cannibals. They are chiefly celebrated for the number of white men and other islanders whom they have murdered and eaten. The latest victim was a man named Fletcher, in the employ of Mr. Henry, and from all that we can gather both from the traders and their not-very-good-friends the missionaries, it was a most treacherous and unprovoked murder; caused only by their hostility to white men, and their desire to eat his flesh and possess themselves of the articles of trade he had with him.

He had gone to the neighbourhood of a chief, named Narai, to trade and get sandalwood, who by treachery induced him to

---

79 An island in the Vanuatu group.

80 Meade does not mention it, but Brenchley made note of Dillon Bay's other major export — women. £5 could secure a "damsel" all ready to be shipped offshore "in spite of her tears, entreaties, and her father's wishes." (Brenchley, p.321)

separate himself a little from the body of Tannamen and Vatese who accompanied him, and then tomahawked him, and afterwards destroyed in like manner a number of his native escort.

They cooked his body and that of his dog in the same boiler or oven, stuck his head on a bamboo, and sent portions of his flesh to neighbouring tribes. Narai was unable to give Mr. Gordon, whom he met on neutral ground, any reason for this barbarous deed. This Mr. Gordon is a brother of the missionary who, with his wife, was murdered here, as I have already said.

It was here also that Mr. Williams, one of the very best missionaries who have worked in the Pacific, and Mr. Harris were murdered. Later also they murdered a whole boat's crew, splitting their skulls as they stooped to lift up the sandalwood.

After a long discussion of the *pros* and *cons* of the localities and means of transporting guns to the village between the Commodore and the traders, two landing parties were prepared and told off — one of a hundred men, marines and small-arm men, and a field-piece, under Captain D________, H________, and P________, to land next morning, and destroy Narai's village, situated on a mountain side some five miles inland; the field-piece being carried by natives in separate pieces. Later, another party under my command, of forty or fifty men, were to land, and, making a slight detour of three or four miles, take up a position in rear of the village of Warris Nangri, lying down on the top of the ridge just clear of the bush which covers only the slopes of the table-land, on the sea face of which the village is built. There we should, from the lay of the ground, be unseen by the inhabitants until they emerge from the bush but being visible from the ship she would immediately commence shelling the village, and drive the natives up to a warm reception from us in the flat open terraces above — altogether a very promising place. But towards evening the Commodore became more and more uneasy touching the expedition to Narai and a cross-examination of the guide as to the road and strength of position of the village, did not add much to the Commodore's stock of information.

About nine that evening the Commodore threw out an indirect hint as to the advantage of having the opinion of an officer who should have seen the road himself.

The Commander and I offered our services, and it was arranged that I should go. It was, of course, out of the question for the Commander to go scouting himself, as I had endeavoured to point out to him before he went in to the Commodore.

August 15th. — The gig having been placed at my disposal, I landed with the guide at half-past two this morning, he having remained on board in the meantime.

His enthusiasm for the little proposed excursion diminished rapidly as the time for starting approached; and he made two attempts to get a guard of men sent with us (without my knowledge), applying first to the Commander, and then to E_______, whose "first" watch it was, but of course without success.

There was a good moon. We set off at once, so as to have the first of daylight to return with; for if anyone should meet or see us by the way, the alarm would immediately be spread that we had passed, and scores of cannibals would be waiting our return behind every bush and rock.

They have plenty of muskets, and usually carry their arms so that any natives we met, if more than two or three strong, if we allowed them to pass us, would probably follow stealthily and shoot us from behind, even if they did not wait to spread the alarm in the villages. And capture by a sudden attack of overwhelming numbers, would entail the additional inconvenience of baking alive in a native oven. We were, therefore, well-armed he: with a carbine and tomahawk; I, with my breech-loading rifle, a Colt's revolver, and bowie-knife.

For the first mile, the path ran by the river side, through a pleasant valley; there we forded the shallow stream, and continued along the gorge on the other side. We were now fairly away from the few friendly natives and Tannamese, who live near Mr. Henry, and amongst the hostile tribes: so, we advanced with the greatest caution.

We passed close to a small village near the river; but we crept low, and were not seen or heard. Soon after this we came to a *whare,* of which the door was open, and close to the very edge of the footpath — it was impossible to avoid it — and it would be broad daylight when we passed it returning (it was then about half-past three A.M.). If the people who lived in this *whare* should live till daylight, they would see our footmarks; the failure of the service I was engaged in, and the heating of the ovens for our bodies, could be the only result.

The same thing would happen if, from out of the darkness of the house, they were to perceive us passing *towards* Narai's village.

To my great relief, and happily for both sides, the *whare* turned out to be empty, though its owners had left very recently — probably the previous evening. After fording the river a second time — not much more than knee-deep — we found the road gradually rises for three or four miles to the gully under Narai's village, with some really grand mountain scenery.

We were delayed by occasional bush, but nothing like what we had gone through in Tanna. We passed two more settlements all safely, though at one a dog began barking, and for a few minutes we thought ourselves discovered, but all was still again, and we passed on.

A few minutes after five we reached the edge of the gully opposite Narai's village, and about distant 300 or 400 yards at the most. There was no object in going any farther, so I made a very rough sketch of it by moonlight and the help of my binoculars. They had a fire burning brightly. It was here that Fletcher's head was stuck on a bamboo.

We returned all safe without any adventure. Daylight broke while we were on our way back, and we could see through the trees the fires which the natives were lighting for cooking, and at one place could hear their voices talking to one another.

I got on board just before eight this morning and reported that between the first and second miles the path leads over large slippery boulders, where it would be very difficult to carry the field-piece without probably many falls and injury to the gun: flanked on one side by the river, on the other by a slightly overhanging cliff covered with bush, from the summit of which ten determined men could keep back 100 by rolling stones over the brink and using firearms, without in the least exposing themselves. Some of the mountainous part of the path is so narrow as only to allow a passage in single file in places where a slip would dash the gun down 200 or 300 feet; that therefore the project of taking the field-piece into position and back again the same day is impracticable, and that without being covered by an efficient fire from the near side of the gully it would be rash to send small-arm men to scale its sides in face of any resistance from the village, but that a field-piece once in position, the village is admirably placed for being shelled, and the ground on the opposite side clear and well adapted for working artillery.

The expedition to Narai was therefore postponed *sine die*. Warris Nangri, the chief from the other offending village, Sifou, the one by the sea-shore, came on board this morning, and having done or promised to do all that was required, their village was spared, and we sailed this evening at half-past eight for Vate or Sandwich Island.

Little more than a year later Unthank, my guide on this occasion, came to an untimely end. He and three other white men, who were with him on board a trader, were murdered and eaten by the natives. He was a wild sort of fellow, but he showed pluck enough last night when we were once in for it, however unwilling he may have been to start at the last moment. I never heard any details of the slaughter, save that the Tanna and Vate people mutually lay it on one another's shoulders, but probably the Erromangans themselves had a finger in the pie. One account was that a number of professedly friendly natives embarked for a passage, or pretending to assist in the collection of sandalwood, and after getting to sea suddenly surprised and killed the whites, eventually gutting the vessel, the 'Mary Ira.' She was afterwards recovered by another trading schooner, the chief of the nearest village consenting for a consideration.

Thus, Fletcher, who was the last white man who had been to that part of the island before us, and Unthank, who accompanied me, having both found their graves in the stomachs of these wretches, I remain the only undigested white who has been there for years, and I am not very likely to complete the trio.

Mr. Gordon remains at Erromango, and even his most sanguine friends can prophesy no better fate for him than being eaten by the natives; but he is obstinate, or devoted, or whatever the proper word may be. I have since learnt that though Mr. Gordon volunteered originally for Erromango, it, "The Board," with Mr. Inglis at their head, who from the safe and snug residence at Amiteum, and in spite of the Commodore's remonstrance, insists on Gordon's going at this dangerous time to his post; they seem to forget that the very worst use that can be made of a man's life is to throw it away.

Mr. Henry intends to remove his sandalwood establishment very shortly to one of the Loyalty islands, and the Erromangans have repeatedly said, and continue to say, that as soon as the traders are gone they will murder Mr. Gordon as well as every Christian on the island, and every man who wears a "lava-lava" (waist-cloth), which they regard as the mark of their foe — civilization.

We saw no native women here, but we were told that both here and at Tanna they wear a scanty apron of bark-fibre strips.

The houses of these natives, although usually surrounded by fences, are of a low order, the eaves of the roof being seldom more than two or three feet above the ground.

Doors are dispensed with, and the houses are of an oblong shape and of considerable length.

One of the model Christians brought on board by the missionaries to see the ship, quite decently clad in a trade cloth lava-lava, was pointed out to me as having eaten, and boasted of having eaten, part of Fletcher's body the other day. And a treacherous-looking miscreant he was with his one eye.

VATE[81] AND DECEPTION.[82]

August 16th. — Anchored at noon at Vila Harbour,[83] a snug anchorage at the southward end of the island, and almost entirely sheltered by Vate and some smaller islets.

The thickness of the weather only allowed us to see enough of the distant hills to make us wish for a closer acquaintance, and to persuade us that the high praise lavished by Erskine on the beauty of this harbour is well deserved.

In the afternoon a small party, of which I was not one (it being limited to the number who could find room in the missionary's boat to cross a lagoon after landing from the ship), went to the Christian village of Erakor with Mr. Morrison, the missionary, and a friendly chief.

It was at this island that Moafu, in 1842, acting under the directions or on behalf of Messrs. H________ and S________, suffocated a number of Vatese in a cave, by lighting a fire at the mouth. Since then the Vatese have retaliated by several massacres of white men and others, who, by chance or wreck, have fallen into their power.

The Vatese appear to be a finer and better-looking race than those of the two preceding islands.

They are also more decently clothed, wearing a species of *maro*, above which is a stiff waist-belt of matting, about a foot deep, stained red and yellow, and festooned before and behind with folds of *tappa*[84] or trade cloth.

The hair stained yellow, and done up in all sorts of extravagant modes; armlets curiously and carefully made out of tiny rings of shell, ground down with infinite labour, and embroidered in diamond-shaped patterns on to a band about two inches wide.

---

81 Among the Vanuatu islands. Now Efate, previously Île Vate.

82 Moso Island, about 200 meters off the northwest coast of Vate. It forms part of Havannah Harbour.

83 Now Port Vila, southwest side of Efate.

84 Barkcloth

August 17th. — Sailed at eight this morning, and anchored in Havannah Harbour[85] (named after the frigate of that name), in the same island, at a quarter past one.

It is a beautiful harbour, long and land-locked, the entrance being shut in by Deception Island, the abode of a particularly savage people.

The chiefs of this island have been informed that unless they appear on board us tomorrow, before 2 p.m., to answer for past ill-deeds and to promise amendment, hostilities will commence.

Luckily all the villages on Deception Island can be easily shelled from the ship or boats, and the high table-land, which occupies all the interior of the island, is so clear that our small-arm men will have no difficulty in dealing with the natives when driven from the sea faces of the hills by the shell and rockets.

A German or Dutchman, to whom report assigns thirteen wives, came off today, but was not very communicative.

A few canoes came alongside, selling bows and arrows, spears, coconuts, and root fruit. Some of these arrows are poisoned with a gummy substance, said to be very deadly, and these points were brought off carefully covered. The arrows which are not poisoned have their points barbed and elaborately carved out of some hard, black wood. Most of the poisoned points are made of human bone.

These people are all inveterate cannibals.

August 18th. — The chiefs put in a satisfactory appearance this morning, and we accordingly remained on the peace platform. B________[86] and V________ landed this morning early under guidance of a chief, another remained on board as hostage during their absence.

Having had the middle watch, and deeming it a useless risk, I did not care to get up in time to accompany them. We sailed at 3.30 for Banks Islands,[87] where we are to meet the Bishop.

----

85 Northwest side of Vate.
86 Brenchley.
87 In the far north of the Vanuatu group.

The island is from 30 to 35 miles long and about 15 broad.

Population, which is said to be decreasing, is estimated at 10,000 to 12,000.

Climate rather damp, but healthy enough if care be taken.

One village, Erakor, is Christian, and in another are a few favourable to the Faith; but all the other people are up to their ears in paganism, cannibalism, murder of old men, widows, and children, and all the other ills that affect the heathen morals at dead low water.

The cotton plant which has lately been introduced does well.

The government is carried on by petty chiefs, who mostly rule over independent villages. Earthquakes common, sometimes severe; — five are said to have occurred in the course of last year.

August 19th. — Passing through the remainder of the New Hebrides[88] group, we steered between Espirito Santo and Leper's Island. The natives of the latter island have the reputation of being the boldest savages of all in these seas.

August 20th, Sunday. — We are all adrift somehow, and have got hold of the wrong islands. At noon, the chart turned out to be nearly 60 miles out, and at one time we were according to the chart in the centre of Clair Island, which, however, was nowhere visible.

---

88 Vanuatu.

CHAPTER X.

Vanua Lava — Unhealthy climate — "Supwe" club-house — Inspection of ladies — Vanikoro — Graciosa Bay — Active barter — Betel-nut chewing — Solomon Islands — An earthquake — Contrariétés — Land with the Bishop — Remarkable canoes — West Bay, Uji — Pigeon-shooting at San Christoval — Recherche Bay — Fate of native teacher — Marau Sound — Guadalcanar — Florida resembles Norfolk Island — Trade — Rodd's atrocities — Exploring party — Isabel Island — First landing of the Bishop — Ebony tree — Visit to a tree village — Pigeon-shooting extraordinary — Native industry and ingenuity — Man overboard — Return to Dillon Bay — Salutary effect of the Tannese operations — Kaniau and Warris Nangri — They refuse to appear — Bombardment of Sifou — Agreement as to use of firearms — New Caledonia — Good Cove Harbour and Port de France — H.M.S. 'Falcon' with a mail — Reception of the Governor — Picnic at the model farm — Vegetation and scenery — Dinner on board the 'Falcon' — Banquet and ball ashore — Prospects of the colony — The curfew gun — Arrival at Sydney.

VANUA LAVA[89] AND VANIKORO.[90]

August 21st. — Arrived at Vanua Lava, one of Banks Islands, and anchored in Port Patterson.

The harbour, which is a very tolerable one, is sheltered on three sides by lofty hills. It is named after Bishop Patterson, who was, I believe, the first white man who landed on the island.[91]

We came-to about 4 p.m. and were soon surrounded by canoes, roughly made and shorter than those at other islands, and

---

89 Second largest of the Banks Islands in the far north of the Vanuatu group.

90 At the extreme southeast of the Solomon Islands. Closer to the Vanuatu group than the main Solomon Islands.

91 The same Bishop Patterson the author met on Norfolk Island and was later killed in 1871 in the Solomon Islands.

filled with native men entirely naked. We found lying here the mission schooner *'Southern Cross,'* with the Bishop on board.

Both he and T________ soon made their number on board, and in their boat we found some of our young friends from "Norfolk Island." The schooner already crowded with natives of different islands, whom the Bishop takes to Auckland to be educated, but there are many more yet to come.[92]

August 22nd. — Landed this evening for a couple of hours. The two villages are built on a very low flat plain covered with bush, only 3 or 4 feet above the level of the sea, and in every way little better than a swamp.

These islands, and indeed almost all those lying to the north of Erromango, are so unhealthy that Europeans cannot live through the summer. Fever and ague are more plentiful here than in China itself.

There is a shipwrecked English sailor here, whom we have received on board. He is the survivor of two who were wrecked here some thirteen months' past, and remained here while the skipper and the others went by boat to New Caledonia.

Rain and thick mist alternately ever since we arrived.

In the centre of the village is a sort of club-house, which is used as a dining-hall by a species of free-masonry society, to which nearly all the men and lads belong.

There are several fire-places in their houses, each belonging to a separate grade, and no man is allowed to cook or eat at the fire of a superior rank.

The members are initiated, and rise to higher grades by payment.

The rank and titles obtained in this society or "Supwe," as the natives term it, not only hold good in the man's own village, but are recognized in all the surrounding settlements and islands which happen not to be at war with his native place.

------

92 With concern growing around slave trading, one theory is the locals who ultimately killed Bishop Patterson mistook him for a slave trader.

The Bishop has not yet learnt enough about the "Supwe" to decide whether it can properly be recognized and utilized as a means of spreading the Gospel. Bows and arrows, the latter usually poisoned, were the only weapons we saw.

The people are a puny race and suffer much from fever, ague, and rheumatism, or something like it, induced by the dampness of the situation and climate.

The men, though quite naked, do not give the spectator such an idea of indecency as the Tannese or Erromangans. They have also a less unpleasant appearance and expression than those in the Southern New Hebrides.

The women are extremely ugly in the face, which is usually tattooed in both cheeks, and unsightly in their form and shape. Nevertheless, their lords are extremely jealous of them; and when we reached the village we found all the women shut up in the houses, the doors of which were closed with cane blinds or palm leaves.

However, after a short time I drew a line with a stick across the open space in the village, and having mustered my shipmates on one side intimated by signs that we would remain there if they would produce some specimens of the female sex on the other. This idea seemed to tickle their fancy, and amidst much laughter two lovely damsels were trotted out for our inspection.

The only raiment they wore was a grass hand one inch wide passing round their waist and tied in front with two fibres, which joined the two ends into a sort of tassel about three inches long.

We were told that the married women wear their *"hopare,"* as they call these garments, while the young unmarried ladies go without, but my impression is that both sexes usually go entirely naked.

This village being nearest to the ship was continually being visited by us as well as the mission people, who have already some influence here; but in another and more distant village, which some of my messmates explored, they reported that the nearest approach to dress worn by any of the ladies were some fig-leaves, growing on a tree a quarter of a mile off.

In a small cleared space in the jungle near the village, surrounded by a rough wooden paling, and surmounted by a rough cross of the same material, is the grave of _________ Young, who was killed whilst with the Bishop at Santa Cruz last year.

A melancholy-looking place, shrouded in long pendent creepers and weeping parasites. The natives have not disturbed the grave.

August 23rd. — Sailed for Vanikoro at 1 p.m. The *'Southern Cross'* in company.

August 24th. — Off Vanikoro, or La Perouse Island, this day. The entrance to the harbour is very narrow and bristling with reef.

Altogether the appearance of the approaches was so uninviting that the Commodore decided to stand on for Santa Cruz. It was at Vanikoro the 'La Perouse' was wrecked.

SANTA CRUZ.[93]

August 25th. — Off Santa Cruz, the greater portion of the day being spent hove-to or standing under easy sail along the northern coast of the island.

We did not enter Graciosa Bay, where there is an anchorage, because it was there that the massacre of the Bishop's companions occurred last year. On the one hand, the Bishop does not wish us to inflict any punishment on the natives of the Bay; on the other, he promised the friends of the Norfolk Island young men who accompany him, not to land at Santa Cruz this year. I presume that the native inhabitants of the island must have heard of the guilt of the Graciosa Bay men; nevertheless, they showed no diffidence; and though we lay some four or five miles from the shore, they came off in swarms, their white canoes dotting the sea for miles.

---

93 Part of the Solomon Islands Chain, relatively close to the archipelago of Vanuatu.

They were very anxious for barter, and as many of my shipmates were not less so, the scene alongside was very animated. Their nostrils, ears, and arms were decorated with a profusion of rings of tortoiseshell and mother-of-pearl, which they gladly bartered for bits of iron hooping, empty bottles, tins, or anything else they could get.

Each canoe was garnished with several bows and bundles of long arrows, which they seemed to have brought for defence or barter, as occasion might require.

They were a very wild-looking lot, but not disagreeable in expression, and much better-made men than at Banks Islands. Most of them wore something round their loins.

The canoes are made of a light-coloured wood, with a very narrow opening to admit the feet; the ends turned up to throw the water off, and the outrigger shaped like a miniature canoe cut solid, and they seem to be more seaworthy than the smaller canoes at previous islands. The natives here chew the betel-nut, which of course spoils the look of their teeth.

The Clunam is kept in a little gourd, or joint of bamboo, and carried, together with the nuts and green leaves for wrapping up each "quid," in a square grass pouch worn at the back between the shoulders. These bags are generally very prettily worked in divers patterns, and decorated with long fringes and tassels.

SOLOMON ISLANDS.

August 25th. — After communicating with the Bishop, we filled and steered for the Solomon Islands.

At ten minutes past five this afternoon, whilst under sail with a light breeze and no soundings, we experienced the shock of an earthquake. The ship trembled violently for about five seconds, and then came two shorter and slighter shocks. The first impression of those of us who were in the wardroom at the time was that something had gone wrong amongst the brass topsails, but we were not under steam at the time. There were several volcanic islands at no great distance from us, and an earth or rather sea-quake resulting from some movement initiated by them appears to be the only explanation. The event was duly chronicled in our log.

We passed Santa Anna and San Christoval Islands, but had no communication with the shore.

CONTRARIÉTÉS.

August 27th, Sunday. — Off Contrariétés, a small island in the Solomon group. We sent a cutter in to sound, but the only anchorage that could be found was in a small semi-circular bay with 31 fathoms within 200 yards of the shore. We therefore hove-to about four or five miles off, though I hear we might have gone much closer with safety. The schooner under the land was surrounded by canoes, but none came off to us.

It is a well-looking island with soft rolling hills thickly timbered down to the water's edge.

August 28th. — Several of us went on board the schooner to communicate with the Bishop about landing. The boat was taken in tow, and we landed at a small village some miles down the coast. The Bishop got ashore in a canoe, but having no means of getting the cutter through the coral, we awaited his report without leaving the boat. It was a lovely little cove with a coral-bound shore, and almost entirely overshadowed by a wide-spreading tree. The Bishop returned at once, saying that there was nothing worth seeing at that village; so as it was getting late, some of us, myself included, returned on board to dinner, whilst the rest landed for an hour or two at another village, after a visit to the schooner, which they found thronged with natives carrying on a brisk trade in curios.

The canoes here are not fitted with outriggers, but they are by far the most graceful and well finished that I have seen in any part of the world. They usually hold from eight to twelve or fourteen men. The extremities end in high curving peaks, which together with one or more little flagstaffs erected within are profusely decorated with feathers, shells, and streaming pennons of a bright scarlet or purple colour. The bow's quarter and sometimes the broadsides are beautifully inlaid with glittering mother-of-pearl, arranged in symmetrical patterns. At the figurehead on the inner slopes of the curving prows and along the sides fantastic images of birds, animals, and fishes are disposed with no bad taste. The canoes are not hollowed out of a single trunk, but are built of separate pieces of wood, cemented together with a black glue made by pounding the interior of a nut into a paste which hardens on exposure to the air.

The natives are a small race, but are better made than those in the New Hebrides. The costume of both sexes is of the scantiest description, and resembles the primitive dress of our first parents.

UJI.

August 29th. — We filled at two o'clock this morning and stood for Uji, one of the Gulf Islands, where we arrived in the afternoon, anchoring in West Bay at 3.15, when I went ashore with the Bishop. The natives were very friendly and we could move about freely and without carrying arms, which we were obliged to do at the last island.

A large majority of the men and women suffer from a scurfy-looking skin disease, and sores appeared to be very common. In the middle of each village is a large boat-house profusely ornamented with carved images of birds, beasts, fishes, men, and gods, showing no little originality of design. One favourite device was a shark's head and body terminating in a human leg with a fan-tailed foot.

The next day we sailed shortly before one o'clock, and in a couple of hours arrived at the large island of San Christoval, where we anchored off the village of Wango, the most extensive we have seen since leaving Tongatabu.[94]

SAN CHRISTOVAL.[95]

31st. — H _________ and I landed in the forenoon, and bagged a dozen pigeons in about an hour and a half, with only one gun

---

94 Tonga.

95 Now Makira, the largest island of Makira-Ulawa Province in the Solo-

between us. The village resembles all the others in most respects. The boathouse was, however, ornamented with a bunch of skulls of foemen killed in war. Most of them had been smashed in by clubs, and the weapons which had inflicted the deadly blows hung beside the skulls.

Many of the women are perfectly naked, but are more pleasing in form and expression of countenance than those at Banks Islands.

September 1st. — Sailed at 10.30 this morning, and anchored at five o'clock in the afternoon in Recherche Bay, in the same island of San Christoval. A very pretty little bit of a bay, high cliffs on the right and left, nearly covered even on the very face with timber, and in the centre a sward of the most brilliant green, hacked by dense bush and a winding valley containing a small but rapid stream. There are one or two houses here, but the two nearest villages are situated one on either side of the two points which form the bay.

One of the natives, a young lad whom the Bishop had taken to be educated at the college in New Zealand, and whom he left here only two months ago, has been murdered and eaten. It is, however, said that his fate had nothing to do with his being a Christian. It appears that for some reason, as yet unknown, he was given up by the people with whom he was then living to some of a hostile tribe, who made short work of him.

September 2nd. — Some of my messmates landed in the bay, but finding no village and the bush impenetrable, they remained close to the beach. All the natives were armed, and were more "cheeky" than at other places. They even pointed and brandished a spear at one of the party, and threw stones at others who were bathing some little way up the stream. But nothing more serious occurred, and many natives came on board, while others bartered freely in their canoes alongside.

---

mon Islands.

September 3rd Sunday. — The Bishop preached on board and kept all hands wide awake.

GUADALCANAR.[96]

September 4th. — Sailed at 6 a.m. and anchored at one o'clock in Marau Sound,[97] Guadalcanar Island, in 23 fathoms.

The islands here form quite an archipelago. They are densely and variously crowded, the trees overhanging the water, sometimes as much as forty or fifty feet, the whole backed up from successive ranges of mountains, the most distant of which must be many thousand feet high.

A few of our fellows landed in the evening, but found there was not much to be done, the natives not being inclined for barter, the houses shut up, and the women sent away inland. This is probably caused by a mistrust of the intentions of the big ship, for at the Bishop's last visit they crowded the schooner, eager for trade. There were a few canoes alongside us, but their inmates were not very anxious to part with their nick-nacks. In the first watch, however, two canoes came off, and making fast to the ladder astern, listened to the band, nor were they even frightened by the nine o'clock gun. B ________ shot a great many parrots, nearly all having an entirely scarlet plumage.

FLORIDA.[98]

September 5th. — Sailed at 6 a.m., the harbour where we lay having been surveyed by S________ and his assistants, and duly christened "Curaçoa Harbour." We anchored in Mboli Harbour, on the northern coast of Florida, just before sunset, the same evening. It is well sheltered by reefs.

The island presents a very different appearance to any other island we have visited, with the exception of Norfolk Island, which it much resembles, but surpasses in beauty, by uniting the

---

96 Better known as Guadalcanal from its role in World War 2.

97 Extreme east end of the island. The sound is created by a number of smaller islands.

98 Also known as the Nggela Islands, part of the Solomon group.

park-like grassy slopes and hill-side groves of Norfolk Island to the waving palms and brilliant reef-girt waters of more tropical islands.

We were immediately surrounded by countless canoes, many of which had kept pace with us, vigorously paddling on our quarter while we steamed along the land. Many of them were double-banked, with stern peaks rising to the height of ten or twelve feet.

September 6th. — All hands gone mad after trading. Five shillings each offered on the lower deck for pipes of the commonest and cheapest sort, which are in great demand amongst the natives, as well as old hoop iron, together with some of a flatter and thicker description, which is nearly in as great request as tomahawks.

Among the native curiosities, I particularly remarked some flat discs of white shell ornamented with another disc of tortoiseshell carved in an open-work pattern. They are worn on the forehead, and secured by a scarlet head-band. Many of their clubs are worked very neatly with grass in various-coloured patterns, leaving only the black exposed. Others are made of ebony and inlaid with mother-of-pearl. Among their weapons is a spear of a description which I have not met with elsewhere. The point about a foot long, is made of human bone, carved in a peculiar manner, and terminating in a hollow point, which contains some half-dozen long-barbed bone needles, which are apparently intended to remain in the wound after the spear has been withdrawn. The whole is said to be poisoned, and altogether is about the most vicious weapon I have ever seen.

The mission schooner came in this morning, having remained out all night in consequence of there not being either daylight or wind enough left last evening for her to beat up to the anchorage.

No one was allowed to land, because as yet there has been only one white man here before besides the Bishop, one Rodd, who shot two of the natives for trying to pilfer some calico.

This is only one specimen, and a mild one, of the atrocities committed by this wretch in various islands in these seas. There can be no doubt about his identity, as he has lost one eye and one hand in a fight with some natives years ago. The Bishop, however, landed alone, wading ashore as usual, while his boat lay off out of harm's way. He met with a far better reception than he had expected, and five or six young fellows gladly came away with him to be educated with the others at the Mission Central School in New Zealand. The men wear mostly *maroas*, and the women aprons resembling those of Tonga.

I dined with the Commodore, where also was the Bishop. S________ and D________ had gone away in the whaler, about three o'clock, to survey the harbour, and at eight, as there were no signs of her, I was sent away with C________ and an armed boat to look for the absentees, the Bishop kindly accompanying us in one of the schooner's boats. Very little anxiety was felt on board, as the whalers had their rifles, and the natives had shown great confidence in the Bishop this afternoon. Sure enough we had not left the ship more than half an hour, and had just got round the first point of the Creek, when we met the stray sheep returning unharmed to the fold. It turned out that they had discovered that the Creek, instead, of being merely the head of the harbour, as shown in the chart, is in fact a passage which completely severs Florida into two separate islands, with never less than 4½ fathoms of water. The explorers were much impressed with the beauty of the scenery in the Straits, and the enormous numbers of pigeons, parrots, and other birds on the various islands that they passed; on both which subjects they expatiated till a late hour of the night.

ISABEL.[99]

September 7th. — Weighed at 6 a.m., and made all sail for St. George's Bay, Isabel Island, where we anchored at half-past two, with the schooner under the lee of Cockatoo Island.

One gets tired of everlastingly chalking down one's impressions of the beauty of these harbours. Yet this island is no exception

---

99 Santa Isabel, third largest of the Solomon Islands.

to the general loveliness of all the Solomon group. The natives are friendly and confiding. Their canoes are well made, and often beautifully decorated with mother-of-pearl.

We saw great quantities of white cockatoos, numbers of which are to be seen perpetually flitting about the bush, singly and in flocks. Few curiosities were to be got, and trade was very flat.

September 8th. — I landed this morning with a large party under the Bishop's wing. We first went to a spot about two miles down the coast, where there grew, or rather had ceased growing, an ebony tree, about two feet thick, which the carpenters had set to work felling and cutting into logs, which were afterwards dragged down to the sea, and eventually embarked by a working party for the Commodore. Meanwhile we retraced our course to a small bay nearer the ship, which we crossed, and proceeded by a very steep track to the tree village on the summit of one of the mountain ridges, which was the object of our excursion.

It was in this bay that the Bishop, some four years ago, landed for the first time. After pulling round it, he was on the point of leaving, convinced that there were no natives living in that part of the island, when one was discovered peeping round a tree. By offering presents and by pacific gestures he was induced to approach the white party, and at last his suspicions were so far disarmed as to allow him to lead them up the mountain to his home, the tree village.

For the first half-hour, our path led up the course of a rocky stream, but after that it was all climbing, hands and feet, holding on to rocks, roots, and creepers. We were a large party, some six or eight and twenty, but not more than nine or ten of us reached the top. The Bishop is a good pedestrian, and seemed inclined to show it.

We found that the village, of which we had come in search, had been burnt down, together with its castle in the air, by a hostile tribe, who had come by sea in their great war-canoes with overwhelming numbers, and nearly all those who had not been killed were carried away as slaves.

There was, however, another village near the site of the old one, and a tree fort about three hundred yards farther. This latter is built among the spreading branches of a stout and lofty tree. The roof low and sloping, with a balcony running all round the house, from which the defenders shower down stones, arrows, and spears on their assailants. Communication with the ground is held by means of a rope ladder, which is hauled up in time of siege. When a fight is coming off, as many as can find room garrison the tree fort to defend their *whares*, which are disposed around within arrow-shot of the tree, while the remainder of the warriors carry on the regular bush skirmishing.

The houses are nearly all raised on piles five or six feet above the ground, and are carefully built and ornamented, presenting a very picturesque appearance, with their high-peaked roofs and wide-spreading eaves.

We were received with perfect confidence and friendship, no traders having as yet ventured to land here, much less come so far inland. The natives were not, however, so inquisitive as on the Bishop's former visit, when they felt him all over, and examined his many "skins" with the greatest curiosity.

From the summit of this ridge we commanded on either side a beautiful view of mountains and valleys, woodland and rocky shores, sea studded with isles and reefs innumerable. Many of the hill-tops were crowned with these tree castles, looking like giant dovecotes. We were invited into a house, where we rejoiced in a stretch-out on a most comfortable couch, which, though made of wood, was just sloped at the right angle, with ledges to check the feet and head towards the wall, so that many could lie abreast. Here we were served with a hot meal, made in some crafty manner from taro and coconut milk, forming a rather glutinous mess, somewhat resembling arrowroot, but to my taste much pleasanter.

The women were more decently dressed than in the other Solomon Islands, the scanty little fringe, which only serves to call attention to what it is intended to conceal, is here replaced by ample folds of *tappa*, enclosing the fair creatures from waist to knee.

After sketching the village, and slaking our thirst with long draughts of coconut milk, doubly delicious after the heat and exertion of the ascent, we took leave of our new friends, distributing a few fish-hooks, beads, and sticks of tobacco amongst the older men and women, and returned by the way we came, picking up most of our stragglers on the road; but we still had to wait nearly an hour in the boat in drenching rain for two or three of our party who had lost their way or got fagged. But one or two of us improved the occasion by bathing in the bay, where the water was quite warm from the rays of the sun striking on it during the greater part of the day. There are plenty of sharks, and we saw two inside the reefs when we landed with the ebony-cutting party, but the natives do not fear them, and say that, unlike the lords of creation in these parts, they never touch human flesh.

Just as I left the village a bright-looking lad ran after me, and shyly gave me a pair of head plumes, made of hibiscus strips, stained red and yellow; it was, I dare say, all he had. Meeting a native alone, on the way down, I offered him a large fish-hook, but he would not take it, being evidently unable to understand that it was a present, till I laid it on a stone and turned to go away, when he hesitated for an instant, and snatched it up like a dog would a bone, then, seeing that no prompt vengeance followed his audacity, he grinned his gratitude all over his face.

There is an island about two miles from our anchorage which is the roosting place of enormous numbers of pigeons, although it is but two or three hundred yards in diameter. S________ went there at sunset, and got twenty-six birds. The next morning five guns went before breakfast, and brought back 107. In the evening, we went in time to have half an hour's shooting before sunset. We had not time to pick up two-thirds of those we shot, as I had promised to be back in time to hoist the boat in before dark, but we brought away with us forty-two birds. H________ shot a fine brown eagle of a species which Mr. Wahl has never heard of; we might have killed more of them had we wished it. There was some pretty shooting on the beach, as the pigeons came in from the mainland a hundred miles an hour. We were shooting for the pot, being short of fresh provisions on board. I never left the boat, as I always found fresh pigeons perched on the favourite branch by the time my gun was reloaded. They were large, plump birds, with bluish-grey and lilac feathers, bronzed wings, and a large scarlet puff.

The natives of these islands, although nearly all heathens and habitual cannibals, are far more gentle-minded and merciful to shipwrecked sailors than the people of the New Hebrides[100] and Santa Cruz groups. I have known instances where castaway seamen have been fed, housed, and carefully tended through sickness and through health for many consecutive months, with no hope for any possible reward for their pains. They also seem to take to work for amusement in a manner which contrasted strongly with the distaste for employment of any sort evinced by the natives of other islands. It was a common sight to see three or four naked islanders mixed with the working party of Maories, and polishing brass work with the greatest assiduity, or clapping on a whip worked by a party of seamen, by the hour together.

They show far more ingenuity and taste in handicraft than any other inhabitants of the South Seas. Such of their houses as are built on the ground, are very picturesque, having high-peaked gables with broad and slightly-curving eaves, the whole ornamented by some quiet pattern. Their canoes are quite works of art, the larger ones holding forty or fifty persons easily.

On the 10th we sailed for Erromango. On the evening of the following Friday a man named Hill was knocked overboard out of the main-chains by the main-topgallant-yard. The boat was lowered and away in two or three minutes (Clifford's Falls), and we found him quite comfortable in the life-buoy which C________ had found lying on the quarterdeck and thrown overboard. Fortunately for Hill there was a steady breeze blowing, and no sea on.

On the evening of the 20th S________ went aloft and shot a boatswain bird, which fell inboard, and immediately disgorged several squid, which apparently had only just been swallowed;

---

100 Vanuatu.

another wounded fluttered into the water, poor thing! there to starve or drown by inches.

The wise ones, of course, predicted ill luck after this, and sure enough, scarcely an hour had passed when we were taken by the lee in a heavy squall, the first of the kind we have fallen in with since I have been in the ship, and though the hands were turned up to shorten sail, the mast from which the deed of darkness was perpetrated took a clear header overboard, leaving the yard and sail like a flying kite.

ERROMANGO.

We anchored in Dillon Bay, Erromango, about eight o'clock on the morning of the 25th. The brig from which we had removed the skipper for his trial on a charge of shooting his mate, has visited Tanna since the castigation we administered to the natives of Port Resolution. The 'Tannese' would not make known their total of killed and wounded, but confessed that about a week after our departure they were examining one of our unexploded percussion Armstrong shells, when it burst, and killed five or six of the lookers-on. Some of the brig's crew had landed to water at the place on another part of the island called Black Beach. One of the white men was seated on the ground close to one of the native crew, who was leaning on the white man's gun. A Black Beach native came behind and tomahawked the man who held the gun, which he then snatched up and shot the white man, only, however, to be immediately afterwards killed himself by a Tannaman belonging to one of the tribes which we had punished.

The natives here have lately had some more fighting amongst themselves, the pagan tribes against the small, partially friendly, and Christian village near the missionary's house. Narai, the chief whose village I visited by night, has not been giving any more trouble lately; but Kaniau, the chief who organized the massacre of Williams and Harris in 1839, and by whose own hand the former fell, has been misbehaving, as also has Warris Nangri, the chief of the settlement in the neighbouring bay, which would have been destroyed last time we were here but for his coming on board and promising amendment for the future. A great feast is now going on at this village, where Kaniau and representatives from other tribes are being entertained.

It is customary for a chief who is about to make war to hire the services of his neighbour's, as in more civilized countries; the principal currency being a sort of quartz worked down into rings or flat discs together with shells and food.

Nangri is now making arrangements with other tribes to assist him in making war on the friendly settlement, their avowed intention being to kill the missionary and every native who wears a waist-cloth, that is to say, all the "Lotos" or Christians, as soon as the departure of Mr. Henry and his Vate men shall have left them defenceless.

I have little doubt that this is really their purpose, though Mr. Gordon says that he will get on better when Mr. Henry with his sandalwood trading and alien islanders have gone.

Under the above-mentioned circumstances a letter has been written to Messrs. Kaniau and Warris Nangri, calling on them to meet the Commodore this day, either on board or at the mission-house, to answer certain complaints made against them.

After their recent behaviour, there was very little chance of their coming on board, but it was thought probable that they might come to the mission-house; and P________, whose afternoon watch it was, received orders to hold himself in readiness to land with twelve good men, armed with concealed revolvers, stroll up to the house, and bundle the two chiefs into the boat before their surprised followers have time to offer any effective resistance. They are then to be kept on board so long as the ship is in Australia and New Zealand as hostages for the safety of Mr. Gordon, and of any other Englishmen who may touch at the island and give no cause of provocation to the natives.

But, "first catch your hare." The two old foxes whose company was so much desired, up to a late hour in the evening showed no inclination to comply with the Commodore's polite invitation either to take a trip on the water or to have a chat at the mission-house.

The next day another messenger was sent to induce Nangri to come in, but without effect; so, at one o'clock we weighed and came to within 300 yards of the beach where his village is built. There is one other sandy bight between it and Dillon's Bay. Sifou village is built close to the shore, at the mouth of a gully lined with bush, but surrounded by high clear tablelands.

As we approached the shore great numbers of natives were seen leaving the place, and either taking refuge in the caves with which the rocks on the coast are honeycombed, or making off along the shore. We could not see whether any were making up the gully, as had been expected.

Close to the water's edge there was a cave, the mouth of which was defended by a gingerbread stockade of posts and coral surmounted by a flagstaff and pendant.

After veering cable, we went to quarters with the watch and fired on the village. The object of the Commodore was not so much to inflict heavy punishment and slaughter as to show them what we can do, and what will be done next year if they do not mend their manners.

For this reason, we only gave them twenty shells and four rockets, and were in no particular hurry in opening fire, which delay allowed ample time for all who wished to clear out; yet up to the moment when the first five or six shells went crashing amongst the coconut trees and *whares*, several natives were to be seen at the doors of the houses.

I was directed to fire a Moorsom shell, with which one of my guns happened to be loaded, at the cave, and it burst against the rock just in one of the two mouths or openings against the stockade; but one of the Armstrong 114-pounders entered the other mouth and burst right inside, the smoke escaping out of holes in the roof or from the open top of the rock above the cave, so it must have done frightful damage among any poor wretches who may have been inside.

One of the natives had the impudence to fire a shot at the ship with his musket, the ball falling about half way: it looked as if he were chaffing us. It was all over in little more than half an hour, and we returned to our anchorage in Dillon's Bay, leaving Sifou village looking very little the worse for the treatment it had received, the little flagstaff still standing, and only three or four shot-holes visible and a few cocoa palms cut down.

As soon as we had anchored Mr. Gordon came on board, and then sent a native messenger to ascertain the effect of the shelling on the two chiefs and the loss sustained by them. But at eight o'clock, after he had been gone four hours, there being no sign of his return, it was considered that he had been killed, so we bade farewell to Erromango and sailed for New Caledonia.

During the recent inter-tribal fights the natives have agreed to use no firearms, but to fight it out with their old-fashioned and less dangerous weapons.

They have, as yet, adhered to their agreement, and the friendlies have refused the ammunition offered them by the whites, who are naturally anxious for the success of their protectors. The old adage about honour among thieves seems hardly sufficient to account for conduct so incompatible with their usual treacherous habits.

NEW CALEDONIA.

We passed through the Havannah Channel on the afternoon of the 28th, and anchored in Good Cove Harbour at half-past six. The anchorage, though deep (20 fathoms), is well sheltered, and surrounded by other harbours apparently as good.

The scenery around is melancholy in the extreme, grey mountain peaks in the distance, low, barren, red earth hills in the foreground, varied only by patches of yellow grass and empty watercourses. We saw one little oasis of verdure in a bay, where apparently, some little stream finds its way into that silent sea amidst no sign of life save some solitary white crane, seeming to meditate suicide as he sat on a lonely rock, and a stray pair of eagle-hawks circling on high, preparatory to the swoop which would save him the trouble and guilt of *felo-de-se*.[101]

The following day was fully occupied in painting the ship inside and out. A French missionary from a neighbouring settlement

---

101 Suicide.

came on board this morning. Two large sailing canoes also came down to inspect us. They were full of natives clad in European clothes, a tall, well-made race, with good heads and features, if these were fair specimens of their countrymen.

September 30th. — Weighed shortly before twelve o'clock, and steamed through Wodin Passage along the coast to Port de France,[102] where we anchored at half-past three. Here we found the *'Falcon'* with our mail awaiting us; also the French vessels *'Fulton'* and *'Gazelle.'*

October 1st, Sunday. — today the Governor, M. Guillain, a captain in the navy, was received onboard. He was accompanied by M. Matthieu, his *chef d'état-major*, and in the afternoon I went ashore with the Commodore to see the gardens at Government House.

The next day I formed one of a party who accompanied the Governor on a picnic visit to the model farm some three miles off. The farm makes progress rapidly, though the very tools used in its formation had to be made on the spot, under the direction of M. Bouton, the engineer and surveyor. He had also to find the necessary supply of stone and timber in the neighbouring mountains and forests. The soil and climate are said to be very favourable to horticulture, European and tropical fruits and vegetables flourishing side by side. Mr. Veitch, who accompanied us, pronounced the young coffee trees to be finer than any he had seen before, even in Ceylon or in the Philippine Islands.

The situation commands a most lovely view in the direction of the mountains.

After being entertained at an excellent lunch by M. Bouton, we returned by the same road, picking up on our way one of the

---

102 "On shore there are about 800 troops, all, however, marines; about 200 of them being marine artillery. They have six small field-pieces, and three or four larger guns at a fort on the east side of the harbour, close to the Artillery Barracks *(Baie Bayonneuse)*. On anchoring we saluted the French flag with twenty-one guns, and the fort returned it with its pop-guns." (Foljambe, p.230)

gendarmes of our escort, whose horse, after depositing his rider's cap in a ditch, had flatly refused to pass the usual half-way house.

The country much resembles in appearance some parts of New South Wales. A species of tea tree (quite unlike that of New Zealand) abounds, and its white bark makes the bush to resemble in some degree the gum-tree woods of Australia.

October 3rd. — Ashore today comparing our charts with the recent French surveys, of which they gave us some copies.

In the evening, I went on board the 'Falcon,' where a grand dinner was given on the upper deck to the French naval and military officers, in return for one at which the 'Falcon's' had been entertained previous to our arrival. Everything went off well. Our band played, and the guests seemed thoroughly to enjoy themselves.

Nobody was the worse for liquor, but if the number of toasts, two or three at a time, the loyal and enthusiastic songs, or the noise we made be any test of enjoyment, the dinner must indeed have been a success. H________ presided, and produced toasts and speeches in polyglot languages with a rapidity which would have puzzled even a shorthand reporter. Meanwhile his captain with the Commodore and P________ were entertained ashore at a banquet given by the Governor. The next day I dined with the Commodore, and met the Governor and Madame Guillain. At the same time others of my brother officers went to *a "ponche"* provided by the French officers, commencing at 11 p.m. A very heavy wet.

On the 5th we went to a ball at Government House. Dancing took place under difficulties, as the ladies were only nine in number, all told. The following morning the *'Falcon'* sailed for New Zealand.

October 8th, Sunday. — We sailed for Sydney at 7.40 a.m., passing through the reef. The New Caledonia reef is one of the largest of the "barrier" class, being over 400 miles in length.

The colony has not as yet much commercial or any other activity, and relies mainly on the penal element for the development of its resources.

The convicts, as in our own penal settlements, are men who have been convicted in the ordinary criminal courts, but the men who form their guard, the *disciplinaires*, are for the most part men belonging to the regular army, who have committed some offence against military discipline, and have been condemned to serve the remainder of their military service in this distant and *triste* settlement.

It is said that the officers out here in many cases are under a cloud, and this of course puts them all in the Governor's power, and tends to make him more despotic than if he had to deal with men who, not being under probation, were less dependent upon his reports on their conduct.

A curfew gun is fired every night at ten o'clock, all the week round, after which all lights are extinguished, and all doors kept rigidly closed, neither sex being allowed to leave or enter even their own houses on any pretext whatever.

We arrived at Sydney on the evening of the 13th, thus bringing to a conclusion the pleasantest and most interesting cruise which I, or indeed any of us on board, have ever made.[103]

---

103 Here the narrative takes a break. HMS *Curaçoa* is sent back to England, and Meade is transferred to HMS Esk. Cecil Foljambe bows out of the narrative and remains with HMS *Curaçoa*.

CHAPTER XI.

Sail for the Friendly Islands — Tongatabu — Father Lamage and missionary squabbles — Wild ducks and flying foxes — Moafu, father and son — Vicarious punishment — Tongan Stonehenge — Kava-ring at Lifuka — Vavau cotton-growing — Governor David and his son Wellington — Legend of the submarine cave — Difficult entrance — Latte — Fiji group — Mbua products — Waterfall — Rubbing fire from two sticks — Mission policy — Canoe-building.

TONGATABU.[104]

October 27th, 1866.[105] — 8 a.m., in 15 fathoms, off Nukualofa. The consul Captain Jones, V.C, came on board and was saluted. At half-past ten, O________, S________, and I landed to shoot ducks. We found King George away, at Lifuka,[106] but Mr. Moss, who has got spliced, did the honours in the absence of his chief. Since we were here in the '*Curaçoa*,' trial by jury has been instituted, and the severity of some of the laws against immorality have been relaxed, adultery alone being now penal.

By Moss's advice we walked along the beach to Mantaunga, a village about a mile distant, when Father Lamage, of the Catholic mission, provided us with a couple of native guides and a canoe. He remembered my having made acquaintance with him when he came on board the '*Curaçoa*' last year with two of his *confrères*, and was very glad to see us.

---

104 Tonga.

105 Note the year change. This is almost a year exactly since HMS *Curaçoa* arrived in Sydney.

106 An island in the Kingdom of Tonga, northeast of Nuku'alofa.

We had not been many minutes in conversation before the subject of the miserable quarrels between themselves and the Wesleyans cropped up. He spoke of the latter very bitterly, averring that their conduct towards him was, "*Rien que des mensonges et des calomnies.*"[107] I believe that both here and in the Samoan group the Dissenting ministers denounce Roman Catholic missionaries to the natives in terms of unwarrantable abuse and intolerance; but the latter were the cause of the whole scandal, by intruding both here and elsewhere on ground previously occupied by Protestants, who had settled there in days gone by at the imminent risk of their lives, and who now naturally feel aggrieved to find that the first result of their successful labours, which have rendered these islands a safe habitation for white men, is the introduction of teachers of a different creed, who follow in their footsteps to seduce from them a portion of their flock, or others who very soon would have become so. What follows when Catholics get the upper hand in these seas, may be seen at the Loyalties and at Tahiti.

Twenty minutes' walk through the bush brought us to the edge of the lagoon, where we had to wait some time for the canoe, which, the tide being low, had to make a long circuit. S________ and I then embarked with one native, leaving O________ to try the creeks with the other; he did not succeed in making his native understand what he wanted, and so failed to re-join us, and got nothing. S________ and I bagged seven ducks and five other marsh and water birds. Moreover, two more wounded ducks made good their escape amongst the thick roots of the mangroves, for want of a retriever: not such very bad sport on the whole, considering that it was nearly three before we began shooting. Towards dusk we saw many flying foxes — apparently large and handsomely furred — but all circling so high above our heads that it would have been useless to fire at them.

It was dark before we got back to the priest's house, where we supped; O________, who had arrived there before us, having got

---

107 Nothing but lies and false accusations.

tired of waiting, had gone off. The lagoon is full of fish, which rose on every side of us — some of them three or four feet long.

On inquiry for Charley Moafu, the Tongan Adonis, whose acquaintance we made in the '*Curaçoa*,' found that he is stopping with his father, Moafu senior, at Vanua Balavu, the Tongan colony in Fiji. We heard two little stories of this gay young gentleman. A plot had been discovered to take his father's life, and the old chief with singular moderation spared the lives of the conspirators, and sentenced them only to banishment to different islands, for which purpose he embarked them all on board his schooner. Just before weighing, the old gentleman went on shore for something, and the son improved the occasion by informing the plotters that though his father's leniency had spared their lives, they were not going to get off quite so cheap as they expected and forthwith producing a "cat," gave them a sound flogging all round.

On another occasion, having been convicted of a breach of the seventh commandment, he was sentenced to hard labour on the roads, or rather road, of which he was bound to complete a certain portion daily. By eventide his task was always done, till its very regularity awakened suspicion, and a watch having been set he was discovered sitting coolly smoking his pipe under the shade of a tree, while a score or so of his lady-loves, past and present, were hard at work making his allotted task of the road — all their mutual jealousies having been overpowered by their sympathy for the hard lot of the object of their affections.

October 28th, Sunday. — C________ and H________ landed. 4.30 p.m. weighed for Lifuka and steamed until we were clear of the reefs.

I should like to have remained one more day to examine the Tongan Stonehenge, situated about 12 miles from Nukualofa.

From Moss's description, it consists of two perpendicular blocks of stone, about 25 or 30 feet high, supporting a horizontal one about half as long again. In the centre of the latter is a circular hollow or basin, which the natives call the God's or the Giant's "Kava Bowl." He supposes that these enormous weights were placed in their present position in the far-off past, when these islands are deemed to have supported a population of several hundred thousand.

LIFUKA.[108]

October 29th, Monday. — S.E. trade. 4 p.m. at Lifuka Island, in 13 fathoms. Landed with H________ and others to stroll for an hour or two. The island is as flat as Tongatabu. Natives began to run in from all directions as soon as they saw the boat approaching. I made a mild attempt to draw the portrait of a very good-tempered-looking and handsome native girl, which pleased her vastly, but made some of her feminine companions proportionately jealous.

October 30th, Tuesday. — Landed this morning at the village (we having shifted our berth farther in at daylight) with the captain and Jones, and the former having kindly told me to let one of the midshipmen keep my afternoon watch, I stayed ashore to see a "kava-ring," which was got up in our honour by the chief.

It took place in front of the King's house, we — that is, the captain, Jones, the doctor, Mr. ________, a white resident, with three chiefs, and self — sitting in the veranda. The lesser chiefs and "Oi polloi"[109] assembled in a semicircle in front with the kava bowl in the centre. A kava plant with about a dozen stalks springing from the same root having been produced with much formality, the green-jointed or cane-like stems were cut off, and the root distributed among a dozen or two of natives of both sexes for mastication; every little detail, even to the position of the bowl on its legs, being arranged with a nicety of etiquette which was in strict accordance with ancient customs, and the respect due to the chiefs and their "distinguished" guests, but would be only tedious in description.

____

108 An island in the Kingdom of Tonga, northeast of Nuku'alofa.
109 From Greek οἱ πολλοί. Has taken on meaning of the masses/rabble. Literally "the many."

After an interval of about ten minutes the masticators contributed the pulpy results of their labours, wrapped up in fresh banana leaves and as dry as possible; they were placed in the kava bowl simultaneously, and water poured over all.

The "punch compounder unknown," a cleanly and good-looking young native, after thoroughly stirring the mixture, threw over the surface of the fluid a fibrous substance, taken I believe from the top of the coconut trees; with this he skilfully enveloped the kava pulp, and having raised it out of the liquid, expressed every drop of moisture in a series of twists and twirls executed with a practised skill and grace. When a kava-ring takes placed for the discussion of any public matter, the time for speaking terminates with the expression of the kava.

A small quantity of kava having been raised on high, one of the chiefs exclaimed aloud, "The kava is up," and a small bowl made of a bent banana leaf full of the liquor was conveyed to Captain Luce, and then to every one present in succession, first to the white visitors, and then to the native men and women according to their rank by birth; the name of each in proper order being called by one of the principal chiefs after the announcement of the raising of the kava by the other, the recipient answering to his name by twice clapping his hands.

The pig and taro were then divided into equal portions and presented to us, and we having gone through the form of acceptance, requested that our share might be distributed to the natives.

There is a church here larger even than that at Tongatabu, the high arched roof supported by stout lofty pillars of dark wood, — the whole secured and decorated neatly with sinnet, — not a single nail or screw being used in the whole edifice, every part of which must have cost infinite labour. There was more than one canoe lading at the beach with produce of various kinds. Then large double canoes, with their broad mat-sail and tall crescent-crested mast, spacious deck and deck-house crowded with merchandise, and tall natives swaying from side to side as they work the perpendicular scull, have a very picturesque appearance. Some of the largest measure: length, 90 feet; beam, 5 feet; depth, 5 feet; deck, 25 feet square.

Food of all sorts is plentiful and cheap. A fowl or a basket of ten eggs for any one silver coin apiece.

"Sulu," or cloth, in great demand here, as elsewhere. 5 p.m. weighed under steam for Vavau.

Not long ago King George, hearing of the advantage reaped in Fiji by cotton planting, made a law that every man in Tonga should plant 100 cotton trees; this was done, but the letter and not the spirit of the law was adhered to, and when the trees fructified, these unthrifty islanders let the cotton lie about the ground and blow far and wide, till it covered the whole island and the very high roads like snow. On this being represented to the King, he made another law, that any man on whose ground cotton should be found lying at the end of the week should be fined. So the cotton was gathered, but it became so soiled and spoiled, that it fetched a very small price. Better luck next time.

VAVAU.[110]

October 31st. — Furled sails 3.30, and came-to off Nuafou, Vavau, in 19 fathoms. I landed in the evening to arrange with one-eyed old David, the Governor or Viceroy, for a couple of natives and a canoe for duck-shooting tomorrow. He remembered me at once, and we got on famously. He is heir-apparent to the King of Tonga, being his son by a wife who was discarded on his embracing the Christian religion, his proper son and heir being defunct. He is a very tall dignified man; he has lost an eye and two fingers. These latter are said to have been cut off as mourning for the death of some relations. He is said to have lost his eye by the kick of a horse, but more likely it was lost in one of his many fights in the Fijis. I took a great fancy to his son, a bright-looking boy about ten years old — Wellington Ngu. The chief's blood in

---

110 Modern Vava'u. Not an island but a group of islands. Neiafu is the main settlement on the largest island. It has a deep-water harbour and is well sheltered.

the little fellow's veins made his good lineage as plainly visible, in spite of his colour, as that of any youthful swell that ever went to Eton or Harrow.

Roads are being pushed on with considerable energy. They are constructed by offenders against the laws, either as punishment or in payment of fines. The enactments against adultery are very severe, and supply the great majority of criminal labour. These laws were passed at a great meeting held at Tongatabu, on the 4th of June, 1862, when civil liberty, a constitutional monarchy, and the abolition of serfdom were proclaimed throughout the Tongan dominions.

The people appear more industrious here than elsewhere, and the not unpleasant sound of the *tappa* mallet gave notice of the proximity of the villages before they could be discovered, through the thick foliage literally smothered in creepers, which here attain an extraordinary luxuriance of growth.

The bark of the *tappa* plant, which furnishes the greater portion of the inhabitants with waist-cloths, is beaten out into a sort of tough paper by being moistened and hammered on a beam of wood by a small square-sided staff or mallet, of which the surfaces are slightly furrowed to facilitate the expansion of the *tappa*, which is said to be the same as the Chinese paper mulberry.

In every village were two or three large troughs looking like small canoes, filled with the white of the coconut, scraped small, and slowly exuding the precious oil under the influence of the warm sun.

Great quantities of *beche-de-mer*, and even yet more repulsive-looking animals, something between a sea snake and a slimy centipede, are found lying in the pools left by the receding tide on the flats.

There are two resident Wesleyan missionaries who claim the bulk of the population, leaving only a very small proportion to the Catholics.

They appear to give way to the usual narrow-minded bigotry which in these islands almost appear to be the prevailing characteristic of their sect, and the manner in which they spoke of their Roman Catholic colleagues afforded an unfavourable contrast to the charitable expressions of the latter. The total population is said to be 4800, showing a considerable decrease of late years. The thermometer averages 90° in the shade, and the climate appeared to us much more bracing and agreeable, and seemed much drier compared with the Samoan group but the missionaries do not speak favourably of the healthiness of the place.

November 1st. — Soon after daylight, O________, D________, and I left the ship in the jolly-boat, accompanied by our two natives in a canoe, and after about three-quarters of an hour's pull, landed at a place where there was a canoe-shed; here we left both boat and canoe, and about a mile's pleasant walk brought us to the village of Hihifu (The West), where after a little delay we procured a canoe. The village is built close to the edge of the lake where the ducks are.

The waters of the lake are brackish, and are contained in a large basin which appears to have been caused by the crater of a volcano now extinct for ages; for the margin of the lake is formed by almost perpendicular volcanic rocks rising to the height of 100 to 300 feet direct from the water's edge, but covered from base to summit with the most luxuriant foliage. A small portion, however, of the shore nearest the sea is flat and swampy, covered with mangroves.

The doctor went by land and got a brace of ducks and two small plovers; but we found afterwards that he had spent most of his time in the village.

O________ and I, with one native, skirted round the edge of the basin, which is really beautiful, the woods rising in rolling terraces one above another from the cliffs, which reach the water's edge to the crests of hills a mile or more distant, and suggesting the idea of some vast amphitheatre.

The ducks were very numerous; but though they rose conveniently and generally in pairs from under the shade of the foliage hanging from the rocks, we shot quite disgracefully, and when we had expended all our powder found that we two had only bagged sixteen ducks — whether from our powder being damp, as we thought, from our never succeeding in killing a duck on the water, and the shot falling short, or from our own extraordinary bad shooting, scarcely one barrel in six brought down a duck, and we lost four wounded birds in the thick roots of the mangroves.

November 2nd. — C________, H________, and S________ went to the basin today, where they suffered various griefs and shipwrecks, and only brought back five ducks and one pukeko, or red-bill.

Young "Welenitoni" was on board all day, and I amused myself by trying to sketch his head, to which he subscribed his name. A monkey we have on board is a source of never-failing wonder and terror to all the natives who visit us, and Finnic being perfectly aware of it, the little brute takes a delight in occasionally driving a crowd of them over the stern or gangway. The little chief evidently did not like to show the same fear of the monkey as the common people, and with a view of making friends with Finnie, he made one of the natives fetch him some Cape gooseberries. Thereupon Finnie made overtures of peace, and in a minute or two was seated in his lap, stuffing herself with gooseberries in the most amicable manner, till the very last was gone, when she bit her benefactor and ran away.

David says he is going to send his son to Sydney to be educated (as he fears the cold of the English climate) and as he says he will gladly pay £300 a year: I hope he may get his money's worth. The last thing I saw before leaving the shore for the last time was old David, surveying with his one eye and all a parent's pride, his son arrayed in all the glory of a midshipman's dress tail-coat — and little else.

November 3rd. — I went for a ride this morning, as I had arranged last night, with my latest thing in friends — Julie — a very pretty little half-caste Tahitian girl whom I had met the first night of our arrival; she rode well and spoke a little French with a pretty little South Sea Island accent.

We weighed about one, having on board the two Wesleyan missionaries, Messrs. Stevenson and Watkins, with the chief and other natives, and their boats in tow. At the mouth of the harbour we stopped, and went in the galley and cutter to examine some caves. The first was well worth inspection; the mouth was broad enough to admit both boats easily, and then water enough in nearly every part to float a frigate. The stalactites and columns under the high-domed roof resemble Gothic arches. The bright sunlight streaming through the narrow gateway of the cave — through the singularly clear water — and reflected up from the sparkling stones and coral at the bottom — full 5 fathoms deep — shed a beautiful series of lights and tints, shades of delicate blue and green, over every part of the walls and vaulted roof. At the innermost end of the cave there is an upward slanting passage over rocks and under arches, the farthest end of which is lighted by some direct communication with the open air above. And one or two of our men scrambling up to explore the place, now in sight, now hidden from view, almost comically reminded one of the "Robber's Cave" business in an opera. The next cave we visited was smaller and less remarkable.

We then made sail before the wind to a cave with a submarine entrance.

This is the scene of the romantic adventure in Byron's poem, 'The Island,' wherein it is well described under the name of "Neuha's Cave."

The native tradition is, that the family of a certain chief having been condemned to extermination for rebellion, one of the daughters, a very beautiful girl, was prevailed upon by her lover to accompany him by night to this cave, which he had accidentally discovered not long before while diving for turtle. Here he kept her concealed, visiting her nightly with food and fresh water, till an opportunity occurred of escaping together by canoe to the Fiji Islands, where they remained undisturbed in their connubial bliss till the death of the Tongan viceroy enabled them to return to Vavau.

Two sticks placed crosswise over a ledge of rock marked the position of the entrance to the cave, which would have otherwise been very difficult to discover; for above water there was no sign whatever of an opening — nothing but an unbroken and almost overhanging cliff. When the water was still for a second, becalmed by the boats, or when the fierce glare of the sun, being kept off the glancing surface of the waves by the overhanging rocks, made the sea transparent, then a darker patch than usual amongst these coral-covered rocks was seen some eight or ten feet deep. This was the entrance.

One of the natives — skilled divers — who accompanied the chief, went overboard from the galley with the end of the boat's lead-line. The first time he seemed to fail, and rose again almost immediately; the second time he disappeared in the direction of the cavernous darkness, and remained out of sight for eight or ten minutes, when he returned, after having made fast the end of the line in the cavern, and rose again to air and daylight.

The chief (David), who had talked so glibly of taking down one of us in each hand, now did not seem very anxious to distinguish himself in that line; so, the captain, who, whether in the hunting field or elsewhere, is always "to the front," persuaded two of the most expert to take him down into the cave.[111]

After entering the passage, the skipper became unable to withstand the natural tendency of his body to rise, thereby repeatedly striking against the sharp projections which form the roof, of the passage, and the natives grasping him one by each arm, had to keep forcing him down through nearly all the length of the passage, which the lead-line showed to be about 30 feet. This to a man not accustomed to protracted diving was rather exhausting, and on reaching the surface of the water within the cavern he had to be helped across the short distance which separated them

---

111 "The officer referred to was Captain Luce, of H.M.S. '*Esk*,' to which ship Lieutenant Meade was transferred soon after the arrival of the '*Curaçoa*' at Sydney." (Brenchley, p.99)

from a ledge of rock, just visible in the dusk, whereon they sat and rested. The little light there was within the cave was derived solely from the reflexion through the mouth of the submerged passage, save when the waters within were disturbed by the swimmers, when the phosphorescent light displayed was more beautiful and brilliant than anything of the sort he had ever seen elsewhere, and he induced the natives to cross the cave in all directions for the sake of admiring the streams of liquid fire which followed every motion of their limbs.

In returning after having passed the lowest point of the passage, the glare of light shining downwards through the waves from the open air beyond repeatedly caused him to attempt too soon to rise, thereby coming into collision with the rocks overhead. The natives now refused to take anyone else down; they said that "the men of the sea are too short-winded," and that after the difficulty they had had to keep the chief of the great war-canoe clear of the roof of the passage, they feared lest an accident might happen should they attempt it again. And in truth the appearance of our worthy chief was such as in a great measure to cool the ardour and lessen the disappointment of those who had been most anxious to follow his example, for his exhaustion for a minute or two was such that on showing above water he had to be helped to the boat, only a yard or two distant; his complexion had turned to a colour of blended yellow and green, and after having been lifted into the boat his first act was to appease the fishes, whose sanctum he had invaded, by feeding them most liberally.

The natives said the correct way to proceed is to dive in the ordinary manner to the entrance of the passage, and then, turning on one's back, keep off the roof with hands and feet till the cave is reached.

By the captain's account, the interior of the cave, as far as he could judge by the fitful light, fully bore out Byron's description.

The legend that we heard agreed with that given in Mariner's 'Tonga' in the main, but some of us were told that, whether from want of air or anxiety during her stay in this submarine or subterranean prison of refuge, the young bride's hair turned grey.

At the time of our visit I had never read 'The Island,' nor, oddly enough, was I, nor most of my messmates, aware that this was the cave described by Mariner and the theme of Byron's poem.

And diving being at all times not only disagreeable but painful to me, I had not concealed the fact that the retiring modesty of my nature would prevent the cave from ever being inconveniently crowded by my adding to the number of its inmates.

I fancy that if I should ever revisit the spot I should feel inclined to try the experiment of letting a deep-sea lead slide down the line, which would lodge at the lowest point of the bight, and so afford a fair leader to keep one clear of the rocks above.

November 4th, Sunday. — Standing off and on Latte, a small and nearly circular volcanic island, to the west of Vavau. The highest part of the mountain, the lip of the crater, is rather under 1800 feet in height. As only one boat was to land, orders were given that three only should land from each mess; and from our mess the parson, purser, and H________ were the three — selected by the simple process of self-election.

The volcano was *volcaning* a little in a pretty, snivelling sort of way, but I hear it relieves its feelings occasionally with a good sneezing eruption.

Our messmates returned late in the afternoon (they had landed at eight) in a very draggletail and dishevelled condition; H________ looked as if he had lost his backbone, the parson looked, if possible, limper than ever — and he always was a very limp man. Wild pigs and pigeons, and remains of a native village.

By careful inquiry I elicited from the explorers that this volcano is very like any other volcano, but it is rather a one-horse concern on the whole.

Water was found in cavities cut for the purpose in live coconut trees, fed by two converging gutters cut down the surface of the trunk above.

Filled, and made sail for the Fijis. No particular service today.

VANUA BALAVU.

November 6th. — 11.45, came-to under steam off Lomaloma, Vanua Balavu Island, Fiji group, in 12½ fathoms.

H________ and others landed at the village, which is under the dominion of the Tongan chief, Moafu. They reported the chief and his son both away, and the place dirty and uninteresting. H________, however, managed to get me seven opercula (green), which he bought from a white beach-comber. These are almost the first that I have been able to get.

Vanua Balavu (Long Land) is the largest of one of the easternmost clusters of islands in the Fiji group, sometimes termed "The Exploring Isles."

VANUA LEVU.

November 8th. — 11 a.m. came-to off Savusavu — a settlement in a great bay on the southern coast of Vanua Levu, the northern large island.

This village was burnt by the *'Esk'* last time she was here, to punish the inhabitants for a series of robberies, and for refusing to give up the principal culprit, who was, I believe, a chief.

These people, as well as others on the northern coast of this island, were formerly Protestant, but when Pritchard, the late consul, quarrelled with the Wesleyan missionaries, he persuaded the chiefs at these places to turn Roman Catholics, with their tribes *en masse*, simply to spite the Wesleyans; at least this is the version I heard from a Church of England layman.

Thakomhau was on board at the time of the *'Esk's'* former visit, and his authority was exerted to endeavour to get the offending chief given up, but without avail; several thieves "of low degree" were given up and flogged on board, but not the chief. While one of the boats, unarmed, was waiting ashore at the white settlement, the midshipman was told that the offender was at Mr. Wilson's place, and sent the coxswain up to secure him. But the latter, who was a small man, found he had caught a Tartar, and the chief was on the point of killing him with an axe when a white blacksmith, who was present, saved his life by knocking down the chief with his fist. But even after they had got him down they failed to secure him, and he made good his escape. The next day the threat of burning the village, having failed to procure his surrender, was carried out.

November 9th. — 6 a.m. weighed under steam. Stopped to take in an Irishman named Cadogan, who comes to pilot us. 3.40, anchored in 5½ fathoms off the mouth of the Mbua river, in Sandalwood Bay. Low land, covered with a great expanse of mangrove bushes, shuts in the horizon, and shelters the bay on three-quarters of the circle, and from the mangroves rise a long, curved chain of lofty and well-timbered hills, whose warm tints and shades from softly rounded ridges looked exceedingly well in the rays of the setting sun.

November 10th. — Jones (the consul), O________, and I accompanied the captain this morning in the galley; we soon found the passage through the mangroves, and then a quarter of an hour's pull brought us to the true mouth of the river, which we ascended for about two miles to the village of Mbua. Here we got out and stopped a little while in a native house belonging to a Mr. Swainson, who seemed to be above the average run of whites loafing about these islands. He is now employed in cotton-planting. He has to find his native labourers in food, which he buys, mainly yams and rice, and he pays them wages at the rate of about £2 a-year, in "trade."

The Fiji cotton is of a very high quality, and when cleaned will fetch as much as 4*s*. alongside the ship in the bay, or 5*s*. at home.

This was the first, or nearly the first place from which the sandalwood trade, then in the hands of the East India Company, derived their supply; and years ago, as many as seven large East Indiamen have been seen lying in the bay at once. But the trees were felled with the same reckless improvidence as in the other islands, and today we were shown a solitary sapling, which had been planted by a missionary, now the only living sandal-tree for many miles around.

Now, I am told, though rather too late, a *tambu*[112] has been laid on the trees for a certain number of years.

In a few minutes Mr. Wilkinson, the king's minister or secretary, an intelligent sort of man, made his appearance, and introduced us duly to his liege lord, Tui Mbua, a middle-aged chief of observant manner, but reserved and gentleman-like. Tall and closely-shaven, except on the upper lip.

He bears the character of a good warrior, and of being, of all the chiefs of the group, the most enlightened and the most anxious for the advancement of civilization amongst his people. Even in the jolly old cannibal days he never was much of a glutton, and only had three wives — an instance of moderation very rare among chiefs.

We all started again together in the galley, as soon as the cutter made her appearance with the other officers, to visit a waterfall. At almost every little bend of the river, which at times was scarcely broad enough for the oars, we flushed one or more couple of duck, but neither of us had a gun in the boat, and, moreover, the river is *tambu*-ed for duck from the falls to the shore-edge of the mangrove bushes, and they are consequently very tame. Fish, good eating, and three or four feet long, are caught up this river, and sharks ascend almost as far as they can swim — in the Wai Levu at Ruva they have been known to take men as far as 30 miles above the mouth.

Twenty minutes' pull brought us to a fork in the river, one branch flowing past the mission-house in sight ahead of us, the other from the waterfall.

We were here joined by Messrs. Brookes and Horseley, in the Wesleyan mission boat, and ascended the tributary in company as far towards the falls as the water and rocks and snags would allow, when we disembarked, and leaving the galleys to get their dinners while we were away, walked on about a mile and a half to the spot where the river, here a mere brook, falls over a cliff of black rocks 60 or 70 feet high into a deep pool, full of little fish with prominent eyes. Here we all stripped eagerly and enjoyed

---

112 Similar to Māori "tapu" — i.e. to be sacred or set aside.

a delicious swim and shower-bath. Then lunch and baccy, and a lesson in the art of making fire by rubbing one stick against another. By Tui Mbua's orders one of the natives went to look for two suitable sticks, and in two or three minutes returned with one about a yard long and a couple of inches thick, and another a third of that length and thickness, which he cut to a rough blunt point. Of course, both were dead and dry wood. There are many species which will serve, though some are better than others. The natives then cut a small slice off the top of the larger stick so as to leave an even surface for five or six inches, with the last half-inch of shaving still attached to the wood, but erect, so as to form a sort of little screen to catch the smouldering dust. He then squatted with the larger stick resting on the ground between his legs, the screen end of the groove from him, and the farther end beyond, steadied firmly against the ground by means of his feet; then clasping the short stick or rubber with both hands, one covering the other, and his work well under his chest, in such a manner as to make the weight of his body assist with the least exertion, he worked it steadily along the pared surface backwards and forwards till the point had worn a groove all along. In a very few seconds the groove began to blacken and smoke, and a little heap of black dust collected at the end against the screen. He began quite gently, and gradually increased the speed, taking care to make each stroke a fiftieth part of an inch shorter than the last, so as not to knock away the accumulating little heap of dust.

The dust caught fire in forty-four seconds from the first application of the sticks, and the sparks having been transferred to a wisp of dry grass, a flame was almost instantly produced. When there are two natives, one will work the rubber and the other steady the lower stick, and help to preserve the dust with a couple of blades of grass.

The captain and I each tried twice, but got no farther than smoke enough to make our eyes smart i and the last time a drop of provoking perspiration fell on the dust at the critical moment.

But next day I tried on board, standing over a table, a position which seems more convenient to any European but a tailor; a messmate steadied the end of the stick, and I produced permanent fire at the very first trial, and in less than a minute. I have since seen a native get fire in fifteen seconds.

We afterwards visited the mission-house, where Mrs. Brookes entertained us with cool water-melons and pine-apples. In the course of conversation, Mr. Brookes nearly persuaded me out of my conviction of the narrow-minded impolicy of insisting that the chiefs and others who had been living in polygamy before the introduction of Christianity, should turn all their wives adrift except one, before admission as Christians. He pointed out that the natives are not converted singly, but *"loto,"* or turn Christian *en masse*, a whole tribe or settlement at once, by the permission and example of the chief, and that as their conversion is often hastened or retarded from political motives, the self-denial required to give up the services and companionship of perhaps a score or two of wives, is their guarantee and test of sincerity. The change is generally an improvement in the condition of the younger women, who can easily find husbands after their own heart among the bachelors of the tribe, and are happier with them than as the concubines or slaves of the chief, who could take as many women of his tribe as he chose to fancy, to the manifest exclusion from marriage of many of the inferior men of the tribe. But, to the elderly ladies, the dear old tabbies whose magnetic charms have lost the loadstone of youth, their fate seems hard indeed.

The mission-house is coolly situated on the crest of a pleasant hill, commanding in rear a good view of the mountains and in front, of the broad and fertile plains, winding river, and distant sea with the corvette riding at anchor, a mere speck on the waters.

I learnt from Mr. Wilkinson that Tui Mbua has established a sort of constitution (I suppose by the former's advice), under which public affairs are dispatched by an assembly, composed of two members from each district, one of whom is named by himself, the other by the inhabitants. The principal punishments are hard labour and flogging, the latter most frequently inflicted for absconding from the former. The instrument of flagellation was formerly the stalk from which hang the coconuts on the palm trees, and the punishment was barbarous, each blow laying the flesh open and after a sentence of thirty or forty stripes the greater portion would be inflicted on an insensible body, the prisoner having fainted perhaps at the fifth or sixth stroke. Mr. Wilkinson has prevailed on the chief to substitute the more merciful cat.

Mbua is now independent of Ban. We examined a large double canoe building under a shed, its length was 24 paces. It is now in the third year of construction, and the fourth will probably see its completion. At the time we saw it, only one man was at work, he being the only man in the neighbourhood possessed of the necessary skill.

The canoe being of too great a size to allow of its being scooped out of a single tree, the parts are joined by scarfing with a bevelled rabbet at the juncture, a raised rim or ledge, is left all along both edges of the join (inside of the canoe), perforated with holes through which sinnet is passed and the scarfing lashed together; not a single nail or screw or anything resembling thereto is used in the construction of any Fijian canoe or house. It being necessary to keep the outrigger always on the weather side, the mast is made to work in a socket at the heel, the greatest dependence being placed on the stay or backstay, which is of great size and strength (5 and 5½ in.). The matting for the sail is sewn together by long bone needles, made from the legs of their enemies. Tui Mbua and Mr. Wilkinson embarked to accompany us to the northern coast. The chief was dressed in a handsome woollen shirt, confined at the waist with folds of white and flowing *tappa*. He sleeps in the captain's fore-cabin and dines at his table. It is surprising to see with how much greater ease these native chiefs fall into the etiquette of the dinner-table than do vulgar whites.

Sheep as well as pigs and fowls were obtained in Sandalwood Bay.

CHAPTER XII.

Tui Mbua on board — Nanduri girl — Expedition against Ritova — Village burnt — A sign of disgrace — Search for opercula — Sharks and swordfish — Strangers' house at Mbau — Cannibal fork — Sacred tree and the braining-stone — Departure of Messrs. Jones and Thurston — Kandavu — Mosquito tree — Tree ferns — Mr. White's station.

November 11th, Sunday. — 6 a.m. weighed under steam for Nanduri. Tui Mbua much struck with the wonders of the engine-room, where the strange sounds and motion impressed him deeply with an idea of irresistible and terrible power. "What strong hearts," said he, "you whites must have here are these men (the engineers) as much at ease as if they were in their own homes, while I tremble in every limb!"

The coast all along here very fine, three ranges of hills, with high mountains beyond, capped with sugar-loaf and other remarkably shaped peaks. Later we neared a point where the scenery changed completely, and instead of the rolling hills and woodlands, the view was cut off by a chaos of dark and barren rocky mountains; cliffs and gullies disposed in the strangest and most melancholy manner and most fantastic shapes, without a blade of vegetation, save the tiniest possible belt of green at the very edge of the sea, which served only to make the remainder seem yet more dismal or as M________ put it, "Here surely must be the approach to the castle of the Giant Despair!"

About five o'clock we passed between the populous island Mathuata[113] and the village of Ravi-ravi on the mainland, miscalled

____

113 Macuata-i-wai; an island north of Fiji's second largest island Vanua Levu.

in the charts Nanduri, and anchored about 6 p.m. off the true Nanduri, six or eight miles farther to the northward and eastward along the coast.

NANDURI.

November 12th. — Landed this forenoon for an hour or two; found the town small but crowded, the houses being confined within a ditch and embankment surmounted by the remains of a stockade. The women outnumbered the men four to one. I wandered away a little distance from the town in search of something to sketch, but I had scarcely got clear of the houses when five young girls of 14 to 18 years of age came and took charge of me altogether, one holding fast to each hand and the others anyhow, laughing and chattering away like wild sprites. The young lady who had boarded on the starboard quarter was just one's idea of what a regular wild island girl should be — teeth and lips like pearls and coral well-shaped feet and ankles finished off a pair of legs which looked like pace-goers by land or water, a smooth and transparent light olive-bronze-coloured complexion, a laughing face, and a pair of flashing black eyes; her sole costume, a couple of wild flowers in her hair, and a *"liku,"* or belt, with narrow streamers of orange-coloured *tappa* hanging nearly down to her knees.

My fair (?) companions had even more than the usual amount of curiosity allowed to their sex; they insisted on examining every article in my pockets and haversack, and unfastened my sleeve-links and shirt-studs to make sure that the rest of my skin was the same colour as my face and hands; my watercolour box especially struck their fancy, and two of them would not be satisfied till I had transferred to their dusky mugs every hue of the rainbow. We soon came to a deep brook, and they nearly all took to the water like ducks. I could not help observing that that portion of their persons which is supposed to be concealed by the *"liku,"* is most elaborately adorned, both before and abaft all, with chaste designs in tattooing, and it is obvious that this operation must be long and painful, but *"Il faut souffrir pour être belle."*[114]

The girls at this place were more forward and confident, and less modest than in any other part of Fiji that I have seen yet, and the men were less watchful and jealous.

I returned on board about twelve, to allow C________ and H________ to land.

Ritova, chief of Mathuata, and Bonavidongo and ________, were sent for to come on board; the two latter complied, and a *korero* was held in the captain's cabin, but the former gave us the slip, getting away in a small canoe after securing time to make himself scarce by giving evasive and temporizing answers. There are, I hear, many complaints against Ritova, who bears a bad character, though supported as a good customer by some of the whites. Bonavidongo, who seems to have been rather a wild cur, is often mentioned in Jackson's "Narrative" (Erskine).

MATHUATA.

November 13th. — 5 a.m. weighed under steam. 6 a.m. anchored off the island of Mathuata. I was sent with two cutters armed, to seize Ritova, or failing that to destroy his property. One cutter was lowered before we anchored, to stop a large double canoe which was making tracks under all sail. She was brought alongside, but the chief was not on board her, as was half expected. It was decided, however, that she belonged to him, and she with her contents — a few muskets and axes — was ordered to be destroyed.

To the eastward of Mathuata lay a small island, divided from the larger by a very shallow passage. We lay between these two islands and the mainland. While the first cutter was making sure of the canoe under sail, I shoved off in the second cutter to intercept another which lay in the passage between the islands getting ready for sea.

---

114 Commonly translated as "You must suffer to be beautiful."

This required careful steering to save the boat's bottom from the coral. Meanwhile the canoe slipped and got away round the other side of the island, where we found her getting provisions, &c., on board; so, I seized her, as well as a whaler, with a white man and a snuff-and-butter-coloured vagabond of no particular breed, whom I suspected of assisting the escape of the chief, or, at all events, of helping to remove his property. Brought these two craft with me round the other side of the island, to make sure of there being no more canoes, &c., afloat.

Meanwhile I learnt that the chief had skedaddled before the ship arrived, and was supposed to have gone to the mainland. About ten o'clock the captain and consul, in the galley with the first cutter, landed and joined me ashore. They had been over to Ravi-ravi in bootless search for Ritova.

I then left G________ in charge of the boats, canoe, and boat-keepers, and took the remainder of the men up to the village. As soon as we had made certain which were the two houses belonging to Ritova, we collected all his property that we could lay hands on, and having piled it in a heap in the middle of the larger house of the two, set them both in a blaze. There were a number of the finest mats that I have seen in all Fiji, which it seemed quite a pity to destroy; but it was better so than to give him an excuse for saying that we came more for the sake of looting than punishment. I fired them myself, so as to make sure against the men looting, and did not even examine the contents of the boxes, which I was sorry for afterwards, as I heard that one of them was supposed to have contained a bag of about sixty red whale's teeth — articles of great value in these islands, each representing to a Fijian, according to Mr. Wilkinson, what a £5 note does to an Englishman; and I should like to know whether they were destroyed or not.

The houses, all of wooden scantling, with very thick thatched roofs, as dry as tinder, burned furiously and when the cross-beams gave way, and the roof fell in, there was a "bully" blaze, which set the tops of the coconut trees and two or three of the nearest houses on fire. We assisted the natives, or rather showed them the example of checking the flames from spreading to the other *whares*, and we then destroyed Ritova's canoe, which was found hauled up on the beach.

The captain then gave a white man who was living under Ritova's protection a letter for him, and we all returned to the boats. Just as we were going to shove off, we saw a fresh burst of flame and smoke in the direction of the village. So, I ran back with a few hands to see what could be done.

I found that the wind having changed, nearly the whole village was ablaze. The natives, most of whom had fled from the village before our approach, were now running down the hill in considerable numbers to try and save some of their property.

Altogether it looked rather grand — every house a perfect sheet of flame; the tall coconut trees, with all their feathery tops in a flame, stood out like gigantic torches against the black darkness of the smoke-thickened groves beyond, the bamboo bursting on every side, from the expansion of the heated air within the joints, with a sound like repeated explosions of gunpowder.

We cut off the fire from a few of the houses furthest to windward, by destroying the intermediate ones and then, seeing that there was no chance of saving the rest of the village, I left. But, before doing so, having told the natives that I was thirsty they immediately provided me with coconuts, husked and opened. It was curious to see the natives swarming up the trees, which almost overhung their blazing domiciles, to give cooling drink to the men who had brought fire amongst their homes. The Maories or even Tannamen, would have looted us out more sharply.

Noon on board — much beer — got the anchor up, and then breakfast. 2.30, anchored off the mouth of the river Crakete, in 4½ fathoms. The captain, consul, C________, Mr. Wilkinson, and Tui Mbua ascended the river in the galley to Nambukava, a town built on a fortified island in the midst of the stream. There is no indication of this river in the chart, though it seems to be one of the largest in Fiji: they went on in the galley, passed Nambukava, to another island five or six miles from the mouth, and never found less than 4 fathoms, and no indication of lesser soundings farther on for some distance. A vessel of 90 tons crossed the bar for cargo not long ago but I did not hear what water there is on the bar.

This district was once under Tui Mbua, but was lately given up by him to Ritova, for the purpose, I believe, of avoiding war. The inhabitants, however, find that it is a change for the worse; and today they received their late king with great rejoicing and giving of presents, pigs, &c.

OVALAU.

November 7th. — The captain, consul, and Mr. Horseley, and the consul's clerk, Mr. Thurston, accompanied by the cutter and six marines under a sub-lieutenant, went away at daybreak on a sort of demonstration or visit to the Livoni, a warlike tribe of mountaineers who inhabit the centre of the island, and have always held their own against the repeated attacks of Bau and Levuka. I believe one of the complaints against them now is their refusal to give up a robber.

Everything went off satisfactorily, except that Jones and some of our men were considerably knocked up with heat and fatigue. They had had to climb for three or four miles after landing.

Some of the whites at Ovalau seemed to think there might be a chance of resistance being attempted. If so — or whether or not — it seemed a pity to go away with so small a party. Every successive time that the captain has landed on service in Fiji, he has taken a smaller party; this seems only tempting a collision.

At present the Fijians have a great idea of our prowess and power — they seem to think us invincible, and that nothing could induce a Briton to run away. This simple creed should be encouraged by all means; for I fancy that if once, taking advantage of the weakness of a small party, on a burning expedition, for instance, they were to succeed in thrashing us, our prestige would be gone for ever, and there would be the devil to pay all over Fiji.

O______ and I landed to bathe and sketch and stroll about. On the beach, we fell in with a white man, who called himself M______, or some such name. He favoured us with his views in general, and (according to him) those of all the English in Fiji in particular, on their relations with the native race; drew a touching picture of the pitiful moderation shown by captains of our men-of-war compared with the vigorous proceedings of those commanding Yankee war-vessels — if a cent of an American's property was touched, didn't "they blaze it into them" and make them pay through the nose? As for us — here his feelings became too much for him — "what's the use of burning their houses down? — they don't care for that — shoot them and hang them — that's the way" — &c., &c., &c.

They're a lively lot — some of them whites.

Burning a chief's house down just is the thing that "touches him where he lives;" it is the sign that he has been conquered, that he has passed under the yoke.

In the late war up the Ruva river one of the conquered chiefs implored Thakombau not to burn his house, whatever he did to those of the common people, but as he was bent on destroying his lodgings, to do so by other means, such as cutting it to pieces, or throwing the materials into the river. But the request was refused, and the chief disgraced.

O________ and I went to the missionary's house on the little hill overlooking the settlement, and called on Mr. and Mrs. Moore, whose house is the neatest and prettiest we have yet seen, commanding a beautiful view of the little town beneath, the breaker-bound reef with its many tinted waters without and within, and the distant islands beyond.

I had made acquaintance with Mr. Moore when here in the '*Curaçoa.*' He impressed me very favourably, being free from the bigotry which seems the distinguishing characteristic of so many of the Wesleyan missionaries. He was able to talk to me for half an hour without saying a word against his Roman Catholic colleagues.

After our visit was concluded we went to bathe at the waterfalls, about a mile from the white settlement. On the way, we passed through the native town of Levuka, one of the dirtiest in

Fiji, and surrounded for defence by a stinking ditch and a ragged stone wall; Tui Levuka getting half-seas-over as usual.

We found the people uglier, dirtier, more mean-looking, and in every way more repulsive than those of any of the other islands visited by us; their pastor even assigns them a lower position in the scale of morality than any in the group.

The whites complain much of thefts committed by the natives, for which no redress can be obtained, as the chief Tui Levuka is a drunken vagabond, who will not take the trouble to keep his subjects in order. Levuka is a tributary of Bau.

The bathing-place pleasant and pretty — a succession of three falls with deep pools under them, so situated that one can jump down all three in succession without danger.

Here it was that I first tasted kava. I had landed rather more than a year ago, when in the '*Curaçoa*,' with D________, one of my then messmates, intending to take a stroll and bathe in one of these pools.

We followed the stream for two or three miles, more or less, finding the taro cultivated in every practicable space, the sides of the ravine being cut into innumerable little terraces, constructed so as to prevent the water from the mountains escaping readily, and thus forming a muddy soil for the taro to grow in.

Crossing the ridge of a little ravine, we suddenly dropped on a party of mountaineers, who were resting under the shade of the trees and brewing kava. Most of them were pagans, and had their faces painted in black and red stripes, perpendicularly from the chin to the top of the forehead, and their hair frizzed out into an enormous "Turk's head," some two feet in diameter, and in a few instances enveloped in *tappa* cloth, to prevent the hair being shaken out of shape, or torn by the bushes they passed through.

Their only garment was the *maro*, and altogether they were the wildest-looking savages I have ever seen.

There were a few women and girls with the party, and in their costume an apron of leaves or *tappa* replaced the still scantier *maro* of the men. We were received with a yell of welcome; and offers of kava tendered in banana leaves folded so as to contain liquid.

I had never before been able to bring myself to gratify my curiosity by tasting kava but this day, having only witnessed the manual straining of the kava through the coconut fibre, and being very, thirsty, I swallowed my disgust and a long drink of kava simultaneously. In appearance, it resembles very weak *café au lait*, in taste something between soapsuds and quinine, but not so disagreeable as this would imply; its effects resemble those of a narcotic. I had heard and read that a person who has drunk kava goes off into a delicious dreamy state, though retaining consciousness long after losing all power of speech or motion. My companion had only tasted half a mouthful, but having all day in the woods before me if I chose, I was willing to try the effects of this marvellous liquid. Yet hour after hour passed in sunshine and in shade, we bathed and basked on the warm rocks, and basked and bathed again, yet not a symptom of the narcotic influence appeared, and when I returned to the ship I thought I was clear of the kava. At dinner I drank very moderately, even more so than usual, but immediately after swallowing a glass of wine I felt that the kava so long inactive was beginning to take effect, and retired to my cabin as soon as dinner was over. The sensation was that of extreme buoyancy and hilarity of spirits, followed by total insensibility.

Next morning the feeling was that of having been refreshed by very sound sleep, and all the disagreeable results which would follow the too free indulgence in liquor were entirely wanting. The details of the first part of the preparation of the kava, the mastication, are not quite so nasty as would appear at first sight, for those employed are exclusively young girls with good teeth, who are forced to be very careful about washing their mouths out at the commencement, so that the amount of saliva which finds its way into a gallon bowl of kava is infinitesimal. It was perhaps in some measure the circumstance of our not having seen the kava prepared that accounted for our having been able to overcome our disgust sufficiently to taste it. The great majority of the lower class of whites residing in these islands become very much addicted to drinking kava, and not always in moderation.

Later we went with Mr. Horseley's son and a party of natives in the mission boat to look for opercula on the reef. I had hitherto ascribed my want of success in obtaining these beautiful little things to the natives being too lazy to go out on the reef in sufficient numbers to search for them; but today I found I was wrong. We remained wading about on the reef till the tide had risen almost to our waists and darkness had come on, without getting a single one of the right sort, though the natives found two shells evidently belonging to the same family (Turbinidae), but the opercula were of a white and pink or brownish colour, instead of the beautiful bluish-green, and quite destitute of the vitreous polish possessed by those of the latter colour.

We left because the water was getting too deep and the twilight too dusky for us to distinguish small objects on the bottom; but the natives were also anxious to go because they say that at this time the sharks come over the reefs. There is another fish called, I think, "Ogo,"[115] which the natives fear even more than the shark (though not more than half the size of the latter), because it bites in very shallow water.

There is a species of sword-fish which is also very dangerous to fishing parties. Mr. Nettleton, one of the missionaries at Kandavu, told me afterwards that a woman was brought to him not long ago for surgical treatment, having been mortally wounded by a sword-fish, whose weapon had completely transfixed her body above the waist.

These fish frequently find themselves enclosed within the ever-narrowing circle of fishing women, and terrified at the sight of so many foes splashing and wading towards them, make one desperate dash for liberty, skimming along the surface with the speed and piercing impetus of a javelin. Then woe to the luckless fisher who may chance across its path.

As far as I can judge (not much in this instance) Mr. Jones sometimes finds it necessary for the preservation of law and order to administer rather sharper remedies than suffice for the matured constitutions of older communities, and has found the

---

115 Great Barracuda.

"cat" a peace preserver of no little virtue. There are plenty about these seas to whom pussy is the sole convincing argument.

In some cases, he is supported by the chief, who becomes by the consent and wish of the consul the direct agent of punishment: thus, at Ovalau a nephew of Thakombau has been deputed as flogger by his uncle. So, if at any time a prosecution or action were commenced against the consul by a culprit whom he had caused to be flogged or sent to hard labour, he could reply that the punishment was inflicted by the lawful government of the country where the offence had been committed.

I am speaking, of course, of the whites. Amongst others, a fellow named also Jones (his latest English name), *alias* "Papalangi-Jonah-Pokahorse,"[116] *i.e.* "Jones, the white horse-gelder," has lately "married the gunner's daughter." This last warning (for his shoulders showed marks of a previous flagellation) induced him to transfer his talents elsewhere, and I hear he has since been drowned on a bar in New Zealand — poor devil!

November 18th, Sunday. — After service, at which by the captain's invitation most of the white residents attended, we weighed for Bau, and anchored at that place, or rather about two miles from the island, and half that distance from Viwa, the original mission-station, soon after four, in 5½ fathoms.

November 19th. — Landed in the afternoon for an hour or two. Mbau has an air of much greater solidity and age than any other town in the South Sea Islands, the houses being much larger, loftier, more carefully finished, and more densely packed. The landing-places, the church, and some of the principal buildings are flanked with broad slabs of stone, many of them over 10 feet high.

---

116 "This self-styled Briton, from whose lips issued more lies than truths, told us he had been in the islands four years, the fact being, as we were not long in learning, that he had only been there some weeks, having been expelled for theft from some other island where he had been living." (Brenchley, p.96)

I went to Thakombau's house with the intention of seeing the celebrated old cannibal — now one of the best friends of the missionaries, at least so say most of them — but he was engaged in a korero with the skipper and the consul, so I did not go in. It appears that he is somewhat riled at our having punished Ritova without having first referred to him, as he claims to be his liege lord.

Thakombau by Julius Brenchley.

Thakombau has now two white men on his staff, one a sort of secretary or minister for home, and the other for foreign, affairs.

He has, moreover, a sort of steward or factotum, a black man, named Beriouk, who showed me all over the place.

The strangers' house is a curious sight; it is the largest building in the group, broad, lofty, with many doors, and divided inside by little fences a foot high into a great number of mess-places, each with its own fire-stones, for the accommodation of the many other tribes who are continually visiting Bau, either as tribute-bearers or as allies for a war-party.

Several long sail-needles made from the leg-bones of their enemies were offered me for sale, and I bought a couple. I tried to get a cannibal fork, such as are used solely for eating human flesh, but failed, though there are already several on board. They are made of wood with four prongs, but not all projecting in the same plane, as with ours. The church's exterior is the most imposing that I have seen in these seas — though that is not saying much. There is a hillock in the centre of the island on which is the mission-house (Mr. Langham), and below is the dancing-ground, where, in the old time, were held war and licentious dances, accompanied by the murder of prisoners and by cannibal feasts. The ground, smooth and hard from the tread of thousands of feet, is overshadowed by a great banyan tree, called the *"Akau tambu,"* or sacred tree, into whose thick trunk a slab of stone four or five feet square is sunk, and forms a sort of table.

Behind this are a row of slabs of stone erect, with their lower ends embedded in the ground, one of which was used for dashing out the brains of the victims. Thakombau, before his conversion, has been known to amuse himself by catching up by the heels the children of his enemies and flinging them at the slabs with his own hands. The same merry old fellow on one occasion cut out the tongue of a captive chief, who had used it to beg for a speedy death, and jocosely[117] ate it before his face.

We were shown another braining-stone, in the same town, used by the fisherman tribe, something like a milestone, but too sharp at the top to be used as a seat. The mode of braining was this: the victim was seized by two natives, one on each side grasping an arm and a leg, with the head foremost; they then run him as hard as they could across the dancing-ground, increasing their speed till his head caved in against the stone, a part of which, about two feet above the ground, has been worn smooth by the thousands of heads which have been knocked against it. Near the stone are a double row of raised seats on slabs of stone, where sat the chiefs to direct the massacres and enjoy the spectacle. It is impossible to form an estimate of the number of those who have been put to death in this manner; but it is a common saying amongst the Fijians, that all the waters of the ocean could never

---

117 In jest.

wash away the blood with which that soil has been saturated. We sailed at four for Kandavu, Jones and Thurston leaving us shortly afterwards in their boat for Ovalau.

KANDAVU.[118]

November 20th. — Went to general quarters in the forenoon, firing at a cask, and anchored soon after four this afternoon in Ngaloa Bay (named after the island Ngaloa which lies in it, black duck). We are close to the isthmus which connects the northern and southern parts of the island, but we are on the opposite side of the isthmus to that where the '*Curaçoa*' anchored.

It is named *"Na-yara-mbali,"* "the hauling over," i.e. of canoes across the isthmus. It was here that Jackson saw the great war-canoe dragged over living rollers, formed of poor wretches bound hand and foot to soft stems of banana trees to keep them square in their places.

While furling sails, steaming in for the anchoring, Bacon, ordinary seaman, fell overboard from the fore-topsail-yard, slightly striking the after-guy of the fish-davit in his descent; luckily for him in going astern he caught the lead-line, or the lead-line him, just under the main-chains, and the ship only going easy at the time, he was able to hold on and so got hauled on board, very little the worse for his fright.

November 21st. — W________, B________, and I landed today, taking S________ with us to try and get some grub for the mess. There is here also an *"Akau tambu"*[119] as at Mbau. We landed at the head of the bay to the right, astern of the ship as she swung nearly always, the spot for landing being marked by four coconut trees (the last of a double row) near the water's edge. Half-a-miles walk hence through a pleasant valley brought us to a village on the northern side of the isthmus, where we found a gentleman-like young trader named Paine, who has recently established himself here for the purchase of oil from the natives. He produced some

---

118 The fourth largest of the Fijian islands.
119 Sacred tree.

cool and grateful beer, and then procured a guide to take us on to Tavuki, the mission station in the next bay. The path was not a very pleasant one on so hot a day, commencing with a tough unbroken ascent of about a mile, leading over a lofty mountain ridge. Old Ward's stout corporation showing signs of melting away altogether, he very soon gave it up, and went back to the village.

We had read in the same "Jackson's Narrative," alluded to previously, of a certain wonderful tree near Rewa which attracted to itself all the mosquitoes in the whole country-side for miles around, so that so long as the tree remained undisturbed, Rewa was free from mosquitoes; but should anyone shake its branches, the insects spread far and wide in myriads. Jackson says that he saw this tree, and that the insects covered it in such swarms that scarcely an atom of the trunk, leaves, or branches was visible.

We had taken this story with a grain of salt, deeming it rather a traveller's tale.

But today, soon after passing the highest point in our path, we came upon a tree whose branches, overhanging the track, were completely covered in the manner described by Jackson; obviously a suitable *"Akau ni namu,"* or mosquito tree. The appearance of each separate leaf was very singular, being completely covered with a thousand little grey wings and bodies, all pointing in the same direction, pulsating with lip, and so closely packed that not an atom of the green surface of the leaf itself could be seen. On closer inspection, however, we found that the insect is not a true mosquito, though it has a close resemblance. They did not seem to be feeding, yet they were not easily disturbed.

Later we came to some of the most beautiful tree ferns that I have ever seen, growing in great profusion and in the open sunlight.

Descending into Tavuki Bay we had to wade across a portion of it to reach the mission-house. Here we found Mrs. White alone, her husband having gone off to the ship, together with Mr. Nettleton, of Richmondi, in the next bay beyond — a mission station, and the Fijian Wesleyan college for native ministers and teachers. Mrs. White's is a cosy little house, with veranda and garden, close to the sea-shore. She was much surprised at our having come over the hills, but remembered me in the '*Curaçoa*,' and regaled us with fresh milk and butter, home-made cake, and other luxuries which we had not seen for a long time, and insisted on my accepting a few green opercula which she had collected.

The natives did not seem much inclined to trade for livestock, and S________ was unable to get anything for the mess, but we had the promise that some should be sent as soon as the chief then absent could be got hold of.

We had to take another road for the first part of the way back, the tide having risen too much to allow of our wading back. On gaining the summit ridge on our return the view was rendered very pleasing by the sunset shadows in the hills, and the grand looking mountain, Buki Levu, in the distance, to the northward.

The *"Akau ni namu"* was much as we had left it. The return was far less fatiguing, as the steepest part was all down-hill.

CHAPTER XIII.

November 22nd. — Mr. White and Mr. Nettleton having left a very pressing invitation for me yesterday, I accompanied the captain ashore in the galley. This time, instead of landing where we did yesterday, we steered to the left up to the head of the other bay, leaving the island of Ngaloa (black duck) on our port hand and then astern of us, till we came to the mouth of a narrow creek, which we ascended, for the most part completely roofed over by the branches of tall mangrove trees. This brought us within a few hundred yards of the opposite shore of the isthmus, whither having proceeded on foot, we found Mr. Nettleton's whaler awaiting us with a crew of four sturdy Fijians in white shirts and *"maros."*

We nearly run over a good-sized turtle, lying sleeping or basking on the surface of the water.

The natives were much amused at my attempts to pick up sentences in their language. As soon as we were well round the first point and under sail, they entertained us and themselves with a hymn, or half-religious song, with an European tune to it. They evidently sang for their own amusement, rather than for the purpose of airing their piety. In crossing the mouth of Tavuki Bay we saw the 'Western Star' brig, which came in here yesterday from Ovalau, lying very much where we did in the '*Curaçoa*.'

We found Mr. Nettleton very snugly quartered in a commodious house, surrounded by a very extensive garden, and perched on the crest of a little hill, commanding a charming view and drinking in the coolest of the fresh and life-giving sea-breezes. Mr. Nettleton met us on landing at Richmondi, and took us up to the house, where his wife and B________, our Padre, were awaiting breakfast.

We then went down to the school-house, where the students to the number of sixty or seventy — grown men from all parts of Fiji — had been assembled by beat of drum to give us a specimen of their reading and chorus singing. The former was clear and fluent, the latter given in very good time and with great heartiness. They are taught singing by Mrs. Nettleton. The students were then dismissed to fetch their writing materials to enable us to worry them in the other two R's, while we accompanied the skipper, who had to decide on a charge of theft brought against the son of the chief and others, names unknown, by a harmless-looking old settler, who had spent half a lifetime among them with his native wife, she having proved, we hear, a very good wife to her husband, who in days gone by frequently required "reorganizing." The accused pleaded guilty, and promised reformation, for which his father, the old chief, vouched. It being the first offence brought home against him, and the complainant not being anxious for severity, the captain decreed ample restitution and a fine of livestock to be paid immediately. All went well, and the chief as well as the accuser seemed much puzzled at the captain refusing to keep the forfeited pigs himself.

The native town is neat and regularly built, and the little streets are clean and swept.

I was much struck with the nattiness and decency of the dormitories for the students. Each one has a little cabin to himself, divided off from the others by a partition of wainscoting made of cane-like reeds like the Kakaho. In all the bed and floor were covered with new and sweet mats, and often with a mosquito curtain. A Bible, one or two other books, and writing gear, a print, and a scrap of looking-glass in some, with perhaps a few flowers, completed the furniture. Such of the students as have no relatives in the town — and many of them come from the most distant isles of the group — are allotted to discreet matrons, who wash and "do" for them.

The cause célèbre of the stolen pigs having been settled to the satisfaction, or at all events to the acknowledged sense of justice, of all concerned or not concerned, we returned to the schoolhouse to examine the students in geography, writing, and arithmetic. They could point out places in the map pretty easily, though the names were all printed in English, which is not attempted to be taught them; their writing was upright, and stiff and formal, but round and very easy to read; in arithmetic they managed long division and subtraction with ease, but a long addition sum of pounds, shillings, and pence produced a few mistakes. Of their proficiency in the main part of their education — the Holy Scriptures and the Christian doctrine — we had no reason to doubt; having declined, with some alarm, an invitation to try to puzzle them with questions in sacred history. The captain said a few timely words to them through the missionary, which appeared to please them; and then, after making the tour of the large garden, wherein vegetation of all climates seems to flourish, we returned to the house to dinner; and a first-rate dinner it was. Then a little music (a fair piano) and singing from our hostess, followed by a cigar in the cool veranda, which gave me leisure to reflect on all we had seen, and to conclude that such martyrdom as this would not necessarily shorten life. How many an English clergyman's mouth would water at the sight of such a parsonage, with the ample garden and well-filled larder under his lee — so neat a parish, so docile a congregation, and all this free of rent, rates, taxes, and churchwardens!

Mr. Nettleton has devoted some little attention to objects of natural history in his neighbourhood — a subject of which many of the missionaries in these seas seem to be singularly ignorant. Kandavu does not appear to be so free of poisonous vermin as are most of the South Sea Islands. There are a few small scorpions, but centipedes abound. There is, moreover, a species of slug, of a black colour, whose slime is so venomous that if allowed to crawl over the hand, or any other exposed part, the skin under its trail turns black, and eventually comes away. Goats and other small animals have been killed by getting one of these slugs into their mouths, or by swallowing one whilst browsing. Mr. Nettleton has a perfect specimen by which he sets great store, the animal not having got rid of its "heel" before capture, as is usually the case.

Mrs. Nettleton would not let us depart till she had persuaded some of us to accept a great part of her store of rare shells, &c.; we then went on, or rather back, to Tavuki by sea. The Tavukians descried us long before we approached the shore, and we could hear the soft sound of the *"lali,"* or drum, once the signal for a cannibal orgy, summoning the natives to the church to receive us. From every direction we could see them streaming in, arrayed in their best or Sunday suit, which, however, varied from a white shirt, &c., for men, and a gown with short skirts for the women, to a simple *"tappa"* waistcloth.

By the time we reached the church door the congregation had a song or hymn in fall blast — a song of exultation expressive of satisfaction at the high-pressure state of Christianity and civilization at which they had themselves arrived, and of commiseration and hope for the future of the benighted niggers in the neighbouring isle.

They stop with a jerk on seeing us enter, though singing with great energy and accompanying themselves at what we presume to be the chorus, or the most telling points of the melody, with clapping of hands.

In an instant the whole congregation, of all ages from infancy to extreme old age, were squatting on their hams — the Fijian attitude of respect.

The usual daily service for the evening followed, consisting of a hymn, short prayer, and a few verses from the Gospel expounded by a native teacher, under the direction of the missionary.

After prayers, the children of both sexes, to the number of about 120, were examined, to show us their proficiency in reading, &c. It was curious to see a lot of little wretches, who in England would have been scarcely out of arms, reading aloud with clearness and assurance. It was only the girls of the budding age of twelve or fourteen who seemed at all shy in showing us what they could do. We were struck with the natural grace of their bearing, whether still or in motion, and the good taste shown in the selection of the colours of the simple dress they wore.

The natives are called for worship or instruction by beat of drum, but within the building silence is proclaimed, or the signal given for rising or squatting during service, or for the cessation of a hymn, by sound of pipe or whistle.

Thence to the hospitalities of the mission-house, where Mrs. White regaled us with many little homely, home-made, home-reminding creature-comforts, which tasted strangely welcome on these outlandish shores.

Mrs. White had also kindly caused the girls of her school to procure for me a few of the shell-fish (Turbinidae) with the beautiful green-blue opercula — *ai songo ni nga ni vivili karakaráwa*, or *ni nga ni vivili lanu moana* [spelt in each case as it is pronounced]: *ai songo* — the cork or stopper; *la* — one of the scales which covers the buds of the breadfruit leaves, calyx? *ni* — of; *nga* — shell; *vivili* — shell-fish, or sea-snail; *karakaráwa* — blue or green; *lanu moana* — colour of the sea.

It was nearly dark before we left, returning to the isthmus with Mr. White in his boat, a good wholesome whaler, manned by a lusty crew. I took the stroke-oar for a mile or two, to give them a rough notion of our stroke, which is longer than theirs, *"Balavu! Balavu!"* They pulled very well, considering that the canoe and paddle was the only means of aquatic progression to which they had been accustomed.

They were very much surprised to see me take off my coat and fist an oar, and they made the surf boil with their redoubled exertions, saying that they had hitherto thought that rowing was deemed amongst us work fit only for servants, slaves, and common persons, but that now they saw it was a real "chiefly" exercise, when one of the chiefs of the great war-canoe took to it of his own accord — no boat in the Fijis should ever pass them in future, &c., &c. and they certainly made the boat walk till her prow touched the beach. Not long ago they raced Mr. Nettleton's crew for a distance of a little over twenty miles — a killing course — and paid heavily for success with loss of much leather. Great demands on the medicine-chest next day for ointment and balsams for the excoriated hides of the rival crews, and on the carpenter's stores for repairs to the boats, whose thole-pins had been carried away and gunwale sprung in many places by fair sheer hard pulling. These men have the stuff in them, both of physical power and of energy to make seamen but I doubt their standing a cold climate.

Before leaving, we arranged that a chief with two natives were to start next morning for some reefs in the neighbourhood of Buki Levu (Great Yam-mound) — a lofty cloud-capped mountain at the southern end of the island, where the Turbinidae with the green opercula are most frequently found — and return if possible, before we sailed.

A favourite place, according to Tui Mbua, is an island to the westward of Viti Levu, named, I think, Asaua, or some name sounding like it.

November 23rd. — Exercised at general quarters in the forenoon, firing shot and shell at a rock. Tui Ngaloa, the chief of the island of Ngaloa (black duck), abreast of us, with three or four other natives, came on board, and were excessively excited and interested at what they saw. At first, they seemed rather startled and overpowered by the noise of the guns but they were soon sent out on the bowsprit, whence they could mark the practice without being deafened by the sound or blinded by smoke, and then their delight was unbounded, every telling shot or bursting shell drawing from them loud cries of pleasure and surprise. In the afternoon, we expended what remained of our quarter's allowance of rifle ammunition at a target. The chief tried a shot, and did very fairly, much to his own satisfaction. In fact, he was in a continual and ever-increasing state of astonishment the whole time he was on board, and expressed himself in sharp, almost childish, cries of wonder, which could be heard perpetually from the engine-room, the galley, or wherever he was pursuing his investigations. The two things which struck the native fancy most were the grand charge — the boarders with drawn cutlasses after grounding their pikes — and a couple of signal and some war rockets which were discharged after dark.

November 24th. — O________ and I landed together, taking some "kai" with us, and went in the direction of Tavuki as far as the valley where the tree ferns grow which we passed on Wednesday; here we halted and sketched. But the bush was on fire, and the flames soon forced us to travel. For some time, I had heard a distant rushing sound which I could not account for, never suspecting the cause till some light-flying flakes of burnt grass, borne from behind me by the light breeze which was rising, fell on my sketching-block, and then I found that the edge of the burning bush had reached to within a couple of hundred yards of where I sat — the thirsty flames consuming the parched grass and underscrub, and licking off with fiery tongues the light foliage of the trees.

This evening Tui Ngaloa presented two turtle to the captain, both of them of good size. He had sent fishing parties away every day since our arrival, but these were the only two they could get. Turtle are by no means common in the Fijis, and are strictly *"tambu"*-ed to the great chiefs — and to a few only of them so that a turtle here represents a handsomer gift than haunches of venison at home.

November 25th Sunday. — 5.30 a.m. weighed under steam for Sydney, having now completed our tour of the South Sea Islands. We leave on good terms with everyone at all the places we have visited, except perhaps Ritova and one or two troublesome whites at Ovalau. There is a Roman Catholic priest at Kandavu, but we saw nothing of him. According to Messrs. White and Nettleton, the Roman Catholics form but a very small percentage of the population. At almost every island there is the same miserable old story — the teachers of each persuasion accusing their rivals of calumniating them to the natives, of admitting and counting as converts such as are so only in name, of personal discourtesy, and of not being gentlemen. There is no doubt that it is the Protestants only who really civilize the natives; it is they who give them whatever secular education they get; it is they who teach them to respect themselves in their persons and their dwellings. The difference in personal appearance of the two sects is very striking. Before a native has approached close enough to show the little medal or image slung round his neck which marks his adherence to the Romish Church, his slovenly dress, dirty person, and unkempt shock head of hair has proclaimed the communion he belongs to.

It is here that the Roman priests exercise the greatest self-denial, that their ascetic life of wholesale devotion to the cause and the Master whom they serve in all single-heartedness is often a cheerless, hopeless, state of solitary and almost abject poverty which it is not very easy to realize; but in the state of peace and safety both of life and property to which the Fijis, the Tongan, and the Samoan groups have attained, these sufferings and sacrifices are for the most part, if not entirely, thrown away. The exhortations of a teacher of another race whose dwellings, style of dress and bearing, and general habits of life, whether in matters of comfort or refinement, are little if at all above the level of their own, have little weight with a set of savages who are naturally rather gentleman-like dogs in their own way, and take stock with half a glance of such little blemishes as loaded finger-nails and dirty linen.

The mission-house at Richmondi which I have mentioned above is the best appointed one that I have seen in the Fijis, or any of the South Sea Islands. To those to whom the idea of a foreign mission is necessarily associated with various degrees of martyrdom, a well-to-do missionary and a humbug may appear to be convertible terms; but in islands where the heat of the day is passed, where the whole or the bulk of the population are Christians, and the dark old days of persecution and terror are gone by for ever, I cannot see why the missionary and the missionary's wife should not endeavour to prove to the natives that there is something more in the secular civilization of which they are generally and always should be the pioneers, than bad rum and sharp trading.

There can be no doubt of the moral effect on the surrounding natives of the example shown by such a *ménage* as that presided over by Mrs. Nettleton at Richmondi: the results were self-evident in the orderly condition of the town and native grounds, and the cleanly, neat, and tasty arrangements in the students' bedrooms and other apartments, than which I have seen few pleasanter sights.

These students remain at the college till they are considered to be thoroughly well-grounded in Scripture history, the teaching of the Gospel, and all such questions of Christian doctrine as are likely to be attacked by heathen disputants; then, if they have also made sufficient progress in the other branches of their education and have maintained a good moral character during their whole time of residence in the college, they are sent to distant villages in the interior of the main island or other places which cannot as yet be furnished with a white missionary. The Pagan chiefs occasionally make it lively for these teachers — or *deadly* I may say, for some of them have or had an awkward trick of shutting up a too logical expounder of Christian doctrine by splitting his skull with a club. But when these little misfortunes do take place there never lack zealous men to take the vacant places.

A few of these teachers who have shown special aptitude, and have been tested in the course of teaching in some heathen village, return to the college to be developed in a higher course of education, and ultimately get rated full parsons.

Before we left, we received, addressed to the captain, a naïve letter of thanks (of which a translation is subjoined) from the Richmondi whaler's crew, for a small present of necessaries and baccy we had sent them.

RICHMONDI, KANDAVU, FIJI,
November 24, 1866.

SIR,

I write away to inform you that the things which you kindly sent for us — the boatmen of Mr. Nettleton — arrived safely, and we have each received our share, for which we greatly thank you. We rejoice greatly that you thought of us kindly, and sent us things that will be very useful. We rejoiced much on the day that we pulled the missionary to Galoa to see the man-of-war and its captain. When we got to the side of the ship, we saw the great land guns, and admired them. When we looked about, we saw the officer standing at the gangway, and we said, "Oh, that one would speak for us to him, that we might be allowed to look over the vessel." Then I spoke to him, and he nodded his head; so we then got on board, and looked over the hold, and saw the men, who were in great number, and very industrious at their work. We beheld them, and respected them greatly. Then we looked around us, and saw the very great guns and the swords in great numbers. We saw the chiefs of the ship, and reverenced them greatly. Then we went again on deck and talked among ourselves, and said, "We young men of this generation were born in blessed times to see such a ship as this. Our fathers saw no such sight. We are living in better times, and we are very thankful for it."

My letter is finished.

We send our love to you, sir — all of us — the boatmen.

I am,

THOMAS NATHEMBA,
Your Friend.

To the Chief of the Man-of-War
Steamer '*Esk.*'

It was my forenoon watch today. At one bell, we stopped the engines and made all plain sail. We were steering S. W. ½S., having shaped course, going six knots, with the wind on the port quarter, and the land some 10 or 12 miles off on the starboard beam and quarter. There were no dangers marked in the chart, but the chart is very imperfect, Kandavu having been omitted from the detailed American survey; and even in better surveyed parts of the South Sea Islands we found (in the '*Curaçoa*') several shoals of which no indication was given. C________ with a party were hard at work surveying all day and every day of our stay at Kandavu.

About half-past eleven, I suddenly saw, stretching along our port bow, as well as right ahead — still at some distance — some irregular but connected streaks and patches of bright-green water, as of a formidable reef, or very shallow shoal. I sent down for the captain, and at the same time calling up the quartermaster (and hard-a-porting the helm), asked him what he thought of it — he said it was a reef. At this time, I thought it was fish-spawn, having seen something like it, though of a different colour (red), in the West Indies, off Trinidad, ten years ago. By this time the captain, startled by the unusual summons to come on deck for some unknown reason, was by my side on the bridge, and pointing to the discoloured water, I asked him whether I should take the canvas off her. The effect on his mind of what he saw showed itself by an expression on his face which I had never seen there before. He did not answer at once, so I piped "Hands shorten sail," and hove her to on the starboard tack.

Before she came to the wind, we passed the green water which had first attracted my attention, leaving it on the port hand at the distance of less than a quarter of a mile; but we seemed to have only escaped Scylla to fall into Charybdis, for there was another patch which there was no avoiding, an extensive one which had been on our starboard bow, concealed from my eye by the foresail and rigging, &c., and the nearer we drew the nastier it looked. Few doubted now that we were facing a hopeless reef.

There are some situations which produce a queer sort of hidden feeling, experienced, I take it, rarely save by men in charge of ships, or perhaps by the guard of a night express when a collision is imminent; a feeling in which no sense of personal risk has any part whatever, being swallowed up entirely by the knowledge that the safety of your charge, your professional hopes and reputation, and may be the lives of hundreds hang by your breath. This occasion was in a mild way one of them.

There was nothing more to be done: the ship was answering her helm as fast as we could make her, with the mizen topsail braced round flat aback, the head sails down, and the men hauling up the foresail. The captain had called the leadsmen to the chains; but no soundings could they get the flying boom and then the ship herself passed through and over the seeming reef like Philip's craft through the phantom ship — there was no reeling shock, no sound of crashing timbers the illusion was complete.

After heaving-to and shortening sail to topsails and jib, a boat was lowered, and C________ went away to examine the patch we had passed. He found no bottom at 20 fathoms, and that the illusion of colour and appearance was caused by the presence of a minute, almost microscopic, substance in the water, of which he brought a bucketful on board.

On examination through M________'s microscope, this substance — which whilst allowed to float on the surface of perfectly still water had presented to the naked eye the appearance of a dirty brown or grey scum almost impalpable — showed itself to be composed of myriads of little objects resembling infinitesimal hair chopped up very short and almost all perfectly straight. M________ thought that it was a vegetable substance belonging or akin to the Oscillatoria, a genus of Algae, of which a description and illustration are given in the Cyclopaedia. I ventured to disagree with him, because the genus described is at least thirty times as large as that we saw because there is no mention of its being found in salt water, but in warm and fresh water springs and because I could see no traces in the specimens under examination of the common central body to which the filaments of the "oscillatoria" are attached.

We left Mr. Jones in great hopes of being relieved before long, and getting sent to some more civilized part of the world than the South Seas. He had been as a boy a cadet in the Austrian Cuirassiers, afterwards in our own army, and whilst serving in the 7th, in which regiment he went through the Crimean campaign, and got a well-earned Victoria Cross and several severe wounds, he tried to get his brevet majority, which had been given to the others under similar circumstances — but failed, got riled, and sold out.

He seems well suited to the kind of work and the wild characters he has to deal with, and inclined to show no partiality to colour, or rather its absence — a quality which has not, perhaps, endeared him to a few of the more vicious class of whites who still infest these islands — men who, having found their previous civilized neighbourhoods getting too warm for them, have moved on, and keep moving on, to wherever the absence of civil law and authority, their influence with ambitious or rebellious chiefs (whom they supply with firearms and rum), and the occasional threat of a terrific ship-of-war, may enable them to live in defiance of all laws human and Divine, debauching themselves and the natives with whom they associate.

FINIS

BIBLIOGRAPHY

These books were used or referred to in the text:

Brenchley, Julius Lucius. *Jottings during the Cruise of H.M.S. Curaçao among the South Sea Islands in 1865.* London: Longmans, Green, and Co, 1873.

Foljambe, Cecil George Savile. *Three Years on the Australian Station.* London: Hatchard and Co, 1868.

Meade, Herbert. *A Ride Through the Disturbed Districts of New Zealand; Together with Some Account of the South Sea Islands.* Edited by Robert Henry Meade. London: John Murray, 1870.

INDEX

www.ingramcontent.com/pod-product-compliance
Lightning Source LLC
Chambersburg PA
CBHW031957050726
47590CB00006B/1939